Problem-Based Learning in Teacher Education

Margot Filipenko • Jo-Anne Naslund
Editors

Problem-Based Learning in Teacher Education

Editors
Margot Filipenko
Department of Language and Literacy
  Education
University of British Columbia
Vancouver, BC, Canada

Jo-Anne Naslund
Education Library
University of British Columbia
Vancouver, BC, Canada

ISBN 978-3-319-02002-0   ISBN 978-3-319-02003-7   (eBook)
DOI 10.1007/978-3-319-02003-7

Library of Congress Control Number: 2015958792

Springer Cham Heidelberg New York Dordrecht London
© Springer International Publishing Switzerland 2016
This work is subject to copyright. All rights are reserved by the Publisher, whether the whole or part of the material is concerned, specifically the rights of translation, reprinting, reuse of illustrations, recitation, broadcasting, reproduction on microfilms or in any other physical way, and transmission or information storage and retrieval, electronic adaptation, computer software, or by similar or dissimilar methodology now known or hereafter developed.
The use of general descriptive names, registered names, trademarks, service marks, etc. in this publication does not imply, even in the absence of a specific statement, that such names are exempt from the relevant protective laws and regulations and therefore free for general use.
The publisher, the authors and the editors are safe to assume that the advice and information in this book are believed to be true and accurate at the date of publication. Neither the publisher nor the authors or the editors give a warranty, express or implied, with respect to the material contained herein or for any errors or omissions that may have been made.

Printed on acid-free paper

Springer International Publishing AG Switzerland is part of Springer Science+Business Media (www.springer.com)

Foreword

This foreword is coloured by two perspectives on Problem-Based Learning (PBL). One stems from direct experience with PBL and related scholarship in a setting indigenous to the roots of this pedagogy – that of medical education. The other is informed by a senior educational leadership experience within a large, research-intensive university and an intimate knowledge of the Faculty of Education at UBC experimentation with the PBL paradigm: from the early days of interest in the use of cases in teacher education to the contemporary history of the Teaching English Language Learners-PBL cohort (TELL-PBL). What brings these perspectives together, however, is a shared enthusiasm for the value of professional education that situates learning at the intersection of theory and practice in ways that draw on real-life experience and require students' active, reflective engagement.

We have long considered it an interesting paradox that one of the most innovative pedagogies that galvanized practice in professional education in several fields critical to societal progress and well-being – most notably in health sciences and engineering education – has not been extensively explored in the field of teacher education, within a discipline responsible for providing leadership in pedagogical and curricular research and scholarship. While Problem-Based Learning has certainly been informed and benefitted from educational research – including theoretical insights derived from work of education scholars – the drive and ability to transform theoretical premises asserting the value of learners' active engagement, critical reflectiveness, problem-solving and the emphasis on connecting the process and outcomes of learning to real-life situation emerged and have been modelled outside of education faculties. Consequently, while literature abounds in contributions speaking of the rationale, practice, successes, challenges and future possibilities of PBL, this book is unique in relating this topic to the field of teacher education and thus provides valuable, new insights on how a pedagogy that has been successfully deployed in educating doctors and engineers can be adopted, refined and reflected upon in a context of educating educators. It provides a springboard and an invitation for further investigation of the phenomena embedded in PBL practice in a setting that so profoundly impacts on how teaching and learning are understood;

what beliefs, skills and competencies are developed to support novice teachers in their practice; and how these eventually define experience of children in the schools.

The first PBL teacher education cohort at UBC was introduced in 1999 in a context where the Faculty of Education's mainstream teacher education programmes for both elementary and secondary teachers already heavily relied on the use of case studies in the Principles of Teaching Course. This required component of the programme combined traditional lectures with small group tutorials – the latter exclusively focused on the student exploration of a custom-written collection of case studies[1] to facilitate reflection and model how theory and practice can come together in helping students understand educational phenomena and develop research-informed strategies for addressing practical realities of the classroom. The intention was to capture, for the benefit of novice teachers, the space 'between theory and practice' and deploy it as a platform for their personal deconstruction of classroom situations with the benefit of insights gained from lectures and readings and with assistance of experienced mentors in facilitating tutorial sessions. Consistently with this emphasis, the assessment in the course was fully based on the case studies' analysis that replaced traditional mid- and end-of-term examinations. This pedagogical framework created a middle ground between the traditional university approaches to teacher education and PBL. The former tended to separate the academic and practical learning and parcelled out content to be studied in discrete, sequential chunks. The latter, as originally developed at McMaster University in the late 1960s, centred learning on the realities of practice in the profession and required students to take a fully engaged, active approach to the construction of their knowledge, beliefs and attitudes, always with a premise that what had to be learned was complex, intertwined and multifaceted.

Interestingly, the UBC Faculty of Medicine introduced PBL as a key pedagogy in its undergraduate medical and dental programme in 1997, just 2 years before the PBL cohort in teacher education was established. The approach taken by Medicine followed a hybrid curriculum model. The tutorials were designed and implemented in ways that closely mirrored the traditional PBL model in all aspects of case design, structuring of the learning environment, approaches to assessment as well as training of tutors and the roles that they performed. However, the Faculty decided to complement PBL with traditional lectures and laboratories. Consequently, while student experience included learning in small, highly interactive groups, the entire programme did not fully rest on this pedagogy.

It would be a stretch to argue that this temporal alignment in the Medicine and Education's interest in PBL in the late 1990s was anything but coincidental. At large, comprehensive, administratively complex universities, it is uncommon to see curricular and pedagogical innovation initiatives purposefully and strategically aligned across a spectrum of separate faculties for a coordinated implementation. Yet, it is quite reasonable to assume that this alignment reflected a growing interest

---

[1] Kindler, A. M.; Badali, S.; and Willock, R. (1998). Between theory and practice: Case studies for learning to teach. Pearson Education Canada: Toronto

and shift towards constructivist approaches to learning in post-secondary education and in particular in PBL at the turn of the twentieth century.

Although the PBL model, as embraced by the Faculty of Education in its PBL cohort implementation, framed the entire programme experience for the participating students around the PBL approach and the Medicine's hybrid curriculum incorporated PBL sessions into a more traditional programme structure, both faculties chose to draw on a heterogeneous pool of tutors who represented academic as well as professional/clinical backgrounds. On the one hand, involvement of practicing clinicians, teachers or professional leaders as adjuncts, preceptors or practicum supervisors has long been a feature of professional education in both fields. On the other, the PBL framework has explicitly asserted the value of contributions of these practitioners in the mainstream of student academic learning and assigned roles to them that paralleled those of tenure track faculty.

Problem-Based Learning in Teacher Education constitutes an extensive case study of over a decade and a half of PBL implementation in teacher education at UBC. The diversity of contribution that has been encouraged, valued and supported in the delivery of the PBL curriculum is well reflected in the book through the voice given to the wide spectrum of stakeholders who have been invited to offer their accounts of experience with the programme and to reflect on the effectiveness and challenges of PBL, as a means to support initial teacher education. Contributors to this volume include academics: senior as well as emerging educational scholars; tenure track research faculty as well as a member of the new, UBC-pioneered tenure track professoriate with responsibilities specifically focused on teaching and educational leadership; and an academic librarian. They also include members of the profession: experienced and pre-service teachers, current and former district and school-level leaders and administrators and a counsellor and an educational resource coordinator. Very importantly, the book incorporates a voice of a graduate from a PBL cohort whose perspective on the experience in the programme is now shaped by his professional practice as a teacher.

Collectively, these authors present a broad perspective on the theoretical and contextual underpinnings of PBL in teacher education at UBC and offer a comprehensive, sophisticated account of the history of its implementation. They reflect on how, over a decade and a half since PBL was first introduced in this context, the ways of thinking about and implementing the PBL approach have evolved and how this has led to the development of the TELL-PBL – a cohort specifically focused on supporting Teaching English Language Learners through PBL-based curriculum and pedagogy.

Given the richness of the backgrounds of the authors, it is not surprising that much of the book is devoted to the topic of collaboration in PBL and ways in which it is structured, enacted, supported and reflected on – not just as an account of the past experience but with a view of continuing enhancement of practice. Partnerships required to develop and revise cases and to implement their use in a PBL instructional setting are examined through the lens of a search for best practice to respectfully and effectively draw on and incorporate professional practitioners' perspectives in the development and governance of an academic program. While some of the areas that the book engages with, such as the challenges experienced by tutors who are called to replace their traditional instructional roles with those of PBL facilitators – and the tensions and difficulties that arise in the process of this adjustment from a lecturer to a cognitive coach – have received considerable attention in PBL literature[2], they are presented here in the context of an education faculty which frames these challenges in unique ways. Similarly, the topic of assessment in PBL – well researched and described in both medical and general education literature[3] – emerges in this book problematized by the exercise of an educational merger/transformation of the TELL-PBL cohorts that adds an additional dimension to the negotiation of the new evaluation protocol.

The book also offers, however, some less researched, unique perspectives on PBL – including an extensive elaboration of the role of student information literacy in supporting PBL learning. Another area explored in the book that will likely capture the special interest of those concerned with PBL in teacher education focuses on how PBL, as a means of professional learning/formation, creates an opportunity for the student to discern aspects of this pedagogy that could be relevant to professional practice of an in-service teacher in his or her own classroom. A detailed overview of the chapters and backgrounds of contributors is offered in the introductory chapter of the book which also alerts the reader to the ongoing challenges and questions surrounding PBL.

Is PBL more effective as a teaching pedagogy than traditional lecture-based models? In the field of medical education, this debate has been raging for decades. Although compelling arguments have been presented by both 'yes' and 'no' camps, most reported data seem to indicate that there are no significant differences in the medical knowledge base among students who graduated from a programme based on either pedagogical model. Such similarities persist as long as the investigated variables are of a 'student-related' variety, such as student comprehension of content or student reasoning skills. On the other hand, the investigations of some of the institutional variables, which can also be measured to assess the effectiveness of a particular pedagogy, resulted in quite different outcomes. Among such variables, graduation rates have been shown to be higher and duration of study lower for PBL graduates, when compared to students who completed more conventional medical programmes. This line of evidence points to active learning environments of PBL and the greater engagement as well as more active participation in learning that they encourage, behind the overall improvement in academic performance and, consequently, decreased attrition rates[4].

---

[2] Leary, H.; Walker, A.; Shelton, B.E.; and Fitt, M.H. (2013). Exploring the Relationships Between Tutor Background, Tutor Training, and Student Learning: A Problem-based Learning Meta-Analysis. *Interdisciplinary Journal of Problem-Based learning.* 7(1). Available at: http://dx.doi.org/10.7771/1541-5015.1331

[3] Gijbels, D.; Dochy, F.; Van den Bossche, P.; and Segers, M. (2005). Effects of Problem-Based Learning: A Meta-Analysis From the Angle of Assessment. *Review of Educational Research.* 75(1): 27–61.

[4] Schmidt, H.G.; Cohen-Schotanus, J.; and Arends, L.R. (2009). Impact of problem-based, active learning on graduation rates for 10 generations of Dutch medical students. *Medical Education* 43:211–218.

Not surprisingly, the arguments supporting the benefits of PBL in teacher training presented in this book align very well with the evidence from other disciplines. It is also clear that the implementation of the PBL model in teacher education at UBC described in the chapters that follow is constantly evolving, as its leaders and contributors seek to offer an approach that can most effectively address most current, ever-changing needs and expectations of professional preparation for new teachers in British Columbia. This responsiveness, flexibility and adaptability of PBL are among the many valuable features of this educational framework.

Ultimately, however, many successfully implemented PBL programmes, even those as dynamic and innovative as the one described in this book, eventually face challenges. For example, large PBL programmes, such as those offered by most medical schools throughout the developed world, are frequently delivered in the context of a broader institutional rigidity, making timely adjustments to improve the quality of learning difficult. Other factors may include difficulties with maintaining adequate training of new tutors or lack of proper attention to the feedback obtained from stakeholders. Finally, challenges may involve persistent misunderstanding or even resistance from peers and/or administrators who are less familiar with the concept of PBL and who may question a multitude of factors that characterize this model, from cost efficiency to relevance of cases and appropriateness of assessment strategies. In the absence of conclusive research evidence of the superiority of the PBL model as assessed against a full spectrum of desired educational outcomes, these considerations problematize PBL as a mainstream pedagogy of choice, even in programmes that have relied on it for considerable periods of time.

In fact, the recent curriculum renewal process of the UBC undergraduate medical programme has resulted in moving away from PBL to case-based learning (CBL), delivered in the context of a spiral curriculum. Although this decision, prompted by several factors, eliminated PBL sessions that have long defined student learning experience in the program, lessons learned from PBL have allowed to articulate aspects and possibilities embedded in PBL pedagogy to meaningfully inform the redesigned framework, including its new context for small group learning. PBL-embedded innovations into teaching paradigms, such as recently piloted at UBC concept of peer-led tutorials[5], illustrate how reflective PBL practice can evolve and propel innovative, effective teaching.

The same is and will continue to be true about PBL in teacher education, where the PBL cohort model, as operationalized in the UBC Faculty of Education, has opened the door to further improvement in educational experience and its lasting impact on future teachers. The collaborative, inclusive and academically rigorous ways in which the PBL teacher education cohorts have been implemented – and reflected on in this book –bring together a wealth of experience and insight that can inform and elevate teacher education in many of its manifestations. Consequently, this book will speak not only to PBL enthusiasts but to all who are committed to

---

[5] Kindler, P. M. and Jang, K. (2010). Second year medical students as peer facilitators in PBL tutorials: a recipe for success? *Proceedings of the 14th Annual Meeting of the International Association of Medical Science Educators (IAMSE),* New Orleans, USA (p. 112).

excellence in teacher education; who seek inspiration in innovative, unconventional practice; and who are keen to learn from unique experience of their peers.

University of British Columbia, Anna M. Kindler
Vancouver, BC, Canada Pawel M. Kindler

Anna M. Kindler is professor in the Department of Curriculum and Pedagogy and senior advisor to the provost and vice president academic at the University of British Columbia in Vancouver. Between 1995 and 2001, she served as the coordinator of Principles of Teaching at UBC and co-authored *Between Theory and Practice: Case Studies for Learning to Teach*. Since then, her career has primarily focused on academic leadership as dean of the School of Creative Arts, Sciences and Technology at the Hong Kong Institute of Education and, for the past 10 years, as vice provost and associate vice president academic at the University of British Columbia. She has recently stepped down from this role to refocus on educational research, teaching and artistic practice.

Pawel M. Kindler is senior instructor in the Department of Cellular and Physiological Sciences in the Faculty of Medicine at the University of British Columbia in Vancouver. Since 2001, he has been directly involved in the delivery of PBL curriculum at UBC, including leading tutor training, serving as a block chair and contributing to case development. Dr. Kindler has also carried on inquiry into difficult incidents in PBL in a cross-cultural perspective and has developed, implemented and studied peer-facilitation-based tutorials as an alternative to their traditional format.

Contents

1 Discovering, Uncovering, and Creating Meanings: Problem Based Learning in Teacher Education 1
Margot Filipenko, Jo-Anne Naslund, and Linda Siegel

Part I Dispositions for Inquiry

2 Exploring Theoretical Frameworks of Problem Based Learning Through Aoki's *Curriculum-as-Plan* and *Curriculum-as-Lived* 11
Jeannie Kerr

3 Dispositions for Inquiry 23
Jo-Anne Naslund and Lori Prodan

Part II Collaborations: Working Together

4 Knowledge Mobilization and Innovation in the Development of a PBL Cohort for Teaching English Language Learners: Successes, Challenges, and Possibilities 41
Steven Talmy and Margaret Early

5 Negotiating the Content of Problems in Tell/PBL 57
Margot Filipenko

6 Finding Good Governance: Collaboration Between the University of British Columbia and the Richmond School District 73
Kathyrn D'Angelo, Gail Krivel-Zacks, and Catherine Johnson

7 Collaboration: The Heart of the School-Based Practicum 85
Carolyn Russo and Nicky Freeman

Part III Fostering Inquiry and Active Learning

8 The Multiple Roles of the Tutor in a Problem Based
Learning Cohort in a Teacher Education Program 103
Frank Baumann, Monika Tarampi, and Lori Prodan

9 "I'm Not Allowed to Tell You": What Does
It Mean to Be a Problem Based Learning Tutor? 123
Lori Prodan

10 Investigating Cases: Problem-Based Learning
and the Library 135
Jo-Anne Naslund

11 Investigating Social Justice Education Through Problem Based
Learning: A Subject Area Resource Specialist's Perspective 151
Anne Zavalkoff

12 The Place of Problems in Problem Based Learning: A Case
of Mathematics and Teacher Education 173
Cynthia Nicol and Fil Krykorka

13 Measures of Success in Problem Based Learning: Triple Jump
Assessments and E-Folios 187
Anne Zavalkoff

Part IV Reflections

14 Continuing Challenges and Resistance 205
Margot Filipenko, Jo-Anne Naslund, and Lori Prodan

Afterword 223

Contributors 229

Index 233

Chapter 1
Discovering, Uncovering, and Creating Meanings: Problem Based Learning in Teacher Education

Margot Filipenko, Jo-Anne Naslund, and Linda Siegel

Introduction to PBL: Problem Based Learning in Teacher Education

By discovering, uncovering, and making meaning of our experiences as teacher educators and preservice teachers, it is possible to begin to share ideas about the roles and practices of problem based learning in teacher education. The following chapters reflect the close relationships between colleagues and preservice teachers who are involved in a problem based learning (PBL) teacher education cohort at the University of British Columbia. Our writings point to some critical understandings, programmatic realities, and professional dispositions of problem based pedagogy as they pertain to the education of new teachers. For over a decade and a half, a group of teacher educators at the University of British Columbia in collaboration with many school partners have initiated, led, and guided a cohort of preservice teachers in their ongoing explorations. Over time what has evolved and continues to evolve is a teacher education curriculum that not only supports the knowledge needs of future teachers but one that offers meaningful opportunities for them to develop dispositions for inquiry, engage in collaborative learning, and exercise critical thinking, reflexive practice, and professional judgment.

M. Filipenko (✉)
Department of Language and Literacy Education, University of British Columbia, Vancouver, BC, Canada
e-mail: margot.filipenko@ubc.ca

J. Naslund
Education Library, University of British Columbia, Vancouver, BC, Canada
e-mail: joanne.naslund@ubc.ca

L. Siegel
Department of Educational and Counselling Psychology, and Special Education, University of British Columbia, Vancouver, BC, Canada

Each September 36 students enter the PBL cohort for their 11-month elementary teacher preparation program. In keeping with the PBL philosophy of student-centered learning, preservice teachers are assigned to small group tutorials of twelve students. The goals of problem based learning include the ability to identify critical issues, to be self-directed, to integrate knowledge from different disciplines, to evaluate ideas and research, and to develop content knowledge. To achieve these goals our preservice teachers are put into small group tutorials where they have opportunities to work together to analyze problem(s) routinely faced in professional, educational practice. Our current class of PBL preservice teachers will complete their Bachelor of Education degrees in 2015, and for over 17 years of the PBL cohort, graduates have worked with a host of faculty, school advisors, school coordinators, university instructors, researchers, and librarians. Although there have been some annual changes in our membership, a core group of faculty has continued to be involved with the cohort. We have a rich storehouse of experience and shared values and vision that has enabled us to sustain the program and more importantly reflect on our practices as teacher educators.

Our book *Problem Based Learning in Teacher Education* came about as many of our projects and initiatives have since our beginnings in 1998. During one of our bimonthly meetings, a question was raised regarding how we might reflect on what we know about problem based learning as it pertains to teacher education, how we might share our rich experiences with this particular approach to teaching and learning, and what we might learn about our own practice(s) as teacher educators in a problem based learning cohort. Specifically, we were interested in the perspectives of those working within this cohort and the ways in which these perspectives are interwoven to create our PBL teacher education program. As an introduction to our experiences shared in this book, we *set the scene* by exploring both the beginnings of the PBL teacher education cohort at the University of British Columbia – including the rationale, inspiration, and design of that first iteration of our program and the focus of our cohort today.

A New Vision for Teacher Education: Problem Based Learning in 1998

In 1998 Linda Siegel a faculty member in the Department of Educational and Counselling Psychology, and Special Education in the Faculty of Education at the University of British Columbia (UBC) launched the first year of the PBL cohort in the teacher education program at UBC. The following are her reflections on her introduction to PBL as an approach to teaching and learning and her work to implement PBL in teacher education at UBC.

In the Beginning: Linda Siegel

My introduction to PBL was as a faculty member at the McMaster University Medical School. When I first heard about it, like most people I was very skeptical. I knew that physicians were required to develop factual knowledge about the bones, muscles, and organs of the body, diseases, medications, treatments, etc. I wondered why medical students were required to go beyond lectures and textbooks. However, as I became involved in the PBL program, I realized that medicine was more than facts. As an example, I remember one of the original problems used in the program. It was the case of a 3-year-old girl who experienced second-degree burns. Of course, the students needed to learn about burns and how to treat them. That was the sort of information that could be obtained from textbooks. However, there was a 3-year-old girl who had to be in the hospital and separated, at least part of the day, from her parents. The students had to consider this 3-year-old girl and her thoughts and feelings. They had to learn about separation anxiety. The hypothetical girl became a "real" 3-year-old, with whom they would need to interact if she was one of their patients. They had to think about the way that they would talk to her and explain what was happening. The students needed to reflect on why this accident happened and how it could be prevented and what their role was as physicians. The students were encouraged to understand the perspective of the parents – what counseling might they need and how could they be supported. The students developed an understanding of the treatment of burns and who was responsible in the hospital system. The role of the tutor was to guide them to recognize the issues and where to find information about them. They learned about the role of other health professionals, psychologists, and social workers. These issues are just some of those variables that were part of the problem. I quickly recognized the value of this approach to learning; it was more than just facts; there was a context for learning, opportunities for the development of dispositions for inquiry, and an understanding of the importance of working collaboratively.

When I became a member of the Faculty of Education at the University of British Columbia, I was convinced that the PBL approach to learning was not only appropriate for teacher education but also essential for helping new teachers develop dispositions for inquiry and collaboration: essential in the increasingly diverse classrooms emerging on the cusp of the twenty-first century. In the existing traditional programs of that time, the preservice teachers spent much of their time in large classes and had relatively little contact with schools and classrooms. Additionally, little time was given to discussion of educational issues that they would be facing as new teachers. My experiences with PBL at McMaster University convinced me there must be more time for discussion, interaction, and collaboration and more time for the preservice teachers to participate in the life of school communities. Thus, with the support and encouragement of Charles Ungerleider, the Associate Dean for Teacher Education, and Nancy Sheehan, the Dean of the Faculty of Education at UBC, we were able to launch the first problem based learning cohort in teacher education in the fall of 1998.

The Proposed PBL Program

The PBL option in the UBC Teacher Education program used a case-based tutorial approach to develop preservice teachers' abilities to identify and address issues involved in teaching in the elementary school grades. In the fall of 1998, thirty-six preservice teachers were organized into four groups of nine; a tutor facilitated each group. The tutors included three teachers and a vice-principal from the Richmond School District. That first year there were nine cases/problems that served as the framework for learning. Preservice teachers had two weeks to work on issues surfaced in each case. The tutorial groups met on Monday and Friday of each week, for three hours. There were five faculty members who were specialists in curriculum areas such as special education, mathematics and science, language arts (reading and writing), art and music, and social studies. We had occasional sessions on specialized topics such as phonological awareness and early literacy. The resource people were available during the period September to March. On the last day of the two-week case cycle, the preservice teachers collaboratively presented their solutions to the issues in the case.

Improving the amount of time preservice teachers spent in the school context was also an important consideration as we planned the new PBL cohort. To that end, we introduced a new practicum that required our PBL preservice teachers to be in schools one day a week for the duration of the teacher education program. Additionally, we increased the short two-week practicum to three weeks.

Resistance

There were tensions and some opposition to the establishment of a PBL cohort within the Faculty of Education. These tensions and opposition focused on problem based learning as a pedagogical approach: How could preservice teachers learn without attending lectures and without completing assignments in the subject areas? Additionally, PBL was a new concept for many preservice teachers who were accustomed to the lecture format and working alone. However, over time, most preservice teachers stated their preference for the PBL pedagogy over the traditional model of teaching and learning.

For those instructors accustomed to traditional teaching, it was and is tempting to provide lectures and assigned readings. However, working with the tutors who modeled both how to facilitate the group process and, specifically, how to help students understand and recognize important concepts as they arose in the course of a case issue or problem helped ameliorate this problem somewhat. However, to some extent the problem still remains particularly with new instructors – not really understanding the student-centered nature of PBL.

Moving Forward: PBL Today

In Canada, children from families with linguistic minority backgrounds form a substantial and rapidly growing proportion of the school population. In the school districts in the metropolitan area where we work, more than 148 different language groups are represented in the schools (Vancouver School Board: Planning and Enrolment Trends, 2013). In some classrooms, more than a dozen different home languages are spoken, and in many classrooms, the majority of children speak a language other than English, the language of instruction, at home. The Canadian context in many ways reflects global trends – according to UNESCO (2011), worldwide there are "214 million people now living outside their country of origin" (p. 75), and the movement of people is expected to increase.

Responding to a need to reimagine our teacher education program and to begin to meet the needs of our increasingly diverse student population, the Faculty of Education at our university introduced a revised Bachelor of Education program designed to prepare teachers with the necessary expertise to teach in our challenging and diverse classrooms. This revised program was introduced in the fall of 2012. Concurrently, with the start of the revised B.Ed. program in 2012, the administration of the teacher education program instigated the coupling of our problem based learning (PBL) cohort with another cohort focused on teaching English language learners (TELL). The cohort that resulted from this merger was titled TELL through PBL (TELL/PBL). The focus of this cohort is supporting English language learners through a problem based learning teaching methodology.

Aims of This Book

This book highlights what problem based learning in a teacher education program looks like. We aim to present a view of this constructivist approach to teaching and learning, specifically as it pertains to teacher education. We explore both the strengths and tensions inherent in this approach and offer our PBL cohort in teacher education as an example of PBL in practice.

In this volume, the experiences are drawn from participants in our PBL teacher education cohort at the University of British Columbia: researchers, tutors, resource/subject area specialists, faculty advisors, school administrators, sponsor teachers, education librarians, and preservice teachers. All authors have been or are actively involved in the problem based learning cohort in our teacher education program. The book draws on much practical expertise as well as extensive research literature.

Structure of the Book

The book is organized into four major parts, each of which includes chapters from different perspectives. Some contributors explore the tensions and challenges of working within this particular model of teaching and learning: both on-campus and in the school districts. Others report on research projects conducted with the PBL cohort. All are deeply committed to teacher education and to PBL.

Part I, entitled "Dispositions for Inquiry," examines both our foundation in constructivism and our belief that teachers must develop dispositions for inquiry, that is, a set of attitudes or a particular stance toward the world. Jeannie Kerr, an emerging scholar in Educational Studies who is currently working as an adjunct teaching professor and faculty associate with TELL/PBL at the University of British Columbia, takes up this theme in her chapter by drawing on Aoki's distinction between curriculum-as-plan and curriculum-as-lived to complicate the discussion on the ways that PBL theory and methodology is understood broadly in the scholarship and the ways it aligns and contrasts with the theoretical framework in the TELL/PBL cohort. In their chapter Jo-Anne Naslund, an academic librarian serving elementary and secondary preservice teachers in the Education Library at UBC, and Lori Prodan, an elementary school teacher and adjunct teaching professor in the Department of Language and Literacy Education at the University of British Columbia, discuss how dispositions for inquiry are understood and lived in our PBL cohort.

Part II, entitled "Collaborations: Working Together," offers the reader an exploration of the many and varied ways collaboration has been enacted in our PBL cohort and examines and locates areas of tension between the many and varied participants. For example, when the Teaching English Language Learners (TELL) cohort was coupled with the problem based learning cohort, it required close collaboration between faculty who had been working primarily in the area of teaching English language learners and faculty working within the PBL cohort. The first chapter of this part by Steven Talmy and Margaret Early, two Associate Professors and specialists in teaching English language learners in the Department of Language and Literacy Education at UBC, reports on their study that examined the challenges faced in merging these two cohorts. In the following chapter, Margot Filipenko, a Professor of Teaching in the Department of Language and Literacy and the coordinator of the TELL/PBL cohort, takes up this discussion by describing the ongoing process of designing and revising problem based learning cases to reflect the newly revised B.Ed. program and the introduction of TELL content into cases (a process which, while collaborative, was and is often strained by competing interests). The chapter by Kathryn D'Angelo, a District Administrator in the Richmond School District; Gail Krivel-Zacks, a member of the Faculty of Education at Vancouver Island University and private pediatric and adolescent counselor focusing on children with exceptionalities; and Catherine Johnson, a Program Coordinator of Teacher Education at Simon Fraser University, takes up the broader picture by outlining the development of the collaborative partnerships between the Richmond

School District and the University of British Columbia needed for the governance of the PBL cohort. This part ends with a chapter by Carolyn Russo, a Richmond School District Grade 2 teacher, and Nicky Freeman, a TELL/PBL preservice teacher, on negotiating difference as they developed a close collaborative relationship during the school-based practica.

Part III, "Fostering Active Learning," takes the reader into the heart of problem based learning with chapters reflecting on explorations and inquiries that have been taken up by participants within the TELL/PBL cohort. Frank Baumann, a former elementary school principal, and Monika Tarampi, a teacher-consultant in special needs education, and Lori Prodan, an elementary school teacher and adjunct teaching professor, discuss the multiple and sometimes conflicting roles of the tutors in supporting and facilitating preservice teachers' diverse learning needs. In the next chapter, Lori Prodan explores some of the issues that arose as she transitioned from working as an instructor of traditionally taught courses, a role that posits the instructor as holding expert knowledge, to the role of a tutor in a PBL cohort where the function is to foster student-centered learning. Then, Jo-Anne Naslund examines the academic librarian's relationship with TELL/PBL and how the underlying pedagogies of PBL fundamental for student engagement and case-based learning align with and complement the academic mission of libraries, librarians, and information literacy programs in higher education. In the next chapter, Anne Zavalkoff, a resource specialist from the Department of Educational Studies at UBC, writes a chapter discussing the opportunities offered by PBL in facilitating preservice teachers' explorations of social justice and anti-oppression and demonstrates the power of PBL in facilitating inquiries and learning around these complex issues. Following on, Cynthia Nicol, an Associate Professor from the Department of Education, Pedagogy and Curriculum (Mathematics), and Fil Krykorka, a teacher and graduate from the problem based learning cohort, examine what it means to learn *about* teaching through PBL pedagogy. Specifically, Cynthia and Fil address the questions: How does PBL prepare preservice teachers to teach in contexts or places different from their own personal and practicum experiences? What aspects of PBL for learning to teach can be used in the classroom for learning school subject matter such as mathematics and science? And how can land and place be inspirations for problem based learning and pedagogical inquiry? And last but not least in this part is a discussion about how best to assess preservice teachers in the TELL/PBL cohort (which is an ongoing and evolving conversation). In this final chapter in Part III, Anne Zavalkoff provides an overview and description of the ways in which our TELL/PBL cohort has worked to align our assessment practices with the problem based learning approach and, specifically, the *triple jump*, a unique form of assessment that measures both specific acquired knowledge and the problem-solving processes.

Part IV, "Reflections," is the last part and outlines the challenges and resistance to problem based learning that lie ahead. Specifically, this part articulates the concerns that permeate our TELL/PBL cohort deliberations and our concerns for the continuing existence of our TELL/PBL cohort in the existing political and financial climate.

Part I
Dispositions for Inquiry

Any discussion of problem based learning in teacher education will involve taking into account dispositions for inquiry. Several aspects of inquiry, such as asking questions, finding out, and engaging in ongoing reflection are embodied in PBL. Teachers are not merely technocrats drawing out what is already in their students. Rather they pose difficult questions and introduce difficult knowledge piquing their students' curiosity, creativity, and motivation to learn. Knowledge is not something deliverable in propositional form; rather it emerges from a learner's relation and immersion in the world and their attempts to make meaning through asking questions. As well "dispositions" – the habits of mind and stances – critical for new teachers, if they are to be nurtured, require an ongoing commitment to professional learning, openness, flexibility, and caring relationships with learners and finally enacting professional judgments that benefit student learning. Not only are we interested in why "problem based learning" is a significant pedagogy in teacher education but more importantly to consider the "lived experience" of PBL in the education of new teachers at the University of British Columbia and how the TELL/PBL program aligns and contrasts with the theoretical framework.

Our examination of the theoretical framing of PBL demonstrates it is grounded in a web of practices and commitments to experiential constructivist learning theory and pedagogy with an emphasis on Socratic dialogue and inquiry. In this section, constructivist learning theory, Deweyan experiential learning theory, Socratic dialogue, and other applicable theoretical underpinnings such as the motivational aspects for student learning as theorized through principles of Rogers' client-centered therapy and resonances with Gadamerian philosophical hermeneutics are explored. Our overview will help clarify terms, define positions, and consider relevant scholarship about PBL programs. In addition, we will specifically apply these to some of the critical goals and outcomes of teacher education and in particular within a teacher education cohort at UBC with respect to the complexity of teaching and to the diversity of "learners" in our changing school environments.

Some of our conversations inevitably open up contested areas and especially areas for debate. Is PBL appropriate and most effective for a teacher education program? What are professional dispositions and in what way are they of significance for teaching practice? Can professional dispositions be fostered and nurtured in beginning teachers? If so how? What import do these dispositions have for interdisciplinarity and the messy context of professional practice? It is hoped that by highlighting the research literature, this will contribute to and enrich our thinking as teacher educators as we discover, uncover, and make meaning of problem based learning and dispositions for inquiry in teacher education. Ultimately, does a PBL cohort help fulfill the promise of more meaningful teacher learning and ultimately result in educating more effective teachers? We do know that we have learned immensely from our students. We remain inspired by their commitment to inquiry, to professional collaboration, and to student-centered learning, as well as by their ability to articulate those commitments. In fact, it may be reasonable to conclude that PBL fosters essential dispositions required for professional practice all the while recognizing the complexity of teaching and learning.

Chapter 2
Exploring Theoretical Frameworks of Problem Based Learning Through Aoki's *Curriculum-as-Plan* and *Curriculum-as-Lived*

Jeannie Kerr

Introduction

Before getting to the discussion, it's important for me to be clear about my relation to the subject and the place from which I write. I am an emerging theorist and scholar in educational studies/curriculum theory and have been teaching in the Teacher Education Program in many of the cohorts at UBC since 2010. I consider place and relationships as fundamental to my work in education and acknowledge that I do this work as a first-generation settler on unceded, traditional, and ancestral Coast Salish territory.[1] I generally teach courses that consider the social experience and complications of schooling and education through engaging issues of social equity, cultural and linguistic diversity, and place – as each relates to teaching practice. I am now in my third year working with the TELL-PBL cohort as an instructor teaching a recently developed course *Aboriginal Education in Canada* and this year also teaching the course *Teaching and Learning with English Language Learners*. I accepted a contract position as tutor and faculty advisor in the program this academic year after completing my PhD. Thus I have the interesting position of having multiple roles within this cohort, and specific educational priorities in diversity and social equity, but also a scholarly practice of engaging theory and philosophy in the field of teacher education. From my experiences in the TELL-PBL cohort, I have developed a significant appreciation for the benefits of this approach and a practical sense of the complications of planning and implementing this approach in teacher education. It is from these priorities and experiences from which I write these theoretical considerations.

---

[1] I use the term "settler" following the work of Paulette Regan (2010) to denote my social position as a person that has settled on indigenous lands but also to forefront my educational priorities in decolonization. The Coast Salish people in the territory in which I live and work are the Musqueam, Squamish, and Tsleil-Waututh First Nations.

J. Kerr (✉)
Department of Educational Studies, University of British Columbia, Vancouver, BC, Canada
e-mail: Jeannie.kerr@ubc.ca

Framing the Discussion: Curriculum-as-Plan and Curriculum-as-Lived

Ted Aoki makes this distinction of *curriculum-as-plan* and *curriculum-as-lived* partially to bring into relief the multiplicity and complexity that emerges when educational plans are brought together with real people that breathe life and meaning into what are often abstract ideas (Aoki 1993, p. 258). Over the last 30+ years, PBL has been developing a body of scholarship that consists of both formal curricular documents, as well as the narratives of implementation of these ideas in different disciplinary contexts in real places. This book continues to build on this tradition and engages in a *complicated conversation*[2] of PBL as it is being lived in a teacher education program at UBC. Aoki suggests that to truly understand educational ideas, our formalized inquiries should consider the ways these ideas become artfully lived by people with unique histories, motives, intentions, and orientations (Aoki 1993, p. 257). In my view, this book embodies Aoki's distinctions through sharing the narratives of the people who are living the PBL curriculum here at UBC and the ways they make sense of themselves and PBL theory and methodology as they do so. In this sense, this book is a formal study of the art of living PBL in a specific teacher education cohort at UBC, and therefore I felt the theoretical framework would be best conceptualized in this way to resonate with the structure of this book.

In following through with these ideas, this chapter will be organized into three major sections. In the first section I will look at PBL in a more abstract way and consider the broader discussions of theory and practice that underlie PBL programs as discussed in the scholarship. I will also offer some of my own thoughts on a philosophical grounding for PBL in hermeneutics. In the second section, I will move to the lived curriculum and discuss the ways that teacher education offers a unique venue for PBL. I will also consider how the educational priorities of the people living PBL curriculum in TELL-PBL have influenced a shift in the theoretical framing of PBL. In the third section, I will end this chapter with a brief summary and conclusion and some thoughts on the benefits of PBL in terms of issues of social equity.

PBL: Curriculum-as-Plan

Maggi Savin-Baden (2000) warns that attempting to define PBL and contain it within boundaries unnecessarily tends to position PBL as a progressive approach to learning set in opposition to what are deemed problematic, traditional notions of

---

[2] I use this term "complicated conversation" to draw on William Pinar's original meaning and to refer to the way Anne Phelan positions this term in teacher education as a needed conversation that "can extend current discussions to concerns about subjectivity (human agency and action), society, and historical moment" (Phelan 2011, p. 213).

learning (p. 16). To avoid this sort of dichotomous and limited understanding, she recommends seeing the key characteristics of the approach holistically and then considers PBL as ideologically located in experiential learning discourse (p. 17). In this section, I will consider PBL as emerging from a particular context and set of concerns in higher education, asking more specifically – What is PBL seen *as response to* in an ongoing consideration of the education of adult students for professional practice? In this section, I will provide the structure of PBL as a cohesive set of responsive practices that are initially identified with the work of Howard Barrows in a medical education program at McMaster University in the early 1970s and then assemble a theoretical framework that locates this set of practices.

Howard Barrows is often considered one of the founding promoters of PBL. His work started with a desire to engage medical students more thoroughly with the complexity of medical practice. Barrows' role heading the team "The Project for Learning Resources Design" worked systematically to develop the PBL approach which soon migrated to other medical schools, diverse programs of professional practice, and then moved into to the K-12 education system in multiple subject areas (Barrows and Kelson 1993, p. 6). Howard Barrows and Anne Kelson note that the PBL approach is a total and systematic response to common complaints that students in all levels of education are passive, scoring poorly on national examinations, have little world knowledge, are apathetic and disconnected, and more generally cannot retain and use what they learn in flexible ways (p. 1). The authors identify six practices/dimensions to the PBL process: (1) through posing ill-structured real-world problems, students are engaged with a process of generating, inquiring, and refining hypotheses methodically; (2) through problem design that avoids explicit objectives, students recognize that they require more knowledge/skills to "dig out" the problems themselves, and with experience in the PBL curriculum, students develop a richly elaborated base of "integrated knowledge and skills" and cognitive flexibility; (3) through teacher facilitation rather than lecture or providing answers, students develop self-directed learning skills; (4) through group structured inquiry, students develop collaboration skills and appreciate the value of multiple perspectives to address problems; (5) "overarching" across the experiences in PBL is that all processes are student-centered and geared to being interdisciplinary – having students take personal and group responsibility for their learning; and (6) through posing the question as a continual instigation, students generate self-appraisal and self-reflection habits (pp. 1–2).

A small number of scholars have concentrated on pulling out the theoretical grounding for PBL based on Barrows' commitments. Alastair McPhee (2002) distinguishes a PBL educational approach as one that provides a fully interlocking web of experiences based in *constructivism*, where the problems constitute the basis of learning (p. 62). Similarly, Wim Gijselaers (1996) states that theories in cognitive psychology on metacognition are closely aligned with PBL-based education programs (pp. 13–14). He draws on the work of Glaser (1991) which highlights that learning is a *constructive and metacognitive* process – one that requires the learner to construct knowledge and also be aware of this in a way that relies on self-monitoring of goal setting, strategy selection, and evaluation (Gijselaers 1996, p. 16).

In this theoretical orientation, the importance of social and contextual factors in learning is emphasized – pointing to the need for learning in higher education to be set in collaborative group situations and to mirror the uneven and ill-fitting nature of the real world in which the curriculum will need to be understood (p. 16). As real-world problems defy disciplinary boundaries, McPhee concludes that PBL necessarily engages an interdisciplinary educational approach (McPhee 2002, p. 63).

Savin-Baden emphasizes the similar theoretical perspective within PBL for complexity and student-centeredness as aligning with the cognitive theoretical tradition but also with the philosophical approach of Socrates and Dewey. Savin-Baden (2000) draws on Carl Rogers' *humanistic* work that marks the importance of the learner having control of the learning context (p. 7). Savin-Baden also draws on the roots of the PBL approach as locating in the philosophical tradition of Socrates via the *Socratic method*. As she notes: Socrates presented problems to students through questions, which "enabled him to help them explore their assumptions and values and the inadequacies of their proffered solutions" (p. 3). Savin-Baden also makes meaningful theoretical links to PBL through John Dewey's (1938) philosophical writing on the active requirements of knowledge generation in *experiential learning theory*. She notes we understand knowledge in this perspective "not as something that is reliable and changeless, but as something we engage with and do" and is "bound up with activity" in real-life complex contexts (pp. 4–5). In this sense, to learn with complexity is not to engage in straightforward answers but to make real-life connections to the area of study and the complexity of the ways it manifests in the world.

The focus on Dewey's *experiential learning* theory is taken up in a more detailed way, as well as linked to Carl Rogers' *client-centered therapy* (CCT), by Kareen McCaughan in her theoretical exploration of the guidelines Barrows established for PBL tutors. McCaughan (2013) points out that within Dewey's theory he explicitly addresses the behaviors of teachers that promote student inquiry, problem-solving, and self-direction and that Rogers aligns and extends Dewey's theory within a therapeutic context (p. 12). She argues that Barrows emphasized that teachers in PBL are tutors that require a mix of direct and nondirective facilitation techniques built on humanistic attitudes (p. 13). McCaughan asserts that the list of techniques Barrows suggests for tutors invites the student to self-assess by engaging more deeply using questions that probe a student's metacognition combined with statements that challenge the student to confront her own understandings. Although McCaughan points out that the focus in CCT is learning about the self, emotions, and psychological issue, CCT as considered in PBL would be focused on learning concepts in a curriculum and metacognition (p. 20). She finds the PBL tutor guidelines align well with Rogers' CCT where the therapist uses careful listening, acceptance, empathy, and reflection, and the client is encouraged to take the lead and be able to "explore and seek answers to his or her own problems" (p. 15). McCaughan notes that CCT also aligns with PBL in that there is the assertion that learning occurs for the client when a dilemma causes disequilibrium, and the client is then motivated to reorganize her thinking to regain equilibrium (p. 17).

McCaughan also finds that PBL aligns with Dewey's vast works in educational theory and philosophy – particularly commitments to scientific inquiry and within experiential philosophy. She points out that PBL methods are strikingly similar to Dewey's inquiry and problem-solving process (p. 18). She particularly notes the observation and collection of data, developing a reasoned hypothesis or ideas, experimental application and testing, and a conclusion and evaluation (p. 19). McCaughan also argues that Dewey's experientialist philosophy is based on the idea that individuals learn "truths" through this kind of structured experimentation in social groups (p. 19). McCaughan compares the focus in Dewey's ideas on the qualitative value of the freedom of the individual within democratic social contexts with PBL's student-centered, collaborative approach. For Dewey, experiential learning is significant, but it needs to be aligned with the quality of the learning experience – in this case a respect for the autonomy of the learner and avoidance of undue control (p. 19). For McCaughan, it is the student-centered and nondirective approach within the systematic PBL structures that focus on real-world messy challenges, approached systematically in collaborative (social) groups, that aligns strongly with Dewey's theoretical and philosophical ideas.

Within a broad consideration of *constructivist pedagogy*, Virginia Richardson (2003) takes a comprehensive look at the common features of educational orientations that fall under *constructivist learning theory*. From her work it is possible to locate PBL firmly within a constructivist orientation – where constructivism is generally understood as "a theory of learning or meaning making, that individuals create their own new understandings on the basis of an interaction between what they already know and believe and ideas and knowledge with which they come into contact" (Resnick 1989 in Richardson 2003, pp. 1623–24). The pedagogical practices that Richardson (2003) identifies as emerging from a comprehensive consideration of constructivist theory (student-centered, facilitative dialogue, metacognitive awareness) are also completely consistent with pedagogical practices identified in the PBL scholarship (p. 1626).

Through considering theoretical scholarship linked to PBL in its broader sense, some of the theoretical commitments are quite distinct, but I would argue that it could also be elaborated through hermeneutic scholarship. From the exploration in this chapter, PBL can be seen as grounded in a web of practices and commitments to experiential constructivist learning theory and pedagogy with an emphasis on Socratic dialogue and inquiry. In my view, the resonance of PBL with Gadamerian philosophical hermeneutics is striking. I note that this has not yet been explored in the PBL scholarship, but feel that these theoretical ideas reach out to disciplines in the humanities, and believe it would be worth exploring so as to engage PBL more broadly.

While I do not have the space to get into more depth with Gadamer's position here, I would highlight a key feature of philosophical hermeneutics as the potential for transformation of the subject (in this discussion the learner) through an event of understanding that occurs through experience (Kerr 2012, p. 373). For Gadamer, participating in experience is an ongoing integrative process where an encounter widens our horizon by overturning an existing perspective. In this view, an experience is not a thing you *have*, but something you *undergo* to overcome your subjectivity and be drawn into and changed by an encounter (Weinsheimer and Marshall 2004, xiii). In this sense, knowledge is not something deliverable in propositional form, but emerges from our relation and immersion in the world and our attempts to make meaning through asking questions. Significantly for this discussion, Gadamer emphasizes the example of Socratic dialogue as creating the conditions for the question to emerge in the learner (Gadamer 2004, p. 359). Gadamer's ideas engage the themes of real-world experience, a focus on meaning-making rather than propositional knowledge, the priority of the question to make meaning from experience, and transformational potential of the subject rather than acquisition of propositional knowledge. As such, there is strong resonance with PBL conceptual themes and Gadamerian philosophical hermeneutics, although I would argue that Gadamer would insist that there is no specific method in creating these conditions, as a Deweyan scientific method would suggest, but that setting the conditions for the question is more art than science (p. 359).

TELL-PBL: Curriculum-as-Lived

I introduced this chapter with Ted Aoki's distinction between *curriculum-as-plan* and *curriculum-as-lived* to highlight the idea that PBL will emerge as something quite unique based on the histories, priorities, and interests of the people living the curriculum. In the previous section, I provided a theoretical framework from the scholarship of PBL and provided a brief consideration of philosophical hermeneutics that might lend a philosophical and interpretative emphasis on PBL scholarship. In this section, I will consider the theoretical commitments that have emerged as PBL becomes lived in the UBC Teacher Education Program (UBC-TEP) in the TELL-PBL cohort. As Savin-Baden (2000) emphasizes, PBL has "many guises and differences" that can stem from the discipline or professional knowledge base into which it is introduced and/or the structural and pedagogical decisions that have been made during implementation (p. 16). In this case, I will initially consider the theoretical alignment of this cohort with PBL frameworks as noted in the first section. From this position, I will look more specifically at the disciplinary context of teacher education and the discourses here at UBC, as well as the priorities of the individual instructors and tutors as they are shared in this book, to frame the theoretical distinctions in TELL-PBL.

In a broad sense the theoretical positions that emerge in the TELL-PBL cohort align quite strongly with the theoretical positions identified in the PBL scholarship. The chapters in the book reveal a commitment to the PBL structures as identified in the scholarship and priority on *constructivist* theory and pedagogy and the related significance of Socratic method and the priority of the question. The chapters also reveal a priority of engaging complexity through the structure of the cases themselves as they embody interdisciplinarity through the messy context of professional practice. In this sense, the emphasis on experiential learning theory and collaborative learning is present in the theoretical framing of the work. However, also emerging in the chapters, and based on my own experience, are disciplinary concerns that move the theoretical framework in TELL-PBL beyond the theoretical frameworks identified within the PBL scholarship.

I would argue that implementing PBL into a program of teacher education presents a complication to PBL theory and methodology, not found when compared to other professional programs such as medicine or engineering. More specifically, teacher education programs are not only concerned with the teaching and learning of preservice teachers per se but also can be seen as spaces that seek to *represent* teaching and learning itself. In this way, tutors and instructors engage reflectively with preservice teachers on the process of PBL for their own learning, but also as educationally generative in their practicum placements and their ideas of professional practice. In my view, the degree to which PBL theory might align with their practicum placement, and also the preservice teachers' own educational history and beliefs about education, is something that everyone grapples with throughout the program. The metacognitive dimensions of engaging with PBL, I find, are quite pronounced in conversations with preservice teachers. The professional focus is on teaching and learning, and thus PBL is not only a method to the preservice teachers but becomes an educational commitment to be engaged in both personally and as an emerging professional.

The TELL-PBL cohort is also located within the UBC Teacher Education Program (UBC-TEP) that has recently been entirely reframed emphasizing *inquiry*. I would argue the sense of inquiry in this place emerges from a history of critique in the field of education and the preparation of teachers for practice. From the on-line text of the UBC-TEP regarding inquiry shown below, it is possible to see the commitment to inquiry as moral and intellectual open-ended activity in contrast with more systematic and methodical approaches:

Inquiry Seminar (I) is designed to engender:

- An understanding of teaching as a moral and intellectual activity requiring inquiry, judgment, and engagement with multiple others – students, parents, colleagues, and scholarly community
- An appreciation of the importance of research in understanding curriculum, teaching, and learning
- A desire to engage in one's own educational inquiries – to become students of teaching (Faculty of Education, University of British Columbia. [n.d.])

In my view, the form of inquiry prioritized in UBC-TEP emerges in response to educational discourses that critique technical rationality and forefront teaching as moral endeavor. Donald Schön defines technical rationality as "instrumental problem solving made rigorous by the application of scientific theory and technique" (Schön 1987, p. 3). The idea of teachers' application of formulas, rubrics, and checklists that are derived from a body of *expert* objective knowledge that teachers *possess* had been a widely accepted notion in Western ideas of teaching in the twentieth century (Furlong 2000, p. 17). Philosopher Joseph Dunne takes up Schön's critiques in the context of teaching and teacher education and conceptually links his work to Aristotle and postmodern critique. He focuses on teaching as a complex, moral engagement that resists reductive technical-rational approaches, but instead relies on attentiveness to the particulars and the moral nature of teaching as a human engagement, and an ability to undertake practical judgment anew in each aspect of practice (Dunne 1993, p. 250). Anne Phelan (2005) argues that the intent of inquiry in teacher education "is to make learning to teach, and teaching itself, a complex and uncertain enterprise that demands, ongoing, thoughtful inquiry and discernment" (p. 340). Each new experience invites reconsideration and reconstruction that illuminates many aspects of practice (p. 343).

I would argue that this context and history in teacher education provides a different theoretical orientation to inquiry than the Deweyan method highlighted in PBL scholarship. The inquiry orientation fosters an opportunity for preservice teachers to grapple with a morally based profession that offers no systematic answer to complexity. Within the specific TELL-PBL cohort, the curriculum is interdisciplinarily organized around the cases, which are designed in ways that invite preservice teachers to inquire into key educational concepts as they emerge in the messy context of teaching practice. Concepts return repeatedly throughout the case cycles, thus inviting preservice teachers to reconsider and re-imagine the complications of lived concepts and their own evolving understandings. While there is a somewhat formalized and methodical approach to working with each case, preservice teachers are invited to understand the case in more detailed and practical ways through their questions – not to solve the case. Through the cases, the context is set for preservice teachers to understand the challenges of practice more holistically, understand and illuminate key concepts in practice more knowledgeably and personally, and continually engage with more refined questions in practice. This process is theoretically distinct from the PBL Deweyan-influenced scientific method of inquiry that highlights the steps of hypothesis, experimental method, evaluation, and conclusion.

The TELL-PBL cohort draws on instructors from different departments (Curriculum and Pedagogy, Educational Studies, Language and Literacy, and Educational Psychology), as well as directly through the Teacher Education Program (Aboriginal Education and Inquiry Seminars) for its programming and interdisciplinary instructional focus – thus bringing together many (and at times competing) educational priorities and commitments as embodied by the various instructors. A clear concern among the instructors is negotiating the tension between engaging processes that reproduce current inequitable social relations and identifying and critically questioning such processes (Giroux 1997, p. 108). Throughout the chapters in this book, it is clear that a number of instructors in TELL-PBL identify with the desire to engage preservice teachers in disrupting educational assumptions and engaging critically with cultural and linguistic diversity, issues of social justice and relations to place and the more-than-human others. I too share these priorities emerging from critical pedagogy, critical discourse studies, and indigenous scholarship, but it is at this juncture that TELL-PBL moves from a purely constructivist and experiential pedagogy prominent in PBL scholarship, focused solely on student learning, to reintroduce the role of the teacher more substantively than is present in other PBL frameworks.

Gert Biesta takes on the notion of constructivist theory and pedagogy quite critically in a recent article and ironically reveals to me that TELL-PBL is actually more involved in teaching than I previously would have thought. Biesta acknowledges there is a need to shift from instructional paradigms focused on the transmission of content knowledge but he expresses concern that constructivism implies teachers have nothing to teach and only draws out what is already in the student (Biesta 2013, p. 451). I recognize these concerns and complications within the TELL-PBL cohort, in that the course instructors admittedly have something to teach within their own disciplinary areas that come from complicating those things that preservice teachers feel they already know about education, diversity and society. As Deborah Britzman points out: "Teachers bring to their work their own deep investments in and ambivalence about what a teacher is and does ... [yet] the teacher's work brings new and conflictive demands that well exceed the resources of her or his school biography" (Britzman 2003, p. 2). It is this excess and disruption that the instructors grapple with in their work in TELL-PBL – myself included. In this role, the instructor is not merely drawing out what is already in the preservice teacher but is also intentionally disrupting and complicating the preservice teacher's unacknowledged assumptions and commitments by introducing something entirely new. It is this piece that moves beyond the tenets of constructivism, which holds that learning is within the student.

Biesta points out that the activity of teaching is to introduce something that comes from the outside and adds rather than just confirms what is already present in the student (Biesta 2013, p. 453). He makes the distinction of *learning from* and being *taught by* as radically different phenomenological experiences based on the willingness of the student to engage in what is new and challenging (p. 457). He acknowledges the critique that what is taught is not necessarily what is learned and instead frames being *taught by* as receiving the gift of teaching: "To be taught – to be open to receiving the gift of teaching – thus means being able to give such interruptions a place in one's understanding and one's being" (p. 459). Biesta advocates seeing teachers not merely as instructional resources drawing out what is already in the student but as those who pose difficult questions and introduce difficult knowledge, in a context where they are invited to be open to the gift of teaching and welcome what is at times unsettling (pp. 459–460).

In my view, the course instructors in TELL-PBL seek to open preservice teachers to being *taught by* them in this sense. This is done through activities that seek to cause disequilibrium within course seminars and subject area workshops. An example of this is the Place-Based Relational Educational Autobiography that was developed as a workshop during orientation week and has been in place for two academic years. The goal of this activity is to have the preservice teachers connect to their assumptions and unstated educational commitments and then narrate their educational biographies through text, visuals and audio. The purpose of the activity is to have this biography available for instructors to use with preservice teachers as a way to narrate their emotional/intellectual educational landscape and also document shifts in their educational commitments after having engaged in activities meant to disrupt by introducing something that challenges their ideas. Within PBL scholarship disequilibrium is sought through the cases to inspire motivation and learning. The TELL-PBL program promotes disequilibrium through instructor activities that help guide preservice teachers through what will be presumed to be resisted course content. Although the course instructors commonly use the title "resource specialists" to describe their work with preservice teachers, and as a way to emphasize student activity and responsibility, I would argue there is actually theoretically more going on in terms of teaching than that label would imply.

The centrality of the question and interdisciplinary focus in TELL-PBL is very similar in structure to the PBL model. However, it offers a different twist on the popular idea of Socratic questioning which provides a model of *facilitator* or *guide on the side* rather than teacher. I still find that the language of *facilitator* is used within the cohort but that teaching is more implicitly in play and not as explicitly acknowledged. The continual focus on refining and reframing educational questions is the primary activity within the case structure and tutorial activities. The questions emerge from the preservice teachers through Socratic dialogue with tutors and instructors, but the cases themselves are structured and worded so that specific questions are likely to emerge. Such questions may emerge from those new to specific disciplinary areas; others remain and are reformulated by those who have been deeply engaged for considerable periods of time with these disciplines. The tutors are provided with these *planned for questions* so as to guide the tutorial dialogues. I would argue that this is similar to the ways that Sharon Todd is able to show that Socratic dialogue is in fact *planned teaching* and not simply *facilitated learning*. She argues that the moment where Socrates demonstrates to Meno that learning does not happen through didactic teaching, but through questions he poses to a "slave boy," and this is in fact Socrates teaching Meno of this idea through persuasion and demonstration (Todd 2003, pp. 21–25). It is this meta-level where the questions in TELL-PBL are already known to the "teacher"; yet they are skillfully brought out in the learner through tutorials, activities and in-class presentations that disrupt and complicate the presented texts, and make this process quite unique. It is a PBL approach that brings a more active sense of teaching within a case based context.

Summary and Conclusion

Through drawing on Aoki's distinction between *curriculum-as-plan* and *curriculum-as-lived*, I have attempted to complicate the discussion of the ways that PBL theory and methodology is understood quite broadly in the scholarship, and the ways it aligns and contrasts with the theoretical framework in the TELL-PBL teacher education program at UBC. My review of prominent PBL scholarship revealed a theoretical framework that emphasizes constructivist theory and pedagogy. PBL methodologically is comprised of a mutually reinforcing set of practices that have strong resonance in constructivism but also Deweyan experiential learning theory and Socratic dialogue – as a reflection of the pedagogical priority of the question in PBL. The motivational aspects for student learning were theorized through principles of Rogers' client-centered therapy. I concluded this review by drawing out some resonances with Gadamerian philosophical hermeneutics, to highlight the ways that PBL might have resonance with disciplines in the humanities. In the TELL-PBL cohort, the PBL *curriculum-as-lived* shares these priorities, structures and theoretical framing but also moves beyond it. The disciplinary context of teacher education offers a unique consideration of PBL as both methodology and professional practice for preservice teachers. The TELL-PBL cohort is immersed in an inquiry program, with many instructors forefronting a critical lens on education itself and introducing practices within PBL that resonate with these priorities and context. In my view, these practices influence a shift in the PBL framework to admit a more implicit but necessary role for the value of teaching within the theoretical framing of the TELL-PBL program.

In my *lived* experience of working in various roles with the TELL-PBL cohort, I have found an amazing opportunity to engage meaningfully and interdisciplinarily with preservice teachers. I have taught in other cohorts in an inquiry-centered program, yet in my experience it is this PBL case format that has brought greater opportunities for transformative learning in preservice teachers. The set of interrelated practices resonate with my theoretical priorities. As instructors and tutors in TELL-PBL, we come together around the preservice teachers – we think about how the cases can bring out certain fundamental disciplinary concerns and questions – and also the challenges they may face in trying to understand discourses that will be new for them. This is certainly not an easy process, particularly as the larger structures of higher education tend to perpetuate disciplinary divides and limit instructor collaboration. I am impressed that the TELL-PBL cohort has come up with creative ways to work within the existing structures and implement this program. I am writing this chapter as I see the great potential in PBL methodology to contribute to a greatly needed transformation of our educational system.

References

Aoki, T. (1993). Legitimating lived curriculum: Towards a curricular landscape of multiplicity. *Journal of Curriculum and Supervision, 8*(3), 255–268.
Barrows, H., & Kelson, A. (1993). *Problem-based learning: A total approach to education.* Urbana-Champaign: University of Illinois Press.
Biesta, G. (2013). Receiving the gift of teaching: From 'learning from' to 'being taught by'. *Studies in Philosophy and Education, 32,* 449–461.
Britzman, D. P. (2003). *Practice makes practice: A critical study of learning to teach,* (Rev. ed.). Albany: State University of New York Press.
Dewey, J. (1938). *Experience and education.* New York: Macmillan.
Dunne, J. (1993). *Back to the rough ground: Practical judgment and the lure of technique.* Notre Dame: University of Notre Dame Press.
Faculty of Education, University of British Columbia. (n.d.). *Course outline for EDUC 450-inquiry seminar I.* Retrieved from: http://teach.educ.ubc.ca/students/courses/inquiry/educ-450/

Furlong, J. (2000). Intuition and the crisis in teacher professionalism. In T. Atkinson & G. Claxton (Eds.), *The intuitive practitioner: On the value of not always knowing what one is doing* (pp. 15–31). Buckingham: Open University Press.

Gadamer, H. G. (2004). *Truth and method*, (J. Weinsheimer & D. G. Marshall, 2nd ed., Trans. and Rev. ed.). New York: Continuum.

Giroux, H. (1997). *Pedagogy and the politics of hope: Theory, culture and schooling*. Boulder: Westview Publishing.

Gijselaers, W. H. (1996, Winter). Connecting problem based practices with educational theory. *New Directions for Teaching and Learning, 68*, 13–21.

Glaser, R. (1991). The maturing of the relationship between the science of learning and cognition and educational practice. *Learning and Instruction, 1*(2), 129–144.

Kerr, J. (2012). Promoting dialogue on teacher professionalism: Opening possibilities through Gadamer's aesthetic judgment and play metaphor. In C. Ruitenberg (Ed.), *Philosophy of education 2012* (pp. 367–375). Urbana-Champaign: Philosophy of Education Society.

McCaughan, K. (2013). Barrows' integration of cognitive and clinical psychology in PBL tutor guidelines. *Interdisciplinary Journal of Problem Based Learning, 7*(1), 11–23.

McPhee, A. (2002). Problem-based learning in initial teacher education: Taking the agenda forward. *Journal of Educational Enquiry, 3*(1), 60–78.

Phelan, A. M. (2005). A fall from (someone else's) certainty: Recovering practical wisdom in teacher education. *Canadian Journal of Education, 28*(3), 339–358.

Phelan, A. M. (2011). Towards a complicated conversation: Teacher education and the curriculum turn. *Pedagogy, Culture & Society, 19*(2), 207–220. doi:10.1080/14681366.2011.582257.

Regan, P. (2010). *Unsettling the settler within: Indian residential schools, truth telling, and reconciliation in Canada*. Vancouver: UBC Press.

Resnick, L. B. (1989). *Knowing, learning, and instruction: Essays in honor of Robert Glaser*. Hillsdale: L. Erlbaum Associates.

Richardson, V. (2003). Constructivist pedagogy. *Teachers College Record, 105*(9), 1623–1640.

Savin-Baden, M. (2000). *Problem-based learning in higher education: Untold stories*. Buckingham: The Society for Research in Higher Education and Open University Press.

Schön, D. (1987). *Educating the reflective practitioner: Toward a new design for teaching and learning in the professions*. San Francisco: Jossey-Bass.

Todd, S. (2003). *Learning from the other: Levinas, psychoanalysis, and ethical possibilities in education*. Albany: State University of New York Press.

Weinsheimer, J., & Marshall, D. G. (2004). Translators' preface (xi–xix). In H. G. Gadamer (Ed.), *Truth and method* (2nd ed.). New York: Continuum.

Chapter 3
Dispositions for Inquiry

Jo-Anne Naslund and Lori Prodan

Introduction

A shared belief among many scholars and educators is that teachers need to be "inquirers into professional practice". A teacher needs to have the capacity to consider the effects of their teaching on student learning and to question their own teaching routines, practices and assumptions (Reid 2010). Current conversations about teacher learning and stories of teacher inquiry reveal that *dispositions*, a set of attitudes or a particular stance towards the world, incline professionals to improve their practice (Halbert et al. 2013). Furthermore, the development of social learning networks enables and supports dispositions for inquiry (Brown and Thomas 2008). One question of importance for teacher educators is how to create a "culture of inquiry" and systematically support preservice teachers as they develop these dispositions.

To begin this discussion, we consider research literature about inquiry and dispositions for teaching. As well, we include several findings from a UBC research study of the PBL cohort conducted over 2 years (2012–2013). In the final part of the chapter, Lori Prodan, a PBL tutor, adds to the discussion by means of her reflections on the learning journey she and her tutorial group have been on together. This multi-voiced narrative heightens our understanding of inquiry, especially as embodied in a PBL cohort and how PBL engenders within beginning teachers a clear personal and professional investment in inquiry.

Dispositions for inquiry are an essential "mindset" in learning to become a teacher. When preservice teachers commit to being part of a "culture of inquiry",

---

J. Naslund (✉)
Education Library, University of British Columbia, Vancouver, BC, Canada
e-mail: joanne.naslund@ubc.ca

L. Prodan
Vancouver School District 39, Vancouver, BC, Canada
e-mail: lori.prodan@ubc.ca

their developing professionalism quite naturally gravitates to focus on the impact of teaching on student learning. Within the PBL cohort, both tutors and resource specialists work hard to create such a culture of inquiry. Their primary goal is to strengthen preservice teachers' professional discernment, collegiality and wise judgement (Coulter et al. 2007). By examining those dispositions for inquiry in problem based learning, our discussion invites conversations from other teacher educators, especially from those wanting to find out more about the role of inquiry and dispositions in learning to teach.

Inquiry in Problem Based Learning Teacher Education

A central tenet of PBL is "enacting inquiry", deepening understandings of teaching and learning within specific contexts. Beginning with the work of John Dewey, inquiry can be described as "learning". When teachers engage in inquiry, through the process of questioning and reflective practice, they become alert "students of education". According to Dewey, three dispositions are requisite for reflective action. These include: *open mindedness*, the active desire to listen and give full consideration to different perspectives and alternate possibilities; *responsibility,* the ability and commitment to carefully take into account personal, academic and social consequences of actions; and *wholeheartedness,* a willingness to examine one's assumptions, beliefs and results of actions critically with the intention of learning something new (1933).

Since Dewey, there have been many discussions about inquiry that demonstrate how profound, personal and complex it is (Farrell 2004; Goodman 1984; Cochran-Smith and Lytle 1993; Schon 1983; Zeichner and Liston 1987). Inquiry is not just something a person does nor is it just a technical activity or series of steps. In so many ways, inquiry is a "way of being" and consists of an array of dispositions.

So how is inquiry instrumental in learning to teach? As preservice teachers consider classroom situations presented in their cases, they ask questions, search for evidence and apply several modes of reasoning to synthesise their information and communicate their augmented knowledge. Through their Socratic dialogues about possible reasons for teacher and student actions, they begin to examine theories of teaching and learning in relationship to classroom practices (Friesen 2008; Jordan et al. 2003; Reid & O'Donoghue 2004). They begin to acquire "teaching knowledge" that is applied during their one day a week field experiences and during their practice teaching.

Inquiry provokes "professional meaning making". When a teacher acquires "the knowledge, skills and disposition to theorise systematically and rigorously about practice in different learning contexts and take appropriate action on the basis of the outcomes of enquiry", they demonstrate professional competence (Reid and O'Donoghue 2004 p. 569). Such teaching knowledge mediated within a theoretically framed workplace offers a way for teachers to engage in lifelong learning. They improve their practice by solving instructional problems and also by becoming reflective practitioners with a willingness to engage in open dialogues with trusted colleagues (Giovanelli 2003; Kincheloe 2003; Klette and Carlsten 2012; Naslund and Pennington 2011; Reid & O'Donoghue 2004; Schon 1983; Yinger 1986).

An important aspect of the PBL cohort is that inquiry forms the fundamental core of the program. The process of inquiry is the curriculum, and as the process of inquiry recurs over and over again, it becomes a habit of mind – a professional behaviour. Inquiry in PBL is unlike any employed within other elementary cohorts in the UBC teacher education program. Inquiry is not just a part of one project or a focus for a series of three inquiry seminars. Rather, inquiry is pivotal and plays a powerful role in learning to become a teacher. Therefore, the attributes of a successful inquirer – those dispositions for inquiry – become of critical interest to teacher educators. One needs to learn about how these dispositions and knowledge apply to effective teaching behaviours in the classroom (Giovannelli 2003).

Dispositions and Their Relationship to Professional Practice

The teacher education literature abounds with theoretical and philosophical discussions about dispositions for professional practice. Many programs focus primarily on teaching dispositions (Ruitenberg 2011). The National Council for Accreditation of Teacher Education (NCATE), for example, "lists dispositions, in addition to knowledge and skills, among the requirements that student teachers should meet" (Ruitenberg 2011, p. 41). So what is meant by dispositions? Are they the dispositions referred to by Dewey or something else? Is it possible to assess dispositions and if so, in what ways?

For many, the notion of dispositions is often vague lying between belief and action. According to Katz and Raths, a disposition is "an attributed characteristic of a teacher, one that summarizes the trend of a teacher's actions in particular contexts" (1985, p. 301). This "emphasizes a teacher's tendency to act in a certain way in certain professional contexts" (Ruitenberg 2011, p 42). In the NCATE glossary, dispositions are defined as: "Professional attitudes, values, and beliefs demonstrated through both verbal and non-verbal behaviors as educators interact with students, families, colleagues, and communities. These positive behaviors support student learning and development" (2010). Ruitenberg concludes that there are distinctions to be made between innate dispositions and professional dispositions (2011).

My thinking about professional dispositions was prompted by discussions that took place as part of our orientation to the UBC teacher education program. I began to think less about teacher skills and more about dispositions – that stance or likelihood an individual may engage in the act of questioning – and critically analyse theory and what it means for practice. Phelan talks about how coming together with others may allow us to turn back on ourselves in "order to reflect upon the very ideas and values that ground the (im)possibility of our thought and action" (2007 p. 59–60). Professional dispositions for teaching move well beyond a set of technocratic skills. Framed by reflective practice, critical theory and an action research perspective, professional dispositions are intellectual by nature and involve discernment, caring and wise judgement (Coulter et al 2007).

Dispositions for Inquiry Research Project (2012–2013)

The goal of the *Dispositions for Inquiry Research Project (DIRP)* (2012–2013) was to learn more about "dispositions for inquiry" and, in particular, notions of inquiry held by preservice teachers, faculty and tutors within the PBL cohort at the University of British Columbia. I wanted to find out how dispositions and experiences of inquiry relate to teaching practice and a professional "way of being" (Reid & O'Donoghue 2004) and, finally, to learn what characterizes preservice teachers' information-seeking behaviours, their critical use of resources and how they communicate and share their understandings.

The *Dispositions for Inquiry Research Project (DIRP)*, conducted over two academic years, included preservice teachers (33), three tutors and six resource persons (faculty) in the PBL cohort. All were surveyed to identify and explicate their notions of inquiry and its role in learning to become a teacher. Following the survey, individual interviews with ten PBL preservice teachers were recorded. As well, PBL tutors and resource persons (faculty) were interviewed identifying factors they considered critical for preservice teachers' success. And lastly, the preservice teachers' artefacts (case packages, presentations and e-folios) were analysed to determine some of the ways preservice teachers develop questions for inquiry, identify and critically use resources, represent/communicate their understandings and grow in their professional discernment and wise judgement.

The primary data sources for this study included a survey, transcriptions and coded analyses of audio interviews with preservice teachers, tutors and resource persons (faculty) and coded analyses of their artefacts. Throughout this chapter, the direct quotations of tutors, faculty and preservice teachers' include minor changes in grammar that have been made to their conversational speech for purposes of textual clarity. The purposes of the interview questions were to determine:

1. Preservice teachers' and faculty/tutors' notions of inquiry
2. The ways preservice teachers and faculty/tutors identified and selected research resources
3. Their use of inquiry in practice (during their practicum or school visits)
4. How they represented and communicated their understandings
5. Any missing items that may have occurred in our discussion

Preservice Teachers: Their Notions of Inquiry and Dispositions for Inquiry

From interviews with preservice teachers, their notions of inquiry revealed many similarities to those reported in the literature. They defined inquiry as a very desirable stance necessary to become the best teacher possible. They made links between inquiry and teacher professionalism and viewed inquiry as important in preparing teachers to become "extended professionals" (Schulz and Mandzuk 2005; Stenhouse 1975). Inquiry involved questioning, being curious, having a sense of wonder, being self-directed, being motivated to learn, being open to new ideas, wanting to continuously learn and being comfortable with ambiguity.

In its most basic form, the preservice teachers defined inquiry as questioning "that internal guide that urges you to find out more and that whole piece of wanting to learn … for myself when you are guided by a question when you want to know or solve a question or problem at hand and then that leads you to knowing" (Preservice Teacher (PST) 1, p. 1.2–1.3). It can be defined as "an educational itch that you have a compulsion to scratch. I guess practically speaking it is some sort of gap in your knowledge, or skill set or social sphere or relationships, some gap that is not limited to just information it could be a relationship or it can be some skill you need to do something you can't. Inquiry is filling that gap" (PST2 p. 1.6). "It's a lot about questioning and asking the right questions. From the teachers' point of view it's allowing the questions to return from the students. It is back and forth really with the teacher and the students exploring together" (PST3, p. 1.11). "Inquiry for me is questioning or critical thinking … people who engage in inquiry they tend to be a lot more inquisitive or like questioning. I think to be good at inquiry learning or critical thinking you have to be able to come up with a basic understanding of a concept and then question everything you know. Or everything you think you know, every statement you come up with, goes deeper into it and figure out how you know it's true" (PST4, p. 1.17–1.18).

Many defined inquiry as having the opportunity to create your own learning experiences "not wanting to have things necessarily spoon fed to you. You like to create your own structure of learning and then you'll find your area of interest and you'll go after it" (PST1, p. 1.1.). Several suggested that inquiry as part of their PBL program was nothing like their post-secondary undergraduate education where they may have excelled at textbook reading and the "traditional approach" to learning. "When I went out into the real working world, I think I was shocked by the reality of undefined project goals or expectations. You can't necessarily always have the nice little box if this is what you do then you'll be recognized. This really shaped how I began to approach thinking and problem solving" (PST1, p. 1.2–1.3). "I think you have to be an active learner because you can always just ask questions but you don't always need to necessarily take the initiative to find out. … So finding out for yourself is very important" (PST5, p. 1.10). "I would describe it as a way where you take responsibility for your own learning and even though we are all in the same cohort not all of us are learning the same things because we are finding our own sources and discovering something about each thing we are studying" (PST6, p. 1.12).

Faculty and Tutors: Their Notions of Inquiry and Dispositions for Inquiry

Compared to the preservice teachers, the definitions of inquiry and dispositions explicated by faculty and tutors were more divergent, complex and contextualised according to their teaching experiences and perspectives as teacher educators. Their definitions of inquiry expanded upon the idea of questioning and curiosity to include ideas about "not holding too firm to ideas and assumptions" and "being open to other perspectives" (Faculty1, 2012).

Inquiry was defined as "an activism", "wanting to know other perspectives" and engaging with other people, "challenging ideas" (Faculty (F) 2, 2012). It meant "anti-dogma", "being skeptical in a good way", "not being lazy" (F3, 2012) and having the ability to "challenge your own identity" (F1, 2012). The process of inquiry was described as "an open ended way of learning" and included the "whole aspect of reflectiveness" and "becoming quite good reflective thinkers" (Tutor (T) 1, 2012). It meant having the "willingness to admit you are wrong" and the ability to be flexible where "they need to be ready to go with those things that are coming at them that are unknown ... willing to take risks and sometimes not know ... giving it a name like PBL was great for me it was almost a confirmation and then taking it to another level with people in the education program" (T1, 2012).

Inquiry was described as asking "what am I going to do, what am I going to say, where am I going in order to justify this. When I am challenged about the advocacy of my decisions, the inquiry is looking into the best ideas I could use as tools to communicate with everyone in that educational community" (T2, 2012). "There are a set of attitudes that give life to inquiry" and when you inquire into things it brings things back to "life for yourself" (T2, 2012). Schooling is "an ongoing process" and to be on the "cutting edge of the conversation, be involved in the conversation we all have a need to engage at that level in our profession, we want to know our challenges, possible "outcomes, next steps to do better" (T1, 2012). "I really go back to that point that inquiry implies, we don't know" and the "end point of the inquiry for me is knowing what I am going to do" (T2, 2012).

Enhancing Dispositions: Some Pedagogical Approaches

"The end point of the inquiry for me is knowing what I am going to do" (T2, 2012). Wise judgement and informed professional discernment are the ultimate goals of PBL. Of real import is what Foucault would term as "problematisation" which means approaching all givens as questions and as a consequence enacting a specific work of thought (Healey 2001). Through inquiry, preservice teachers learn to become teachers. They learn to find out and recognise that as an individual, they are situated, interpreted and prejudiced. By exposing preservice teachers to this type of thinking and reflection, their professional dispositions can be awakened so that they embrace and value learning and discovering answers for themselves.

There are a variety of pedagogical approaches that facilitate inquiry and enhance dispositions for inquiry. These are intentional approaches. They focus on trust building, diverse instructional groupings, transferred leadership and shared teaching roles.

One important approach in PBL is to establish an ethos or culture of inquiry. PBL preservice teachers participate as members of a community of learners. Each tutorial group is unique; however, common to all is a code of conduct endorsed by all tutors where preservice teachers are expected to work together, respect and help each other and recognise each other's differences. This environment of trust has been recognised as important in the development of a culture of inquiry.

In addition, tutors employ a Socratic method to provoke thoughtful dialogue. Again an atmosphere of trust is essential, as open discussions are critical. All questions are welcomed and valued. Careful listening is enacted. They are obligated to listen and to hear out opinions and ideas that may be different than their own. During the deep reading of the cases, preservice teachers consider a wide variety of perspectives and feel safe to share their own perspectives. The underlying rules for discussion display civility and respect when conversing with their peers, faculty, tutors and librarians.

Similarly, in their schools, the creation of a safe and caring learning environment for preservice teachers, school and faculty advisors and students is important. The school should be a place where preservice teachers and school advisors may talk openly about their teaching – questioning their actions and reflecting on their practices. Within this workplace, the environment could be described as one where your colleagues are inclusive and tolerant and one that is pervaded by a good and friendly atmosphere. It is constructive, productive and supportive and one where preservice teachers can "ask whatever and whenever" (Klette & Carlsten 2012, p. 76).

Further to that, sharing and collaboration are valued, encouraged and practised in PBL. As preservice teachers create their research packages and even when preparing for their triple jump assessments, they may collaborate and work together. This is encouraged. As they undertake a case, they share their work as the bibliographies and research packages are posted online as part of the course management system.

Grouping for instruction is another pedagogical approach that's intentional and results in preservice teachers having as many opportunities as possible to work collaboratively, as a large tutorial group, in pairs, threes and individually. For specialised workshops and time spent with their resource persons, the preservice teachers come together as a large cohort.

The case cycle reinforces and results in repeated opportunities to practise inquiry over the course of the year. After ten cases, preservice teachers have established routines, research strategies and acquired habits of the mind that should strengthen their growth towards collegiality, professional discernment and wise judgement. By identifying reasons for actions and examining the theory behind their practices as exemplified in their initial bibliographies and subsequent research packages, they become more proficient at analysing situations and from that know how to find out about the underlying issues.

Such practical problem solving though also involves critical theory. By questioning, being alert to other perspectives and possibilities, they have a chance to consider their identity as teachers. They begin to understand their positions of privilege and issues of equity and social justice. The tutors guide the preservice teachers to clarify meaning, identify issues/problems and expand on what seem to be dilemmas/puzzles emerging from the cases. Each week they develop inquiry questions that emerge from each case. These are not scripted but are intended to cover major learning outcomes.

For each case, preservice teachers draw upon and locate research. They post their initial research bibliographies and final research packages and present their research packages with a partner, to their tutorial group. At the conclusion of the case, the preservice teachers prepare an individual synthesis of the case, selecting a format of their choice. Ultimately, they make a decision about their resources and research and present a stance or their take of the issue. They make a presentation and create a research package, but ultimately, they create a personal synthesis that is only submitted to their tutorial instructor. In this synthesis, they make an informed decision about the case.

Examples from the case analyses of the preservice teachers' artefacts – their bibliographies and research packages, from Case I, Case 3 and Case 8 – demonstrate that preservice teachers are capable of asking a wide range of important questions of practise. All of their questions evolve from the deep reading of the case as well as from their own desire to learn more. It was quite clear that their questions related well to teaching practice. The issues were very relevant and once explored more fully, they would provide many opportunities to learn a great deal that could be applied within a school setting.

As the preservice teachers search for information, they find evidence relevant to the question. The preservice teachers displayed resourcefulness and scholarly approaches to their investigations as well as balanced bias, accuracy, currency and a mix of theoretical versus practical works. They located at least fifteen resources for each case, and these included primarily journal articles, ministry resources, books and websites. They displayed proficiency in locating relevant contextualised evidence.

The initial questions for inquiry that arose out of the careful reading of Case I included the following:

Questions for Inquiry for Case I (2012)
How do we build a caring classroom community?
How do we effectively establish and maintain community?
Insights into understanding diversity in the classroom.
How do we deal with respect and diversity?
What is early learning and the primary program?

(continued)

How do young children learn?
What is an effective teacher? A rationale for teaching
To play or not to play?
Play – how do we get children excited about learning?
What does literacy and numeracy look like?
How does early childhood development affect the classroom environment including play-based learning?

After completing their initial explorations of all the questions posed, the tutorial group narrowed down their investigations. Working in pairs, they researched and then presented their research packages to the group. Just to give you a flavour, the following are examples of research packages for Case I.

Research Packages for Case I – One Tutorial Group (2012)
Research Package 1: Shape of the Day – Building a Caring Classroom Community. Table of Contents: Community of Caring Learners; Defining a Caring Classroom Community; Fundamental Skills of a Community Member; How to Foster a Learning Community; Social and Emotional Development; Social and Emotional Learning; Play and Social Responsibility; Building a Classroom Environment; How Teachers Can Create a Respectful Environment; Rules and Routines; Extrinsic Versus Intrinsic Rewards; Community Building Activity; Communication with Families; Why Family Communication Is Important; Activities that Promote Prosocial Skills and a Sense of Community; Glossary and Annotated Bibliography
Research Package 2: Insight into Understanding Diversity in the Classroom. Table of Contents: Diversity; Inclusive Classrooms: Cultural Diversity; Ethics and Responsibility; Approach to Race; Language; Gender; Socioeconomic Status; Why Foster Multicultural Knowledge; The Multicultural Classroom; Questions; Glossary and Bibliography.
Research Package 3: Early Learning.
Table of Contents: What Does an Early Learner Look Like?; How Can Early Education Meet an Early Learner's Needs? What Is Developmentally Appropriate Practice? What Is Constructivism?; Piaget's Cognitive Development Theory; Vygotsky's Sociocultural Theory; Comparison Between Piaget's and Vygotsky's Theories; Additional Developmental Theories; Are Theories of Child Development Relevant to Full-Day Kindergarten? The Primary Program; An Introduction to the Primary Program; Three Goals of Education; Three Principles of Learning; Five Areas of Development Philosophy of the Primary Program; K-1 Literacy

(continued)

> and Numeracy; Literacy Primary Program's View of Literacy; Prescribed Learning Outcomes for Literacy; Numeracy; Primary Program's View of Numeracy; Prescribed Learning Outcomes Numeracy; Glossary; Annotated Bibliography.
>
> *Research Package 4: What Is an Effective Teacher?*
> Table of Contents: What Is an Effective Teacher: Definitions, Behaviours and Characteristics; BCCT Standards; Prime Minister's Award; Planning, Class and Time Management; Assessment; Working with Others; Knowledge of BC Curriculum K-1; How to Maintain Balance; Glossary; Bibliography.
>
> *Research Package 5: Play or Not to Play.*
> Table of Contents: Play and the BC Ministry of Education: Primary Program; Gr. K Curriculum (PLOs); Overview of Play; History of Play; Models of Play Programs; To Play or Not to Play: Understanding the Movement Towards Didactic Approach; The Information Age; Brain Development and Closing the Achievement Gap; What Is Play (Definition); Types of Play; Why Is Play Important: The Role of Play in the Contemporary Child; Play in the Early Primary Classroom; Glossary; Annotated Bibliography.

As a consequence of developing these cases, responding to their peers and then providing a synthesis to their tutor, the preservice teachers develop and acquire some dispositions for inquiry while at the same time deepening their understandings of teaching.

One Tutorial's Learning Journey Through PBL: Lori Prodan

> I am not a teacher: only a fellow traveler of whom you asked the way. I pointed ahead – ahead of myself as well as you. George Bernard Shaw

As a tutor with a disposition towards many of the central tenants of the (PBL) pedagogy – student-centered approach, communities of trust and the value of inquiry – I nonetheless held a high degree of scepticism at the beginning of my first year as a PBL tutor. How could preservice teachers develop understandings for teaching without any textbooks at all? No required readings? Could novices to the teaching profession really learn all that much from each other? How will they know what they don't know?

I wanted to know, how did they see PBL? What lasting benefits, if any, did they take away from learning through this pedagogy? In many ways, these questions are difficult to answer immediately upon graduation. The lasting value of a teacher education program, the depth of the learning, change and development, is more knowable after one has been teaching for some years, when one has a better sense of one's own voice as a teacher.

Nonetheless, at the completion of the one year program, preservice teachers' understanding of their own experience with PBL offers valuable insights into the way in which the pedagogy itself informs their practice and their view of themselves as teachers. Towards the end of the academic year, following the long practicum, I asked my preservice teachers if they would like to speak with me about PBL and their experience in it. Eleven out of thirteen volunteered to talk with me and spoke at length about the role of the tutor as well as about their experiences with PBL more generally and about how they viewed this pedagogical approach. In many cases, their depth of investment in and commitment to PBL pedagogy was unexpected and inspiring. Several themes surfaced, which led me to think that there was additional value in learning to teach through inquiry-based pedagogy. The issues of what content was or was not learned (or retained) aside what became clear was that the *process* of learning to teach through problem based learning helped develop the qualities one might want to see most in a teacher: dispositions towards inquiry, collegiality, an openness to complexity, holistic thinking and a sense of agency as a professional.

Not surprisingly, given their immersion in problem based learning for 11 months, inquiry itself emerged as an enduring value for the preservice teachers. As one succinctly commented, "And I think that's how I grew as a teacher in this program, because there were no answers". The emphasis on inquiry was a new concept for most of the preservice teachers and one that many felt they wanted to take into their own teaching practice; in some cases, a few were even able to implement during the extended practicum. Speaking about education in general, one noted: "How I thought about it was the opposite of my experience during my undergrad. In my undergrad I got lectured to every class. And [in PBL] it was all dependent on what we want to know".

Another preservice teacher went on to do a short practicum at an elementary school which focuses on inquiry-based teaching. The parallels between [her] own learning and her students' were interesting:

> They [the teachers at this school] ask questions and they ask the students to ask questions and then they get the students to answer their own questions. So it was kind of this really interesting experience where I was in September. They're learning how to ask and answer their own questions. And they're in Grade Three!

Another preservice teacher implemented an inquiry-based approach to science during the extended practicum and noticed an important distinction between her own experiences as an adult working with inquiry-based pedagogy and how her intermediate students engaged in inquiry:

> Learning how to use PBL is a big process. It takes a long, long time...and I had a chance to go to a workshop where adults were teaching other adults to use inquiry based learning and

I can see how for adults it can be really difficult. It's a difficult thing to grasp and to think about and to actually use it...And comparing that to my kids, they kind of just went with it. Like it wasn't a big deal to them. They were just like, 'oh, ok'. And they were really engaged with it because they got to learn what they wanted to learn about and honestly... I was so proud of them, and I was so amazed at what they came up with and they were owning their own learning.

In addition to being inquiry based, the PBL program is highly collaborative. Preservice teachers work with different partners for each case cycle to complete two major assignments of the cycle – the research package and the presentation. In addition, they are continually learning from and directly teaching each other in order to complete individual synthesis at the end of the case cycle. Positive social dependency is created and, according to these preservice teachers, valued.

Several preservice teachers commented on the shared responsibility of the case cycle as being highly motivating. As one put it: "It wasn't just about teaching my group of K/1/2 [children] for this year, I was also responsible for teaching my peers about things on a bi-weekly basis". Another honestly reflected about the value of greater sense of accountability with this type of learning: "you always have a group of people...who we are kind of accountable to. During your undergrad you go to lectures if you want to, you study if you want to, you write your paper last minute, but here it's so dependent on each other".

With the cohesiveness of team work comes a feeling of responsibility, which prefigures in important ways what it is to work as part of an elementary school staff. While evaluating the preservice teachers on practicum, I noticed that they worked highly collaboratively in two of the schools in which many were placed. Instead of a sense of competition, they worked together, openly sharing resources and ideas and in many cases actively seeking out opportunities to team teach.

Before I began working as a PBL tutor, someone described the approach as being a good one for independently minded learners, people who were self-directed and self-motivated. Thinking about how PBL actually works and listening to the preservice teachers' reflections, in many ways, I think the opposite may be true. PBL engenders a spirit of cooperation and teamwork, which is so vital to a successful elementary school. One preservice teacher recalled:

> I think a big shift in my thinking was from a traditional sort of individualistic [perspective] – you're getting grades for yourself and you're just working for yourself and not necessarily hiding things from others, but it's always a competition to get grades and so that shift of all of a sudden of not having grades and always working with a group of people or always having a partner to work on something with and shifting and having that support was such a good change. It's weird at first though because all of a sudden you are a team and you're learning together.

Several preservice teachers commented on their colleagues as being of great value in the program and in their own development as teachers. For example:

> There's a lot of smart people and it's nice to hear different perspectives because you always learn. 'Oh, I didn't think about that that way' or 'I don't know if I would do that in that situation'. It's really nice to have that collaborative effect and everyone's so different and

they've all got their own experiences. They can all bring something to the table. So I think it's a really neat opportunity to be able to do that and share.

Another noted that the program depends on group rather than independent work, saying, "It's very dependent on others. And I think that a lot of what we learned is through each other".

With so much emphasis on preservice teachers learning from and through each other, the danger is that the wrong things are learned or that something important is left out. Returning to my initial hesitation with the lack of textbooks and required readings, the question is how will the preservice teachers – complete novices to the field of education – know what they don't know? How will they have the context to understand the information they find or to pose the most important questions?

For one preservice teacher, even near the end of a year of PBL work, this remained a concern and a limitation of this pedagogical approach. Speaking about the overwhelming amount of information about education, she reflected:

> What should I be spending my time on? Sometimes I feel I did miss out on some really important writers and theories because I didn't have an expert to guide me in that direction....I guess I'm on the fence with PBL. I can see some of the benefits of it, but I can also see where it's lacking...I feel that there can be some direct teaching ...when you have someone who has got knowledge and expertise, passing that on, I'm not opposed to that, and I don't think that's a bad thing.

As a tutor, this remains the only significant source of scepticism I have with the PBL approach or with inquiry-based learning more generally. If the person posing the questions doesn't understand the context of the field of inquiry, or the history of debate in that field, is she properly equipped to pose the questions or recognise the "correct" answers amid the mountains of information and opinions readily available? However, perhaps the benefits of the struggle to ask the questions, to feel this powerful sense of agency over one's learning, are vital to the development of teachers who must be continually be posing questions about their students, often based on very little information or context. Using a colourful metaphor, one preservice teacher reminds me, that although her colleagues began as complete novices in the education field, they were not in any way *just* novices:

> I have a picture in my mind that in a traditional school, they give you the ingredients and the recipe and they expect you to come up with something and everyone's got to taste the same, look the same because they gave you the recipe, but for then for us, you gave us the ingredients but we were also allowed to bring in our own ingredients, maybe our background, our own expertise in some areas, languages, different cultures, different beliefs, and then you just taught us how to chop and then simmer and all, and we all came up with different foods at the end at it all tastes different...That's how I see PBL.

An often heard complaint for many preservice teachers is the lack of relevance of the course work or on-campus work. Many openly consider the work at the university to be secondary to the "real work" of the school-based practicum. Perhaps because of the narrative, holistic structure of the cases, the PBL preservice teachers did not report such a split. In fact, when asked about PBL pedagogy in general, many wanted to discuss the connection they felt was inherent in the course work and their own emerging teaching practice developing in the schools. One preservice teacher explained it thus:

> One other aspect of PBL is the case studies, so I really liked| that aspect of it because it's kind of like a mesh of real life with UBC education. I don't think that any other cohort gets that.
>
> I think that they learn situation by situation almost and for us it's a mesh of everything. Like social justice is always in there. It's always ELL and some sort of different learner and there's always these different components within one situation. And that's what happens in teaching. That is what a real classroom looks like and a real student looks like and so I liked that aspect of it. We were able to learn not only about assessment and visuals and first language and learning and all of that, but we were also learning about how there is so much that happens in the classroom. And how to give and take and find what you believe in…I like that because it's not just school.

Preservice teachers were excited by the links they could identify between their practicum classrooms and the case studies. In the words of one, "it just seemed more like reality than a lot of my other schooling did". I posed the question, "if you were to describe PBL to someone now, what you say PBL is?" One preservice teacher, noting that she now considers herself an advocate for PBL, echoes this sense of "reality": "the thing that I stress when I talk to people is that practicality and the experience that you get through diving into these cases and just figuring out what the problems are or how you can go about them". Another echoed this idea, saying of PBL, "it made practical sense. I've never been in school where it was really applicable". The links between theory and practice, between on-campus and in-school learning, were readily apparent to the preservice teachers as they worked through the eleven cases over the course of the academic year. As they created their own self-identities as teachers, from learners to teachers who also learn, they were continually reflecting on learning itself.

Perhaps the most important theme to emerge from the preservice teachers' conversations about PBL was the feeling that through inquiry-based learning, they had learned valuable things about the nature of learning itself. Apart from the external pedagogical theories, they were learning about learning from the fundamental act of posing questions. Comparing the experience to her first degree program, one preservice teacher reported, "…when you're given the thesis, when you're given that question, it's a lot easier. Finding the answer is easier than formulating the question". Another noted the reciprocal relationship between teaching and learning: "I see how multimodal this learning and teaching is because when we're learning, we're always learning but we're also always teaching each other. And each of us has different ways of perceiving things". A third considered questioning to be a thread throughout the program, noting, "I think through PBL the whole aspect of problem based learning, inquiry and asking questions and not making assumptions about what you think this person is learning, but just breaking it down…that was a huge, over-arching theme for me this year". Moving beyond teacher education itself, the process of posing questions and setting the direction for their learning, helped one preservice teacher gain, what she termed, "life skills":

Even besides the learning part, there's so many life skills that you learn in it [PBL]. I think we as adults learned in a way where it's more traditional, more standard but this is something that's so different. So it challenges us in ways to think differently, to do things differently, not necessarily good or bad, but you know what works for you, what doesn't work for you. I think in that aspect it's beneficial.

For one preservice teacher, the insights into learning itself were among the most valuable aspects of the program, saying PBL "taught me a lot too just about how I learn…looking back on it I think it was probably the most valuable way to learn was to figure out how you learn". For another, a large lesson was in flexibility and adaptability, arguably two very important qualities for an elementary teacher. Speaking about how she adapted and changed as a learner through PBL, she stated: "So I think that's one of the big things that the program taught me was just how to go with it and breathe through whatever they happen to throw at you on whatever day it gets thrown".

Conclusion

In our minds, the value of problem based learning lies in its role in fostering professional dispositions for inquiry that last a lifetime. Preservice teachers' learning about questions, flexibility, collegiality and the nature of learning itself, and themselves as learners and as teachers, will inform their lives as teachers, as agents engaging *their* students in meaningful, inspired learning. It is impossible to know if these insights are the result of a year in teacher education generally, a problem based learning program specifically or even of some other concurrent life experiences. When asked about the value of PBL, one preservice teacher aptly noted that "it would be nice for people to live two lives to make that comparison. I don't know. And even if I were to go through another teacher education program that was instruction based, it would be hard for me to say that".

As teacher educators, we are also unable to conclusively answer the question. We do know that we have learned immensely from these preservice teachers and remain inspired by their commitment to inquiry, to professional collaboration and to student-centered learning, as well as by their ability to articulate those commitments. Given that, it may be reasonable to conclude that PBL fosters the essential dispositions required for professional practice all the while recognising the complexity of teaching and learning.

References

Brown, J. S., & Thomas, D. (2008).The power of dispositions. *Ubiquity*, (November 1). doi:10.1145/472987.1472988.

Cochran-Smith, M., & Lytle, S. L. (1993). *Inside/outside: Teacher research and knowledge.* New York: Teachers College Press.

Coulter, D., et al. (2007). A question of judgment: A response to "standards for the education, competence and professional conduct of educators in British Columbia.". *Educational Insights, 11*(3), 1–11.
Dewey, J. (1933). *How we think: A restatement of the relation of reflective thinking to the educative process.* New York: Heath.
Farrell, T. S. C. (2004). *Reflective practice in action: 80 reflection breaks for busy teachers.* Thousand Oaks: Corwin Press.
Friesen, S. (2008). *Effective teaching practices: A framework.* Toronto: Canadian Education Association.
Giovannelli, M. (2003). Relationship between reflective disposition toward teaching and effective teaching. *The Journal of Educational Research, 96*(5), 293–309. doi:10.1080/00220670309597642.
Goodman, J. (1984). Reflection and teacher education: A case study and theoretical analysis. *Interchange, 15*(3), 9–26. doi:10.1007/BF01807939.
Halbert, J., Kaser, L., & British Columbia Principals' and Vice-Principals' Association. (2013). *Spirals of inquiry: For equity and quality.* Vancouver: BC Principals' & Vice-Principals' Association.
Healey, P. (2001). A 'limit attitude': Foucault, autonomy, critique. *History of the Human Sciences, 14*(1), 49–68. doi:10.1177/095269510101400103.
Jordan, E., Porath, M., & Bickerton, G. (2003). Problem-based learning as a research tool for teachers. In A. Clark & G. Erickson (Eds.), *Teacher inquiry: Living the research in everyday practice* (pp. 141–153). London: RoutledgeFalmer.
Katz, L. G., & Raths, J. D. (1985). Dispositions as goals for teacher education. *Teaching and Teacher Education, 1*(4), 301–307. doi:10.1016/0742-051X(85)90018-6.
Kincheloe, J. L. (2003). *Teachers as researchers: Qualitative inquiry as a path to empowerment.* New York: Routledge.
Klette, K., & Carlsten, T. C. (2012). Knowledge in teacher learning: New professional challenges. In *Professional learning in the knowledge society* (pp. 69–84). Rotterdam: Sense Publishers. doi:10.1007/978-94-6091-994-7_4.
Naslund, J., & Pennington, G. (2011). Enhancing volunteer youth sport coaching practices through intergenerational dialogue. *Journal of Coaching Education, 4*(3), 44–64.
National Council for the Accreditation of Teacher Education. (2010). NCATE glossary. In *NCATE unit standards.* Retrieved March 1, 2014, from http://www.ncate.org/Standards/UnitStandards/Glossary/tabid/477/Default.asp
Phelan, A. M. (2007). Enjoying their own margins: Narratives of innovation and inquiry in teacher education. In L. Farr-Darling, G. Erickson, & A. Clarke (Eds.), *Collective improvisation in a teacher education community* (pp. 51–63). Dordrecht: Springer.
Reid, A., & O'Donoghue, M. (2004). Revisiting enquiry-based teacher education in neo-liberal times. *Teaching and Teacher Education, 20*(6), 559–570. doi:10.1016/j.tate.2004.06.002.
Ruitenberg, C. W. (2011). The trouble with dispositions: A critical examination of personal beliefs, professional commitments and actual conduct in teacher education. *Ethics and Education, 6*(1), 41–52. doi:10.1080é17449642.2011.587347.
Schon, D. (1983). *The reflective practitioner: How professionals think in action.* New York: Basic Books.
Schulz, R., & Mandzuk, D. (2005). Learning to teach, learning to inquire: A 3-year study of teacher candidates' experiences. *Teaching and Teacher Education, 21*(3), 315–331. doi:10.1016/j.tate.2005.01.004.
Stenhouse, L. (1975). *An introduction to curriculum research and development.* London: Heinemann.
Yinger, R. J. (1986). Examining thought in action: A theoretical and methodological critique of research on interactive teaching. *Teaching and Teacher Education, 2*(3), 263–282. doi:10.1016/S0742-051X(86)80007-5.
Zeichner, K. M., & Liston, D. P. (1987). Teaching student teachers to reflect. *Harvard Educational Review, 57*(1), 23–49.

Part II
Collaborations: Working Together

> Effective discourse depends on how well the educator can create a situation in which those participating have full information; are free from coercion; have equal opportunity to assume the various roles of discourse (to advance beliefs, challenge, defend, explain, assess evidence and judge arguments); become critically reflective of assumptions; are empathic and open to other perspectives; are willing to listen and to search for common ground or a synthesis of different points of view; and can make a tentative best judgment to guide action.

New times are characterized by cultural and linguistic diversity, and the requirements of new competencies (creative and critical thinking; superior communication skills across a range of modes, audiences, and platforms; and enhanced personal and social responsibility awareness) demand collaborative and innovative approaches to teacher education. Just as a community is needed to raise a child, it could be suggested that it takes a collaborative community to educate a teacher. Since PBL's inception in 1998 at UBC to its transformation to a TELL/PBL cohort in 2012, upholding a collaborative approach and working together have been and continue to be central tenets.

In this part, those attributes that help create a successful collaborative teacher education inquiry group made up of diverse participants dedicated to creating the very best teacher education program possible will be discussed. Shared goals and visions are part of that discussion, and most recently the shared commitments of the TELL/PBL cohort include critical principles for language teacher education, situated programs and practices, responsiveness to learners, dialogic engagement, reflexivity, and praxis. Other factors involve good governance which from the beginning of the PBL program could be identified by the following: shared responsibility, participation, transparency, accountability, responsiveness, and most importantly good will and collaboration between all partners. It is in this type of environment that an open and equitable culture is established where all parties—university and school based—feel valued and respected.

From Mezirow, J. (1997). Transformative Learning: *Theory to Practice. New Directions for Adult and Continuing Education, 74*, Summer 1997, p. 10

Further in this part, the need for a respectful environment is emphasized not only within the tutorial groups but through the interactions between PBL tutors, faculty, and school advisors during their meetings and as part of their daily modus operandi. It is acknowledged that collaborative relationships in the PBL program are subject to change. Often they involve a core group of individuals but over time necessitate inclusion of new members—new faculty, school advisors, tutors, and each year a new intake of preservice students. The administrative merger of two distinct and diverse cohorts, for example, meant that TELL and PBL cohort coordinators, faculty advisors, and instructors had to collaborate and communicate in order to redesign, plan, and implement TELL/PBL curriculum and pedagogy.

However, in PBL collaboration is a given; it is a high priority critical to success. All parties are respected and valued educators, and their focus and dedication is to the delivery of quality teaching and learning for both preservice teachers and students in schools. Collaborations between and with district and school partners are essential. They mean that quality mentor/mentee relationships develop; opportunities for trying and testing new ideas within collaborative relationships within the context of messy classrooms are explored; and best supports offered for preservice teachers' discovery of who they are as educators.

For effective collaborations to occur, the frequency and quality of communications are paramount. Weekly meetings, for example, are an essential part of the collaborative process especially if knowledge mobilization and innovation are to occur. Tutors, faculty, and librarians contribute ideas for the redesign of the cases and to make explicit the objectives embedded within the set of cases to meet the requirements of the teacher education program (through a matrix of outcomes, program themes, and assessments). Clarity, openness, and above all respect for diverse opinions characterize these communications and are critical. In addition, the website and ongoing e-mail communications among stakeholders are instrumental in implementing PBL as individuals can check in with each other, monitor what others are doing, and work to articulate lessons with one another—not just for preservice teachers but among those responsible for the program. Collaboration between school advisors and preservice teachers is enhanced through daily communications and two-way journals.

What is heartening and revealed in this part is that regardless of differences that arise between PBL members, the spirit of collaboration that PBL affords and promotes ultimately triumphs.

Chapter 4
Knowledge Mobilization and Innovation in the Development of a PBL Cohort for Teaching English Language Learners: Successes, Challenges, and Possibilities

Steven Talmy and Margaret Early

Introduction

We live in an era of globalization, internationalization, transnationalism, and transmigration, where cross-cultural and cross-linguistic exchange is at its highest in human history. This is particularly the case in Canada, which has long had one of the highest per capita immigration rates in the world. Between 2006 and 2011, for example, Canada received approximately 1,162,900 immigrants (Statistics Canada 2013b) and an additional 263,000 arrived between June 2012 and July 2013 (Statistics Canada 2013a). Projections indicate that in the coming years, immigration will rise steadily to 400,000 annually. Consequently, there is expanding linguistic and cultural diversity, especially though not exclusively, in large urban areas. In the 2011 census, one in five Canadians, or nearly seven million people, reported a mother tongue other than English or French (Statistics Canada 2012). The impact of globalization and immigration is realized markedly in the linguistic diversity represented in Canadian schools. For example, in British Columbia (BC), 11 % of students Kindergarten-Grade 12 (K-12) are designated English language learners, while in the K-4 range the percentage rises to over 20 %. Overall, some 25 % of BC K-12 students speak a language other than English at home (BC Ministry of Education 2013), and in Vancouver the number is greater than 50 %, with approximately 150 different languages represented in the city's public schools (Vancouver School Board n.d.). Additionally, dramatic transformations in the global economy have occurred that impact schools, particularly in the move from a manufacturing- and industry-oriented economy to a knowledge-based economy. This ongoing change is codeveloping with equally dramatic technological innovations. These forces jointly impact multiple aspects of our lives and call into question language

---

S. Talmy (✉) • M. Early
Department of Language and Literacy Education, University of British Columbia, Vancouver, BC, Canada
e-mail: steven.talmy@ubc.ca

and literacy pedagogies for the twenty-first century (New London Group 2000). In BC, as in other parts of the world, these radical economic and social changes have led to a process of curriculum review and reformulation. In the recent BC education plan, it is noted that:

> our education system is based on a model of learning from an earlier century. To change that, we need to put students at the centre of their own education. We need to make a better link between what kids learn at school and what they experience and learn in their everyday lives. We need to create new learning environments for students that allow them to discover, embrace and fulfill their passions. We need to set the stage for parents, teachers, administrators and other partners to prepare our children for success not only in today's world, but in a world that few of us can yet imagine. (BC Ministry of Education 2011, p. 2)

New times, characterized by cultural and linguistic diversity, and the requirements of new competencies (creative and critical thinking; superior communications skills across a range of modes, audiences, and platforms; and enhanced personal and social responsibility awareness), demand new, innovative approaches to instruction. How best to prepare teacher candidates to enter such twenty-first century classroom contexts is one question that motivated us in part to bring the TELL and PBL cohorts together and to research the process and product of the merger in terms of the knowledge flows and mobilization that can occur (and not occur) in the context of an innovative teacher education initiative.

From TELL to TELL-Through-PBL

The TELL cohort was originally established to respond to the circumstances surrounding the increasing presence of English language learners in BC schools alluded to above. As one of several themed teacher certification cohorts in the Teacher Education Office of the Faculty of Education at the University of British Columbia, TELL adopted an inquiry orientation to developing knowledge about language and second language teaching into an elementary generalist teacher education curriculum. TELL added a 26-hour course to the existing teacher education curriculum, which focused on knowledge about language and second language pedagogy, with a particular focus on integrating language with content-area instruction. Additionally, there was a specific aim toward working to integrate a TELL focus across the 1-year teacher education curriculum, for example, by emphasizing (second) language and literacy issues in the social studies, science, math, and language arts methods courses TELL students were to take.

In 2012, with the implementation of a revised teacher education curriculum and a reduction in the number of themed cohorts, it was decided to merge the TELL cohort with the existing PBL cohort to create a new cohort: TELL/PBL. The rationale was that in addition to ensuring that both TELL and PBL would continue as thematic strands in the TEO with the merger, that TELL would fit well with PBL's original language and literacy orientation, and that PBL would be ideal for the inquiry orientation originally envisioned (and somewhat unevenly implemented) for

TELL: the merged cohort would enable TCs to become ethnographers of language/language use, so they could implement such an approach in their own classrooms, to have their students similarly become more metalinguistically aware and investigate how language was used in schools, their families, and their communities.

Collaborative Professional Conversations: Knowledge Mobilization and Innovation

Three interrelated perspectives inform the conceptual frame of our study: a functional theoretical stance on teaching academic language and content across subject areas in multilingual/ELL classrooms, a critical pedagogical approach to L2 teacher education, and participatory action research. For a number of years, there has been a growing literature on policy, programs, and practices in classrooms where ELL students are learning school subjects in English (for comprehensive reviews, see, e.g., Crandall 1992; Snow 1998; Mohan et al. 2001; Stoller 2004, 2008). Still, in a review that addressed what are commonly termed content-based L2 programs, Stoller (2008) maintained that as yet, "[t]he integration of content and language-learning objectives presents challenges for policy makers, program planners, curriculum designers, teachers, materials writers, teacher educators, teacher supervisors, test writers, and learners" (p. 65). However, while challenges, as well as opportunities, persist, Schleppegrell and O'Halloron (2011) highlight three significant instructional aspects as a way forward in this area. These include: providing support for teachers regarding "how language works in their subject areas," careful unit planning, and scaffolding students' academic language and content learning simultaneously (p. 3). With respect to L2 teacher education, Burns and Richards' (2009) edited volume was important for the theoretical framing of this study, particularly the chapter by Hawkins and Norton (2009), which drew on a wide range of research to offer five principles for critical language teacher education: the situated nature of programs and practices, responsiveness to learners, dialogic engagement, reflexivity, and praxis. A related body of research on participatory action research (Kemmis and McTaggart 2005) was also significant for this study. Research participants met on a two-week cycle to discuss and revise the cohort's cases and to engage in what we considered to be a crucial feature in the merger: the exchange and mobilization of knowledge about TELL and PBL from respective specialists' perspectives. Similar to participatory action research, "[the participants'] principal concern [was] in changing practices in the 'here and now'" (Kemmis and McTaggart 2005, p. 564). As such, we were mindful of the key features of participatory action research, as characterized by Kemmis and McTaggart: as a social process, as participatory, practical and collaborative, as emancipatory, critical, and reflexive, and with aims to transform both theory and practice (pp. 565–568).

The Study

Given the comparative lack of research that examines teacher education initiatives such as the TELL/PBL cohort merger, and in an effort to provide an empirical basis to inform its continued implementation, we formulated a small-scale qualitative case study to investigate its processes over the course of its first year of implementation. There were three research questions for the study; this chapter only concerns the first[1]:

> What successes, challenges, and opportunities resulted from efforts to create a successful collaborative teacher educator inquiry group of diverse participants who sought new and innovative inquiry-based ways, appropriate to changing times, to support teacher candidates in multilingual classrooms?

Participants of the study included the TELL/PBL cohort coordinators, cohort tutors, and several, but not all, cohort instructors.[2] Several forms of data were generated for the purpose of answering this question:

- Audio and video recordings of twice-weekly meetings over the course of the year with cohort tutors and instructors regarding upcoming cases which served as the basis for TELL/PBL. These meetings were a central data source as they were the primary site where efforts to infuse TELL principles into already-existing PBL cases were undertaken. Approximately 16 h of audio/video data were generated from these meetings.
- Field notes and reflections on these meetings.
- One audio-recorded interview each with four of the cohort tutors/instructors, conducted at the end of the first year of the merger by a graduate research assistant (Melanie Wong).
- Email communication over the course of the one-year study period among various research participants.
- The original (PBL) and revised (TELL/PBL) cases and other documents relevant to the cohort merger.

Audio/video data from the instructor meetings and interviews were logged and transcribed for content by Melanie Wong and subsequently analyzed for themes by the authors, who developed a coding scheme responsive to both the data set and research question. Following repeated readings/viewings of the data set, the authors identified and refined two clusters of "semantic" themes (Boyatzis 1998): successes and

---

[1] In fact, due to some of the challenges discussed below, the second research question "What multiliteracies practices are revealed as centrally important in designing learning experiences across the curriculum for teacher candidates in multilingual classrooms?" could not be answered. Due to space constraints, the third research question "What are ways that ongoing, recursive, and reflexive feedback provided to the collaborative teacher educator inquiry group can benefit group relations, interests, intentions, and practices?" will not be answered here.

[2] To protect participant confidentiality, information that might identify specific individuals has been altered or omitted.

challenges of the TELL/PBL cohort. These thematic clusters were in fact topicalized in the research question, and they organize the discussion that follows.

Before we continue, we pause to note that while we have endeavored to represent the perspectives of everyone who participated in this study as fairly and accurately as possible, our backgrounds and expertise in TELL, and our experience as TELL specialists in the merged cohort, have invariably influenced our discussion below of the first year of TELL/PBL. We are confident that a PBL specialist working with our data set would arrive at similar findings as we have; we are equally confident that because no scholar writes from nowhere (Haraway 1988), certain nuances or traces of PBL experience and expertise would shape the representations of those findings, just as ours as specialists in teaching L2 learners inevitably have.

Additionally, we would like to problematize from the outset the rather stark binary between TELL and PBL that might be inferable below, another artifact of this study, its premise, and the institutional realities it aims to investigate (i.e., that there were two distinct cohorts named TELL and PBL; that they were merged; that participants for the study were recruited and/or self-identified as either TELL or PBL specialists; that these categories were mobilized by participants in meetings, email communication, and interviews; and so forth). Because of these considerations, we are aware that it may at times appear in the analysis that PBL specialists had little or even no experience with TELL and, vice versa, that people in TELL had no experience with PBL. However, this is not the case. Our discussion should therefore be viewed in terms of programmatic, administrative, and disciplinary emphases between two distinct institutional entities, rather than the individual people who comprised them.

Successes

The first cluster of themes we generated variously referenced the successes of the TELL/PBL merger, viewed both in terms of how TELL was taken up and extended in the new cohort and how PBL principles and practices were manifested. The data that we have drawn these themes from come particularly from the twice-monthly cohort meetings; they were confirmed informally among participants over the year, as well as in the formal interviews with instructors/tutors.

Infusion of ELL Issues

A distinguishing feature of TELL/PBL was the wide range of issues germane to the education of school-age ELLs that was infused into the newly merged cohort's curriculum and instructional practice. The significance of this most basic success cannot be overstated: there is overwhelming empirical evidence from a range of disciplinary perspectives that demonstrates that ELLs are "overlooked and underserved" (Ruiz de Velasco et al. 2000) in North American schools, from elementary through high school. Reasons for such neglect include the "invisibility" of language and language demands to non-ELL specialists (Early 1990; Harper and de Jong 2004), a belief among subject area teachers that ELL instruction is not their responsibility (Samway and McKeon 1999), the conflation of L2 needs with behavioral, emotional, and cognitive "deficits" (Crawford 2004; Klingner et al. 2008), assimilationist views concerning immigrants and the languages they speak (Cummins 2007; Menken 2013), mistaken assumptions and lay language ideologies about L2 learning and learners (McLaughlin 1992), challenges of adding ELL programming to existing administrative structures (Harklau 1994), and negative beliefs about ELL from ELL teachers and students themselves (e.g., Talmy 2009, 2010). As a result, simply raising the sorts of neglected issues ELLs consistently face in schools in the professional conversations that took place over TELL/PBL's first year was an important development.

The clearest indication of this infusion was how ELLs were featured in the PBL cases that cohort coordinators, tutors, and instructors revised in the twice-monthly meetings. Register, for instance, a key theoretical construct in functional approaches to content-based L2 learning and teaching, was featured throughout most of the cohort's 11 cases, particularly as it related to commonalities in academic language across subject areas (Mohan 1986; Schleppegrell 2004). The concept of register was complemented approximately mid-year with consideration of educational genres, as another means of implementing pedagogy that was responsive to ELLs as well as non-ELL children and youth (see, e.g., Derewianka 1990; Early 1990). An early case concerning how classroom community could be created and maintained was revised to attend to how students' first languages might be incorporated in service of this endeavor (Lucas and Katz 1994). Classroom composition profiles that previously alluded to race/ethnic and cultural diversity were updated to explicitly consider linguistic diversity; relatedly, TCs were encouraged to move beyond an *appreciation* of cultural and linguistic diversity to consider how it might be *utilized* as a pedagogical resource (Cummins 2007). Discussion of the importance of oracy for kindergarten classrooms was expanded to include its centrality for L2 learning as well, particularly among children (Gibbons 2002). Issues concerning English as a second dialect were foregrounded in a case about Aboriginal children in a Northern BC elementary school (Ball et al. 2005; Siegel 2007), focal students in cases were transformed into multilingual youth rather than English monolinguals, bullying was extended to recognize many of the ways that it can occur through language, the advantages of a (post-)process approach to writing was discussed in terms of its advantages for L2 learners (Ferris and Hedgcock 2005), and much more. This is not to suggest that the PBL cases that existed before the TELL/PBL merger were deficient in any way, just to indicate a few of the many ways that ELL issues were infused into the cohort over its first year of implementation.

Integration of PBL Principles and Practice

The professional conversations that stakeholders engaged in as we went about revising the PBL cases for ELLs were exceptionally rich, not just in terms of the infusion of ELL issues, but in PBL's inquiry orientation, as well. Just as specialists in TELL raised topics related to principles of L2 learning, register, genre, and the like, for the merged cohort, PBL specialists regularly pointed to ways that TELL education could be implemented in terms consistent with PBL. As a result, the aims for inquiry that we had always envisioned for TELL were provided both a firm theoretical and methodological basis and, perhaps more importantly, a structure for actually implementing it. This structure was manifest in the PBL two-week case cycle; the recruitment of instructors in the TEO who had background and understanding of PBL principles and practice; the twice-monthly meetings with cohort coordinators, tutors, and instructors; and the unique approach to assessment (the triple jump) that had long been featured as hallmarks of the original PBL cohort. It is fair to say that the merger with PBL provided TELL the means for implementing the stance toward learner inquiry that we had always hoped for, but that remained unattained in our first years; more significantly, PBL *extended* our understanding of just how thoroughgoing that inquiry orientation could be. It also demonstrated to us the significant challenges that had been negotiated by PBL specialists in the years prior to the TELL/PBL merger, to implement a cohort structure that simply did not fit within existing institutional constraints of the TEO.

Time on TELL

In contrast to TELL/PBL TCs' perceptions (see below), the amount of time and attention devoted to ELLs was greater, more variegated, and more dispersed than in previous iterations of the (unmerged) TELL cohort. Although the two-week PBL case cycle meant that the two-credit class concerning ELL education in the TEO (LLED 353: Teaching English Language Learners) met less frequently than in other cohorts, in fact, ELL issues were taken up in the tutorials and, though less consistently, depending on the instructor's awareness of the characteristics of language used in their disciple, in subject area classes. This meant that ELLs were considered in a range of different contexts from a range of different perspectives over the entire academic year, rather than simply one two-hour class per week over a single university term, as in other cohorts. Additionally, workshops, another unique feature of PBL that carried over to the merged cohort, allowed more extended consideration of certain issues concerning ELL education. Workshops offered TC hands-on demonstrations and practical applications in a range of subject, thematic, and topical areas. Considered together, the time and attention that ELL issues received in TELL/PBL cohort via the ELL course, the tutorials, the subject area classes, and the workshops were significant successes that derived from the merger.

Collaboration and Communication

The distinctive characteristics of PBL, both in terms of its pedagogical principles and its programmatic infrastructure, were important affordances in carrying the first year of the TELL/PBL merger through to completion. The twice-monthly meetings with cohort coordinators, tutors, and instructors were central sites where knowledge mobilization and innovation could occur, from discussions about the revised cases and the issues they involved to how teachers could work together around a particular topic to the planning for workshops, and beyond. A web-based learning management system that all coordinators, tutors, and instructors had access to was another important site where stakeholders could check in with each other, monitor what others were doing, work to articulate lessons with one another, and so on. The website, the twice-monthly meetings, and ongoing email communication among stakeholders were instrumental in implementing PBL not just for the TCs, but among all of us involved in bringing TELL and PBL together. Regardless of the differences that arose over the year, and there were several (see below), it was without question done in the sort of spirit of collaboration and goodwill that PBL affords and promotes.

Challenges

Bringing together two teacher education cohorts, with distinct sets of practices, emphases, and foci, different histories and stakeholders, all in a fairly inflexible institutional context, was an endeavor that we knew from the start would inevitably encounter difficulties. Add to this the implementation in the larger TEO of a new curriculum and administrative structure, and the challenges would only multiply. Such was the case with the TELL/PBL merger. Despite the important successes described above, there were several substantive challenges, which led to several stakeholders to in fact question over the course of the first year whether the merged cohort should continue. This section outlines those challenges.

Frontloading

The matter of what we came to term "frontloading" was perhaps the single thorniest and most persistent challenge that those involved in the implementation of the cohort merger grappled with over its first year. By frontloading, what we mean is the a priori provision to TCs of concepts, constructs, and knowledge required to undertake inquiry, specifically, the sorts of inquiry that we as TELL specialists had in mind for them: inquiry into language, how it is used to construct subject area content in schools, and whose interests particular language-constituted representations serve. Frontloading was, in short, aimed at providing both a *provocation* and a *means* for inquiry.[3] What we had hoped to do was require a textbook (such as Gibbons 2002) and related assignments to help TCs learn what it was they actually could inquire about and problematize for their PBL cases (via, e.g., metalinguistic constructs such as register and genre), in addition to some basic texts in L2 learning and teaching (e.g., Lightbown and Spada 2013).[4] This was protested by several PBL specialists, who indicated that prior to the merger, they had not assigned readings or other activities to TCs, that to do so would undermine the integrity of the cohort's inquiry orientation, and that overall, such practice was contrary to PBL principles. Although this conundrum was not satisfactorily resolved over the first year, it was heartening to learn that it is not new to PBL (see Provan 2011).

Working with Existing Cases

The process of working to infuse TELL issues and principles into the existing cases was a rewarding and interesting task for all stakeholders and, as discussed earlier, proved to be a productive site for knowledge mobilization and innovation. At the same time, modifying existing cases rather than creating new ones meant that too often, ELL issues seemed to have been simply "added on" rather than integrated in more meaningful ways. For instance, in a case where bullying was featured, bullying through language was added onto bullying due to gender nonconformity. In a case that featured working in a classroom composed of a substantial number of Aboriginal students, English as a second dialect was added to issues concerning culturally responsive curriculum and pedagogy. As a result of these sorts of additions, tutors and instructors commented that the original issues (e.g., bullying due to gender nonconformity) may have been given less attention than was needed, and it was apparent to us, as well, that the TELL issues were not always attended to in ways we believed they could have been. There were also frequent discussions about the increase in the number of issues per case: with the addition of TELL issues, there was now too much in the cases to be adequately taken up by tutors and TCs.

---

[3] We are grateful to Melanie Wong for the wording of this sentence.
[4] This is not to suggest that teachers need to be applied linguists in order to effectively teach (about) language; on the contrary, it is our experience that a few powerful constructs (such as register) can help teachers become co-inquirers with their students about language (use) in the school, home, and community. Additionally, our experience in L2 teacher education aligns with research (e.g., Richards and Lockhart 1994) that tremendous benefits accrue when teachers of ELLs are offered opportunities to reflect on their own beliefs and ideologies about L2 teaching and learning. See below.

TELL Knowledge Mobilization

The goal of this study was to investigate knowledge mobilization among PBL and TELL specialists and nonspecialists. One of the primary findings of the study was that TELL knowledge mobilization was not robust enough to adequately support the integration of TELL issues across the cases. This was a particular challenge when it came to working with TCs to help them discern the language demands of subject area content; if instructors or tutors were themselves not sure how to inquire about language using concepts such as register or genre, they indicated they were not able to help TCs sufficiently do so either. This challenge no doubt had much to do with structural constraints described above, including working with existing cases, and the non-assignment of a relevant textbook and related coursework. It may also have been due to inadequate support from those of us in TELL to help scaffold understanding of TELL principles over the course of the year: we did not provide as many professional development sessions as we had initially hoped, and several instructors were unavailable to attend those that we did schedule. As a result, the status of language as "an invisible medium" (Diaz-Rico and Weed 2002, in Harper and de Jong 2004, p. 156), its role in learning and teaching implied or even taken for granted, unexpectedly endured in the first year of TELL/PBL cohort, with uptake to ELL issues varying considerably among instructors and tutors. In essence, TELL simply became another "subject area" to be covered, one issue among many, rather than a coherent approach to inquiring into, investigating, and problematizing the registers that are conventionally understood to constitute academic language, across the disciplines.

Loss of PBL Identity

If TELL specialists were disappointed in the adequacy of TELL knowledge mobilization and the inconsistency in uptake to issues of importance in ELL education, several PBL specialists lamented the loss of what was variously referred to as PBL identity, spirit, and its "core" principles. Many factors evidently played a part in creating this sense of loss. They included: the desire of those in TELL to require a textbook and related assignments even though PBL had in the past explicitly rejected such practice; the expansion in the number of case issues that attended the TELL "infusion," which rendered more focused and "organic" inquiry unviable; the recurrence of (TELL) issues that had (ostensibly) been addressed in previous cases, for instance, the repeated appearance of "register" across multiple cases; the pressure to ensure that TELL was discussed in classes and tutorials, to the apparent detriment of other important issues; the diminishment of central PBL practices like Socratic questioning brought on by the need to "steer" TCs toward issues of concern to TELL; and more. Another significant frustration voiced by participating PBL specialists had to do with TCs who had signed up for TELL rather than PBL. In previous years, when PBL was a standalone thematic cohort, TCs explicitly selected it, ensuring a cohort group that knew what they were opting for, and embraced it. Many TELL/PBL TCs, in contrast, had chosen the cohort for TELL; some did not understand or accept PBL as TCs in the past had. Thus, there was an underlying tension among a minority in the cohort who wanted TELL, but not PBL, and who in fact viewed PBL as an impediment to learning more about TELL. There were complaints from TCs about having far fewer of the ELL classes (LLED 353) than their peers in non-PBL cohorts were receiving, even though they were actually receiving more "time on TELL" than other cohorts, in the tutorials, other subject area classes, and workshops. Regardless, the TCs' frustration with the merged cohort was felt by us all as we worked to ensure that we met their needs while adhering to curriculum objectives and the at times competing priorities of TELL and PBL emphases.

Possibilities

The challenges just described notwithstanding, we and other members of the TELL/PBL group remain optimistic that our initial successes can be cultivated to create the sort of dynamic cohort we still believe is possible. To abandon the merger due to the tensions experienced in its first year would not recognize the complexities involved in bringing together two groups with distinct histories, expectations, and emphases. Neither would it honor the substantial amounts of time and effort the coordinators, instructors, and tutors put into making it work. And it would not recognize that the endeavor we all undertook was made far more complicated by the larger TEO curriculum revision, when it was not always clear whether challenges that were encountered were due to the merger or to the newly revised teacher education program.

The first year of the TELL/PBL cohort showed us the promise of what the merged cohort could offer, and it showed us that it will take more work. In order to fashion a cohort that is responsive to the interests of both sets of stakeholders, what follows are a set of recommendations we have produced that is based on our collective experience in the cohort in addition to the empirical record generated for this study.

- Frontloading. We respect the reluctance, as reported in this study, to assign core readings in PBL, but our experience with the first-year cohort underscores that without even rudimentary preparation in knowledge about language, second language learning, and language/content integration that TCs are simply ill-equipped to undertake informed and critical inquiries into academic language and the demands of the language of schooling for ELLs. We do not claim that teachers of ELLs must be experts in language – quite the opposite, in fact – but they must have a basic understanding of how language works in schools in order to *inquire* about it, investigate it, and interrogate it on their own and, more importantly, teach their ELLs how to inquire about it, investigate it, and interrogate it on their own. In this respect, we liken this sort of understanding about language to basic anatomy or pharmacology coursework that medical students in PBL programs across the world must take prior to or in tandem with their cases in problem-based learning. The idea here would not be to take away from learner inquiry, but to *enable* it in ways that TCs in the cohort's first year simply never learned. The ostensible invisibility of language is a major challenge for mainstream teachers working with ELLs; what we would aim to do is to help render perceptible that which has frequently proven indiscernible to the non-ELL specialist.

- A one-week TELL orientation, for TCs and tutors. While this may not be workable in the current context of the TEO, we believe a series of workshops over the first week of the school year, where we introduce in some depth a few basic constructs we believe are essential for successfully working with ELLs in mainstream, subject area classrooms. Key among them is:
  - A perspective on language that goes beyond it serving as a simple means of transmitting information, toward one that acknowledges that language *means*, language *does*, and language is *used* in very particular ways *to constitute* subject area content and academic texts and that language use is therefore inherently *political*.
  - An understanding that ELLs bring with them a range of resources for making meaning, including most significantly, their first languages, but also other modes, modalities, and registers (written, visual, musical, embodied, and so on) that are often not valued in school. These are resources that can and should be mobilized in the acquisition of English registers and genres that are necessary for academic success.
- New cases. We worked in the first year of the merger with existing cases from past years of the (non-TELL) PBL cohort and revised them to infuse principles of relevance to ELL education in K-12 North American settings. While the process of revising these cases was a significant site for knowledge mobilization and innovation, the *product* – the revised cases – was ultimately inadequate for the successful integration of TELL with PBL. Therefore, going forward, we need new cases, cases that will build into them from the start principles of teaching ELLs, which will feature recurrent attention on (meta)language and language-related issues that develops from case to case (e.g., case sequencing of matters concerning register), so that TCs can become informed inquirers into (academic and nonacademic) language and help their own students become ones, as well. This may be the most important innovation for the TELL/PBL cohort moving forward.
- Tutors with TELL expertise (or a strong curiosity and commitment to rapidly developing this professional knowledge and know-how). Tutors are appointed on a three-year cycle, and as such, time is of the essence vis-à-vis "apprenticing" into the culture of this rich and complex cohort. Given the central role that tutors play in the TELL/PBL cohort in ensuring that particular issues are taken up by TCs, and taken up effectively, we believe cohort tutors would ideally have a strong grasp of how language functions in school, and in theories of second language learning, so that they may more expertly guide TCs in their inquiries.

- Finally, the importance of the workshops often meant that there were numerous interests competing for workshop time. We would suggest that additional workshops be taken up throughout the year and in addition to the first week of TELL workshops that will prioritize in them perspectives on these issues as they relate to TELL.

Conclusion

The successes of the TELL/PBL cohort in its first year of implementation, in the context of a major structural overhaul in the UBC TEO, were a tribute to the time, effort, and goodwill of a group of immensely committed university educators. The challenges, some anticipated, many not, were in some senses inevitable given the difficulties of knowledge mobilization and innovation in a setting where tradition, disciplinary insularity, and institutional inertia frequently prevail. As this study has suggested, however, the possibilities of the TELL/PBL cohort demonstrate the power that can result when those who are committed to it will persist. This includes those in the current second year of the TELL/PBL cohort, the cohort coordinators, tutors, and subject instructors who, at the time of writing, are currently working to put a number of these recommendations into practice, with plans for further development, in the coming years.

Acknowledgment Research was funded by a University of British Columbia HSS Seed Grant (#15R07971). The authors gratefully acknowledge this support, as well as the work of Melanie Wong, graduate research assistant, who played an instrumental role in the research.

References

Ball, J., Bernhardt, B., & Deby, J. (2005). *Implications of First Nations English dialects for supporting children's language development*. Presented at the World Indigenous Peoples' Conference on Education, University of Waikato, Aotearoa/New Zealand. Retrieved from http://hdl.handle.net/1828/1440

BC Ministry of Education. (2011). *BC education plan*. Author. Retrieved from http://www.bcedplan.ca/assets/pdf/bc_edu_plan.pdf

BC Ministry of Education. (2013). *Student Statistics – 2012/13*. Author. Retrieved from https://www.bced.gov.bc.ca/reports/pdfs/student_stats/prov.pdf

Boyatzis, R. E. (1998). *Transforming qualitative information: Thematic analysis and code development*. London: Sage.

Burns, A., & Richards, J. C. (Eds.). (2009). *The Cambridge guide to second language teacher education*. New York: Cambridge University Press.

Crandall, J. (1992). Content-centered learning in the US. *Annual Review of Applied Linguistics, 12*, 110–126.

Crawford, J. (2004). *Educating English learners: Language diversity in the classroom* (5th ed.). Los Angeles: Bilingual Educational Services.

Cummins, J. (2007). Rethinking monolingual instructional strategies in multilingual classrooms. *Canadian Journal of Applied Linguistics, 10*, 221–240.
Derewianka, B. (1990). *Exploring how texts work*. Rozelle: Primary English Teaching Association.
Diaz-Rico, L. T., & Weed, K. Z. (2002). *The cross-cultural, language, and academic development handbook. A complete K–12 reference guide* (2nd ed.). Needham Heights: Allyn & Bacon.
Early, M. (1990). Enabling first and second language learners in the classroom. *Language Arts, 67*, 567–575.
Ferris, D., & Hedgcock, J. (2005). *Teaching ESL composition* (2nd ed.). Mahwah: Lawrence Erlbaum Associates.
Gibbons, P. (2002). *Scaffolding language, scaffolding learning: Teaching second language learners in the mainstream classroom*. Portsmouth: Heinemann.
Haraway, D. (1988). Situated knowledges: The science question in feminism and the privilege of partial perspective. *Feminist Studies, 14*, 575–599.
Harklau, L. (1994). ESL versus mainstream classes: Contrasting L2 learning environments. *TESOL Quarterly, 28*, 241–272.
Harper, C., & de Jong, E. (2004). Misconceptions about teaching English-language learners. *Journal of Adolescent & Adult Literacy, 48*, 152–162.
Hawkins, M., & Norton, B. (2009). Critical language teacher education. In A. Burns & J. Richards (Eds.), *Cambridge guide to second language teacher education* (pp. 30–39). Cambridge: Cambridge University Press.
Kemmis, S., & McTaggart, R. (2005). Participatory action research: Communicative action and the public sphere. In N. K. Denzin & Y. S. Lincoln (Eds.), *Handbook of qualitative research* (3rd ed., pp. 559–603). Thousand Oaks: Sage.
Klingner, J. K., Hoover, J. J., & Baca, L. (2008). *Why do English language learners struggle with reading? Distinguishing language acquisition from learning disabilities*. Thousand Oaks: Corwin Press.
Lightbown, P., & Spada, N. (2013). *How languages are learned* (4th ed.). Oxford: Oxford University Press.
Lucas, T., & Katz, A. (1994). Reframing the debate: The roles of native languages in English-only programs for language minority students. *TESOL Quarterly, 28*, 537–561.
McLaughlin, B. (1992). *Myths and misconceptions about second language learning: What every teacher needs to unlearn*. Santa Cruz: National Center for Research on Cultural Diversity and Second Language Learning.
Menken, K. (2013). Emergent bilingual students in secondary school: Along the academic language and literacy continuum. *Language Teaching, 46*, 438–476.
Mohan, B. (1986). *Language and content*. Reading: Addison-Wesley.
Mohan, B., Constant, L., & Davison, C. (Eds.). (2001). *English as a second language in the mainstream: Teaching, learning and identity*. New York: Longman.
New London Group. (2000). A pedagogy of multiliteracies: Designing social futures. In B. Cope & M. Kalantzis (Eds.), *Multiliteracies: Literacy learning and the design of social futures* (pp. 9–37). London: Routledge.
Provan, A. (2011). A critique of problem-based learning at the University of British Columbia. *BC Medical Journal, 53*, 132–133.
Richards, J. C., & Lockhart, C. (1994). *Reflective teaching in second language classrooms*. Cambridge: Cambridge University Press.
Ruiz de Velasco, J., Fix, M., & Clewell, B. C. (2000). *Overlooked and underserved: Immigrant students in US secondary schools*. Washington, DC: The Urban Institute.
Samway, K. D., & McKeon, D. (1999). *Myths and realities: Best practices for language minority students*. Portsmouth: Heinemann.
Schleppegrell, M. J. (2004). *The language of schooling: A functional linguistics perspective*. Mahwah: Lawrence Erlbaum Associates.
Schleppegrell, M., & O'Hallaron, C. (2011). Teaching academic language in L2 secondary settings. *Annual Review of Applied Linguistics, 31*, 3–18.

Siegel, J. (2007). Creoles and minority dialects in education: An update. *Language and Education, 21*, 66–86.
Snow, M. A. (1998). Trends and issues in content-based instruction. *Annual Review of Applied Linguistics, 18*, 243–267.
Statistics Canada. (2012). *Linguistic characteristics of Canadians, 2011* (No. 98-314-X2011001). Minister of Industry. Retrieved from http://www12.statcan.gc.ca/census-recensement/2011/as-sa/98-314-x/98-314-x2011001-eng.cfm
Statistics Canada. (2013a). *Components of population growth, by province and territory* (CANSIM, table 051–0004). Minister of Industry. Retrieved from http://www.statcan.gc.ca/tables-tableaux/sum-som/l01/cst01/demo33a-eng.htm
Statistics Canada. (2013b). *Immigration and ethnocultural diversity in Canada* (No. 99-010-X2011001). Minister of Industry. Retrieved from http://www12.statcan.gc.ca/nhs-enm/2011/as-sa/99-010-x/99-010-x2011001-eng.cfm
Stoller, F. (2004). Content-based instruction: Perspectives on curriculum planning. *Annual Review of Applied Linguistics, 24*, 261–283.
Stoller, F. L. (2008). Content-based instruction. In N. Van Deusen-Scholl & N. H. Hornberger (Eds.), *Encyclopedia of language and education* (2nd ed., Vol. 4, pp. 59–70). New York: Springer.
Talmy, S. (2009). "A very important lesson": Respect and the socialization of order(s) in high school ESL. *Linguistics and Education, 20*, 235–253.
Talmy, S. (2010). Achieving distinction through Mock ESL. In G. Kasper, H. T. Nguyen, D. Yoshimi, & J. Yoshioka (Eds.), *Pragmatics and language learning* (Vol. 12, pp. 215–254). Honolulu: University of Hawai'i, National Foreign Language Resource Center.
Vancouver School Board. (n.d.). *Vancouver school board sectoral review: Our schools, our programs, our future*. Author. Retrieved from http://ourfuture.vsb.bc.ca/report/assets/documents/sectoral_reviews21411.pdf

Chapter 5
Negotiating the Content of Problems in Tell/PBL

Margot Filipenko

Introduction

Problem based learning (PBL) is an instructional model based on the notion of the centrality of cases to learning (Jonassen and Hung 2008; Savery 2006). Dolmans et al. (1997) write:

> Cases are the driving force behind students' independent study in problem-based learning … the nature of student learning in problem-based learning is to a large extent dependent on the quality of cases presented to students. (p. 185)

Well-designed cases problematize the curriculum and engage preservice teachers in learning about theory and pedagogy within specific contexts. Within our teacher education program at the University of British Columbia (UBC), cases are designed to ensure that the PBL program addresses the requirements of the overall Bachelor of Education (B.Ed.) curriculum while at the same time systematically and sequentially developing preservice teachers' learning and understanding of teaching. The process of both designing and maintaining the currency of our cases for the B.Ed. problem based learning cohort is both collaborative and purposeful. A curriculum development team consisting of faculty, tutors, and librarians meet prior to the introduction of each case to ensure content is consistent with the needs of our preservice teachers and the objectives of the B.Ed. program.

This chapter describes the process of designing problem based learning cases within a newly revised teacher education program. It describes how the development of a matrix to identify course objectives drawn from across the teacher education program was used to redesign the cases and to make explicit the objectives embedded within the set of cases developed for the PBL cohort. Seven principles of

---

M. Filipenko (✉)
Department of Language and Literacy Education, University of British Columbia,
Vancouver, BC, Canada
e-mail: margot.filipenko@ubc.ca

effective case design for a problem-based curriculum will be described and illustrate how these principles assisted in crafting effective cases (Dolmans et al. 1997). This review of the case design process employed in PBL to meet the changing curricular requirements of a revised teacher education program at the University of British Columbia, with the design matrix, principles of case design and use of existing cases, may be of interest to and helpful for teacher educators wanting to implement PBL pedagogy or to those engaged in teacher education reform.

Designing Cases for a New B.Ed. Program

A new twinned cohort called TELL through PBL was introduced concurrently with the new B.Ed. program in teacher education at UBC in the fall of 2012. In the informational handbook, of the Teacher Education Office at UBC, the new cohort was described as follows:

> Members of the TELL/PBL cohort prepare to work effectively with elementary-age learners for whom English is an additional language – a population that has expanded dramatically in British Columbia (BC) schools in recent years – using an innovative educational strategy that weaves problem–solving and critical thinking into content knowledge through the use of real world problems and situations. UBC instructors use case study methods to expertly guide teacher candidates to develop inquiries into pedagogy, curriculum, learning, and the profession of teaching.
>
> Additional emphases include ways to use multilingual, multimodal and multicultural ways of meaning-making that learners bring to the classroom; working as a school resource for English language learners; teacher collaboration; and advocacy work for this population. (p. 15)

The introduction of both a new B.Ed. program and a new focus on the teaching of English language learners required those of us working in the TELL through PBL cohort to redesign our PBL cases. This process was undertaken by an interdisciplinary group of academics, seconded teachers, and an education librarian to revise eleven problem cases that make up the PBL teacher education program at the University of British Columbia.

Issue 1: Developing the Matrix

Using a case-based PBL approach engages students in discussions with scenarios (cases) that reflect messy, real-world situations. In the case of our PBL teacher education cohort, cases reflect complex educational scenarios. Dolmans et al. (1997) write:

> Cases are the starting point for students' learning activities in problem-based learning (PBL). A case usually consists of a description of some phenomena, which require some kind of explanation. The task for the students is to explain the phenomena described in the case. While discussing these phenomena, some questions remain unanswered. These questions are subsequently defined as learning issues and are the driving force behind students' self- study. (p. 185)

However, while much has been written about PBL as a *process* through which students take responsibility for their learning by formulating their questions and learning needs in relation to a given problem, it is also essential that students achieve the *content knowledge* required for their profession (Dahlgren 2000, p. 3).

At the University of British Columbia, all preservice teachers in the teacher education program, including preservice teachers enrolled in the PBL cohort, are required to achieve the learning outcomes of all the courses which comprise the teacher education program. These twenty core education courses are offered across four departments and are listed below:

Educational Studies (EDST) – courses include Education, School, and Society; Education and Media; Education, Knowledge, and Curriculum; and Ethics and Teaching

Education Curriculum and Pedagogy (EDCP) – courses include Art, Mathematics, Music, Physical Education, Science, and Social Studies

Language and Literacy Education (LLED) – courses include classroom discourses, Literacy Practices, Teaching French as an Additional Language, and Teaching English as an Additional Language

Educational Psychology (EPSE) – courses include Assessment and Learning in the Classroom, Cultivating Supportive School and Classroom Environments, Applying Developmental Theories in the Classroom, Understanding Diverse Learners, and Development and Exceptionality in the Regular Classroom

In addition teacher candidates are required to complete two inquiry seminars and a course on Aboriginal Education.

Given the importance of our preservice teachers achieving the content knowledge outlined in the course objectives of these twenty-one courses (including EDUC 440: Aboriginal Education), it was determined that we would begin our revision of the cases by outlining the topics and objectives for each of these required B.Ed. courses. This document (the matrix) would provide the material (topics and objectives) from which we would begin revision of the cases.

The twenty-one core courses developed for the new program in the B.Ed. program at UBC were required to follow a common template. This template included identification of the course objectives and course topics to be covered in the course.

Information from the course outlines regarding the course objectives and course topics from each of the twenty-one core courses was added to the matrix (Table 5.1).

Issue 2: Thematic Strands

With the course objectives and topics outlined in a matrix, the interdisciplinary curriculum team turned to the other demands of the new B.Ed. program. The document outlining the new B.Ed. program identified five thematic strands to be woven throughout all aspects of the new teacher education program (courses, seminars, practica):

Table 5.1 Example from the course matrix

Course	Course objectives	Topics
LLED 353: teaching and learning English as an additional language – elementary	Major theories of second language acquisition	The context of language teaching: Ministry Expectations and Guidelines
	Major theories and approaches to teaching English as an additional language	Digging deeper: language teaching approaches
	The role of language as a medium for learning multilingual and multimodal literacy	Language learning and teaching are based on communication
	The role of literate environments and enriched language environments in fostering second language and literacy development	School language and home language
	Integration of language and culture	Integrating language and content
	Tools for second language and literacy assessment	Nurturing the development of oral language
		Reading in a second language
		Listening and putting it all together again
		Diversity as a resource
		Imagining multilingual schools: designing a multiliteracies pedagogy

- *Languages, Literacies, and Cultures*: Recognizes that school is a social language-using community and the importance of developing insight into the relationships that exist between language and learning, language and identity, and language and cultures
- *Curriculum, Pedagogy, and Assessment*: Identifies curriculum as a *complicated conversation* in which educators engage in questions, inquiries, debates, and discussions about knowledge that is dynamic and changing. Thus, pedagogy positions teachers as facilitators of student learning rather than dispensers of knowledge
- *Diversity and Social Justice*: Is linked to the concept of equality of educational opportunity, variously defined as: (a) equality of access to the school system, (b) equality of treatment within school, (c) equality of learning outcomes, or (d) equality of results (e.g., equal access to life chances as adults)
- *Field Experiences*: Identifies the need for preservice teachers to merge the knowledge they develop in university classrooms with the knowledge they develop as they engage in practicum experiences in schools. It calls for preservice teachers to engage with a multiplicity of resources (peers, classroom teachers and pupils, the research literature, and popular culture) to challenge existing beliefs and to deliberate on teaching practice as evolving

- *Inquiry and Dialogical Understanding*: Identifies that dialogical understanding and inquiry are integrally connected. Inquiry being the practice of reflecting on every aspect of professional development and dialogue as being the means for building collaboration through engagement with diverse points of view within a group in order to come to new understandings. It is in listening to others and to oneself that the process of exploration takes place and new understandings are reached[1]

For the purposes of our case development, the curriculum development team identified the strands as being an ongoing emphasis on:

- Inquiry and research throughout the program
- Diversity and social and ecological justice
- Aboriginal Education and aboriginal perspectives
- Linguistic and cultural diversity as resource
- Integration of technology
- Theory to practice links

Issue 3: How to Schedule Content of Cases

The problem based learning academic year the problem based learning academic year is comprised of eleven cases that unfold over 11 months. While the curriculum development team felt it had a good grasp of the content knowledge (course objectives) and strands, which must be embedded in the cases, decisions still had to be made on how best to organize the material to develop the cases both individually and as a series of cases that would scaffold and build one upon another.

The team drew upon the ten existing cases and a dilemma (with a focus on Education Policy). It was decided to look to these existing cases and dilemma for guidance. The existing cases were set in kindergarten and elementary classrooms beginning with the kindergarten classroom and moving in a lockstep manner through the elementary grades. While this had been a successful approach in developing scenarios of the complex and messy world of education, we needed to update the content (provided by the new teacher education program), weave in the strands through the cases, and interrupt the lockstep nature of the cases.

For example, it was decided that Case 4 which follows the short 2-week practicum (during weeks nine and ten of the teacher education program) should be developed by the preservice teachers from questions and issues identified by them during and following their short 2-week school-based practicum. Since preservice

---

[1] These five strands and the summary of each of the strands are taken from a report generated by the Committee for Re-imagining Teacher Education at the University of British Columbia in May 2009. This report formed the basis for the new B.Ed. program at the University of British Columbia and can be accessed at http://teach.educ.ubc.ca/files/2013/07/CREATE-Faculty-Meeting-Sept-2009.pdf

teachers complete their practica across the elementary grades, issues and questions raised and included in Case 4 would be interrogated across the grades rather than focusing specifically on a particular grade as happens in the majority of the cases that occur in the first term of the year. It was felt that this would both shake up the lockstep approach to the delivery of cases and underscore the relationship between *theory and practice* and on *inquiry* – two of the programmatic strands.

Since inquiry and research are at the heart of the PBL methodology, the curriculum development team knew that this particular strand would be amplified within and across all cases. Following the model of the existing cases, five of the cases were set in and focused primarily within and on problems as they are manifested within a particular grade. However, it was decided to amplify one or two of the strands in each of the remaining cases. The focus of each of the cases was as follows:

- Case 1: K/grade 1
- Case 2: Primary grades
- Case 3: Teaching in a resource-based coastal community with a large Haisla First Nations community[2] (grade 3) – Aboriginal Education and ecological justice strands
- Case 4: Student generated from questions and issues following the short 2-week practicum – theory to practice strand
- Case 5: Grade 3/4
- Case 6: Grade 4/5
- Case 7: Grade 5/6
- Case 8: Planning for instruction – theory to practice strand
- Case 9: Bullying – social justice strand
- Case 10: Technology in the elementary classroom – technology strand
- Case 11: Special needs education – diversity strand

While the decision was made to emphasize or *amplify* particular strands or themes in five of the cases, the curriculum development team was committed to embedding *echoes* of the strands in all of the cases. For example, while bullying (social justice) is amplified in Case 9, the issue has echoes in Case 2 and Case 5 (see Appendices).

Issue 4: Developing Effective Problems

Acting upon several studies conducted to establish the effectiveness of cases, Dolmans et al. (1997) developed seven principles to guide the development of effective problems. The following table was developed outlining these principles and implications for designing cases within a teacher education program (Table 5.2).

---

[2] The Haisla First Nations community has lived on British Columbia's North Coast for hundreds of years.

Table 5.2 Principles for designing effective PBL cases

Principles of effective case design for PBL	Implications for problem design
1. Reflect course objectives	Should match teacher education course objectives
2. Simulate real life	Case should represent a context relevant to the preservice teachers' chosen profession of education
3. Lead to elaboration	Case should contain cues that stimulate students to elaborate on educational issues
4. Encourage self-directed learning	Should encourage preservice teachers to generate learning issues that lead to inquiry and research
5. Constructivist	Problems fit and build on preservice teachers' background knowledge
6. Integrated knowledge base	Present relevant basic educational concepts in the educational context of a classroom to encourage integration of knowledge
7. Stimulating	Should enhance preservice teachers' interest in the subject matter, by stimulating discussion about possible solutions and facilitating exploration of alternative explanations

With the matrix, the seven principles for designing effective cases and the existing ten cases and dilemma in hand, the curriculum design team began work on revisioning and developing the cases for the PBL cohort in the new B.Ed. program. Using these documents Case 1 was developed (Box 5.1).

> **Box 5.1: Case 1**
> Congratulations! You are about to begin your first year of public school teaching. You've landed a job as a kindergarten classroom teacher in an ethnically, economically, linguistically, and culturally diverse neighborhood. It's now the third week of August and you're feeling both excited and anxious. Last night, as you lay awake at 3 a.m., you were thinking about how you would build on children's orality.
>
> When you stepped into your school a couple of days ago, a young mother was in the office registering her children. The principal called you over and introduced you as the new teacher. The mother looked you up and down and said, "When my son was at this level, all they did was play. How are you going to make sure my daughter learns to read and write and add and subtract?"
>
> "I, uh, well…please come to the Meet the Teacher Night in September," you replied. "I'll share my plans then."
>
> "I'll be there," she said and returned to the forms she was filling in.
>
> As you turned to leave the office, the principal slipped you a copy of the Full-Day Kindergarten Program Guide and whispered, "Don't forget this!"
>
> Later, in your classroom, you were stapling the word "welcome" in multiple languages around your bulletin boards when a man with spiky gray hair and
>
> (continued)

Box 5.1 (continued)
black-framed glasses poked his head through the door. "Hi, I'm Sid," he said. "I teach in the room next door. Give me a shout if you need anything." Over lunch, you found out that Sid has been passionate about social justice education for 25 years and has lots of ideas to share. He shares with you this piece of advice "Start out with getting to know your kids and building your classroom community." At the end of the day, as you walked out of the school together, Sid introduces you to Sam, the First Nations Enhancement teacher. After a brief introduction, Sam tells you he's meeting with a few members of the Musqueam Nation to plan a school event for next week. "I'll look forward to talking to you about the event at the staff meeting" he says as he heads back in.

Clearly this case meets principles two and six above (simulating real life and integrating across the education subject areas). To ensure the case also met principle one: course objectives (knowledge base), the curriculum development team, using the course matrix, developed the following table to guide the design of the case (Table 5.3).

Table 5.3 Integrating course objectives

Course objectives	Possible research topics	Case issues
EPSE 308	Theories of child development/learning, discovery/play learning	Play-based learning
Explore theoretical perspectives regarding child development and the implications for classroom practice		Kindergarten Program Guide
LLED 350 and 353	Early literacy	Language and communication EAL and language acquisition
Understanding of children's language and literacy development	Orality	
Understanding of the role of language in learning	Nonverbal communication	
EPSE 308	Classroom community/cultural diversity	Building classroom community
Learn about socialization processes and demonstrate an understanding of diversity across the classroom community		
ECED 405	B.C. Ministry of Education Full-Day Kindergarten Program	Ministry of Education Curriculum documents
Gain knowledge about the major curriculum approaches and issues in early childhood programs		
EDUC 440	Indigeneity	First Nations Enhancement Education
Assist those becoming professional educators to make a contribution to transform Aboriginal Education in order to improve educational outcomes for Aboriginal/Indigenous learners	Aboriginal Education	
EDST 401	Conceptions of social justice education	Social justice education
Identify key features of different conceptions of social justice and the implications for schooling		
Explore how teachers have attempted to translate teaching for social justice into practice		

Box 5.2: Questions and Issues Raised by Preservice Teachers in Case 1

1. The Value of Play

   - What is the role of play in the classroom?
   - How do we as teachers or preservice teachers relay the value of play to parents?
   - How is play manifested in the classroom?
   - What forms of play relate to classroom learning?

2. Orality and Language Acquisition

   - What is orality?
   - Should there be an emphasis on orality rather than literacy in the primary classroom?
   - What kind of linguistic support is inside and outside of the classroom?

3. Building Classroom Community

   - How does the term community relate to the classroom?
   - What are the key issues in classroom communities and how might they impact teaching (e.g., social economic status, race, gender, language, culture, class composition, and so forth)?
   - How can a teacher be effective in a diverse classroom setting and are there particular models or theories in place that can act as aids for teachers?

4. Kindergarten Program Guide

   - What is the importance of the program guide?
   - What theories of learning are used to develop the B.C. Full-Day Kindergarten Program?
   - What is school readiness and how can children be prepared for learning both socially and academically?

5. First Nations Enhancement Education

   - What is the role of a First Nations Enhancement teacher?
   - What issues are First Nations students dealing with (e.g., impact of residential school system on families and communities)?
   - What does First Nations education look like in a contemporary school setting?

6. Social Justice

   - What is social justice?
   - What responsibilities does an educator have around social justice and social responsibility teaching for social justice?
   - How do you use social justice education principles to build classroom community?
   - How is social justice education implemented within an elementary school setting?

While it seemed to us (the curriculum development team) that Case 1 (above) provided many opportunities for preservice teachers to elaborate on the issues (principle three), encourage preservice teachers to generate learning issues that lead to inquiry and research (principle four), and stimulate discussion regarding possible solutions and alternative explanations of issues (principle seven), it was not until the preservice teachers had engaged with this particular case that we had evidence that indeed the case met the requirements of principles three, four, and seven. The following (Box 5.2) outlines the ways in which the preservice teachers engaged with the issues in Case 1.

Following identification and discussion of issues, the preservice teachers, working in pairs, developed research packages on each of the topics. Peer responses to these research packages illustrated to the curriculum development team that Case 1 met all seven principles as outlined by Dolmans et al. (1997): course objectives (knowledge base), real-life issues encountered in educational settings, elaboration of educational issues, supporting self-directed learning, building on background knowledge, integrating knowledge, stimulating interest, and concern regarding educational issues.

Preservice teachers' responses to their peer research packages underscore their engagement with the issues (Box 5.3).

Box 5.3: Examples of Preservice Teachers' Responses to Research Packages
Research package 1: Play-based learning

Your resource package is comprehensive in both breadth and depth. I found the section on the differences between child-initiated vs. teacher-initiated play informative and will use the chart you provided in my lesson planning. I do believe a balance of child- and teacher-initiated play fits into a well-rounded, provincially supported, parent-approved, real-world approach for a kindergarten classroom.

Research package 2: Issues of social justice and Aboriginal Education in the kindergarten classroom

Your resource package is very comprehensive and informative. As teachers/preservice teachers, it is very important to address social injustice in classrooms. You have provided us with an understanding of *Making Space*[3] and described the importance of it. You've also highlighted the issue of bullying at schools. It is a big issue that seems to go on and on. Addressing the issue

---

[3] *Making Space: Teaching for Diversity and Social Justice throughout the K-12 Curriculum* (2008) is a B.C. Ministry of Education Curriculum document. Making space is designed to help K-12 teachers to find ways to promote awareness and understanding of diversity and support for the achievement of social justice.

(continued)

Box 5.1 (continued)

starts with teachers and preservice teachers providing lessons to help students understand social injustice in order to minimize and prevent bullying. You have included resources and information on how teachers should approach the issue of social justice. The procedural principles and strategies you have included are a great way to guide teachers and preservice teachers on how to address the issue and incorporate social justice into a lesson.

Research package 3: Building a classroom community

Your introduction of Peck's stages of community[4] is very interesting and actually made me think back to the many classroom and collegial settings that I've experienced. You also incorporate the importance of family in the school community – another aspect of your package that I appreciate: Parents and guardians place their trust in educators, and it is part of the educator's job to be as inclusive and open as possible. I found the study conducted by Hao and Bonstead-Bruns (1998) that you cited identifying family expectations for their children's education very intriguing, and it caused me to think of why expectations benefit some groups of students but hinder others. It puts the issue of diversity in perspective as well as placing an emphasis on continuing education for educators in relation to cultural sensitivity and acceptance. Page 15 of your package is something that I'm actually going to save for future reference.

Research package 4: Kindergarten curriculum

Your resource package is definitely a valuable addition to go alongside the Full-Day Kindergarten Program Guide! It really helps to explain things in an easy to understand way and provides a good introduction to what a kindergarten class could be like. Also, your classroom strategies section was excellent – very informative and filled with wonderful suggestions that can be directly applied to a kindergarten class!

Research package 5: Orality and literacy

Thank you for your resource package on Orality! You distinguish the differences between the oral tradition and structured literacy very well in your package. Your presentation showed me that using all my senses to take in a story through storytelling could be more engaging than simply reading the same story from a book. I can apply this approach to all my lessons across all subjects. I thought your coverage on the history of oral tradition was key in understanding how innate oral communication is to our human nature.

---

[4] In his book, *The Different Drum: Community Making and Peace* (1987), Dr. M. Scott Peck an American Psychiatrist, the community-building process goes through four predictable phases: pseudo-community in which conflict is avoided, chaos in which individual differences emerge, emptiness in which individuals begin to share deep emotions and experiences, and community in which a place of true acceptance and where differences are appreciated.

While I have outlined the development of Case 1 as though it occurred in isolation, in fact, each of the eleven cases was considered to be part of the TELL through PBL teacher education problem *set*, and each case was developed as part of that problem *set*. We used the matrix, seven principles of designing effective cases and considered the existing ten cases and dilemma not only in terms of how that case functioned as a stand alone in facilitating learning but how each case built one upon the other to meet the curriculum needs of the TELL through PBL cohort across the teacher education program (as a set of cases or problems). Thus, issues or topics could be taken up again in subsequent cases deepening preservice teachers' understanding of complex issues. For example, issues of language were/are embedded in the cases as follows:

- Case 1: Developing language-rich classrooms – creating contexts for language learning
- Case 2: Development of oral language through interactive, participatory activities using multiple modes to aid learning
- Case 3: Code switching – English as a second dialect in First Nations communities
- Case 5: School language and home language – developing cognitive academic language proficiency (CALP) and basic interpersonal communication skills (BICS)
- Case 6: Refugee students and language – plurilingual (a range of languages, dialects, and registers) and intergenerational differences in home language, culture knowledge, and affiliation
- Case 7: Eligibility for English Language Learning (ELL) funding and the role of the ELL/resource teacher
- Case 8: Planning for multilingual classrooms – designing multiliteracies pedagogy
- Case 9: Integrating language and content – A student's first language (L1) as a resource for content and second language (L2) learning in the mainstream classroom

Through engagement with language issues across the cases, the preservice teachers gradually build a depth and breadth of understanding of the major theories and approaches to teaching English as an additional language, the role of language as a medium for learning including the integration of language and content, transformative multiliteracy pedagogies, the role of literate environments and enriched language environments in fostering second language and literacy development, and tools for second language and literacy assessment.

Issue 5: Ongoing Revisions

While the set of cases for the TELL through PBL cohort was completed and implemented in the academic year 2012/2013, work continues to review them as to their effectiveness in meeting requirements of the B.Ed. program and in preparing preservice teachers for their practica. For example, while the focus of the PBL cases in the first term of the teacher education program is primarily on the foundations that underpin understanding of teaching practice, the focus changes in the second term to engaging preservice teachers in teaching and learning in the subject or content areas (e.g., Science, Physical Education, Music, Art, and so forth). The subject area resource specialists are actively involved in ensuring issues in the subject areas are covered, current, and pertinent to the needs of preservice teachers about to embark on careers in the very complex North American multilingual/multicultural classroom environment. For example, Case 6 reads:

> This year, you are teaching grade 3/4 for the first time. The school is located in an inner-city neighborhood and most of your students are from low-income families; many of the families struggle to provide basic necessities and a number of the students take part in a district-funded lunch program. Many students have also come from refugee families, speak a language other than English at home, and some have interrupted formal schooling. Here's a recent entry from your teaching journal:
>
> *What a day! The kids were restless and it felt as though I spent the whole day nagging them to do their work. Emil and Tony participated in math class by wandering around bugging people! After school, I talked to Doug who teaches next door and he asked if I would like to do some planning that addresses a common theme across social studies, science, technology, visual art and music. This definitely sounds more exciting than the worksheets we've been doing, but I don't know if my class is ready for it. How can we do interesting things if they can't settle down?*
>
> You've attended several workshops on reading assessment and looked at the Developmental Reading Assessment (DRA), District Assessment of Reading (DART), Reading Assessment District 36 (RAD) and Reading 44. You have decided to meet with your teacher-librarian to develop bins of leveled books for both your guided reading program and students' independent reading.
>
> One of the bright spots in my day was noticing how much happier David seems to be. That workshop on Asperger's syndrome and other autism spectrum disorders (ASD) gave me a lot more insight into his behavior and how I can help him succeed at school.
>
> First term reports are due in two weeks and I'm glad I've learned how to prepare ahead of time. Still, I feel bad giving a "C" to somebody like Brajit who's been working really hard. We had a heated discussion in the staffroom at lunch yesterday – Marilyn was defending letter grades as "great motivators" while Max and Ruta argued that they do more harm than good. People were actually starting to shout at each other – and then the bell rang.

During discussions of the case, the resource specialist in Physical Education suggested that preservice teachers might identify the affordances of Physical Education to address issues of concentration if the following sentence was added to paragraph two of the case:

> *I wonder how I can utilize Daily Physical Activity (DPA) and co-operative games in the gym to support my students' concentration in class.*

Additionally, the Art and Music resource specialists suggested the addition of an additional paragraph (following paragraph four) that focuses on identifying opportunities for collaboration between the classroom teacher and resource teacher. Specifically, in this case identifying the ways in which the resource teacher and the classroom teacher can help a child with autism spectrum disorder participate in music and art activities.

> *I will have to speak to the resource teacher about Mary. Although he has been reluctant to provide EA support for her during a non-academic class, I don't think he is aware of the behavior issues caused by autism that occur during art and music, two very hands-on classes. Yesterday, she flicked paint at the person next to her with her paintbrush and last week, she blew her instrument very loudly into Joni's ear. Perhaps discussing some of the ASD workshop materials would help convince the resource teacher.*

This process is undertaken with each case: Cases are read, critiqued, and edited by the TELL through PBL team. These team meetings are often lively (sometimes loud) as subject area specialists (content knowledge) and tutors (inquiry and process) discuss the merits of a particular case. However, all agree that this process is essential to maintaining the currency and rigor of our cases.

Summary

A curriculum development team made up of tutors, a librarian, and members from each of the Faculty of Education departments (Educational Studies, Language and Literacy, Educational Pedagogy and Curriculum, and Educational Psychology and Special Education) was identified to plan, develop, and write cases for a problem based learning cohort with a focus on Teaching English Language Learners (TELL) in a new teacher education program at the University of British Columbia. The case writers developed a matrix of objectives and topics based on the courses comprising the teacher education program at UBC. There was consensus among the curriculum development team that essential strands identified as pillars of the new teacher education program – inquiry and research, diversity and social and ecological justice, Aboriginal Education and aboriginal perspectives, linguistic and cultural diversity as resource, integration of technology, and theory to practice – be either amplified or echoed across the case set. Existing cases were used to provide direction in the writing of the new cases. Finally, case writers agreed that the seven principles outlined by Dolmans et al. (1997) would guide the writing of the case set.

However, while the development, planning, and writing of the cases were completed in time for the implementation of the new teacher education program at UBC, the cases still needed to be evaluated in terms of whether they successfully engaged preservice teachers in developing both process skills and professional content knowledge. To that end, the TELL through PBL teaching team made up of tutors, subject area resource specialist from each of the Faculty of Education departments, and the education librarian meet every 2 weeks to evaluate the current case in terms of complexity, length, and preservice teachers' engagement with the issues. Additionally, each upcoming case is interrogated by the TELL through PBL team to delete any parts of the case narrative that are unclear, edit the case if it is too long, and ensure that it builds on preservice teachers' emerging knowledge. In short, case writing, revisions, and usage are ongoing and continually scrutinized as part of the TELL through PBL curriculum.

References

Dahlgren, M. A. (2000). Portraits of PBL: Course objectives and students' study strategies in computer engineering, psychology and physiotherapy. *Instructional Science, 2*(8): 309–329. Retrieved February 22, 2014. http://www.diva-portal.org/smash/get/diva2:260015/FULLTEXT01.pdf

Dolmans, D., Snellen-Balendong, H., Wolfhagen, I., & van der Vleuten, C. (1997). Seven principles of effective case design for a problem-based curriculum. *Medical Teacher, 19*(3), 185–189. doi:10.3109/01421599709019379.

Hao, L., & Bonstead-Bruns, M. (1998). Parent–child differences in educational expectations and the academic achievement of immigrant and native students. *Sociology of Education, 71*(3), 175–198.

Jonassen, D. H., & Hung, W. (2008). All problems are not equal: Implications for problem-based learning. *Interdisciplinary Journal of Problem-based Learning, 2*(2): 6–28. doi:10.771/15415015.1080.

Savery, J. R. (2006). Overview of problem-based learning: Definitions and distinctions. *Interdisciplinary Journal of problem-based learning, 1*(1): 9–20. Available at: http://dx.doi.org/10.7771/1541-5015.1002

Chapter 6
Finding Good Governance: Collaboration Between the University of British Columbia and the Richmond School District

Kathyrn D'Angelo, Gail Krivel-Zacks, and Catherine Johnson

Introduction

In 1998 the teacher education program enrolment at the University of British Columbia (UBC) included 538 preservice teachers. 299 were in the 12-month program, 128 in the first year of the 2-year Bachelor of Education, and 111 in the second year of the Bachelor of Education. There were 11 elementary cohorts, and many of these were themed (e.g., Elementary French Specialist cohort that prepared teachers to work in French Immersion, Core French, and Intensive French as well as in Francophone schools; Middle years cohort which prepared teachers for teaching in Middle schools, generally, Grades 6 to 8). All cohorts were under the administration of the Teacher Education Office (TEO) in the Faculty of Education. While we knew that the ultimate responsibility for the problem based learning (PBL) cohort would remain with the TEO, it was clear to us that at the cohort level we needed a fresh approach to governance.

Research in a number of fields has identified the importance of good governance practices in effective organizational performance (Shipley and Kovacs 2008 p. 216). While the term governance can be rather *slippery* in that it may mean different things to different organizations, e.g., global governance, corporate governance, participatory governance, and so on (Gisselquist 2012), in general terms, it simply means a framework and/or a process for decision-making. The concept of "good" governance can be defined as the model of governance that leads to desired results

---

K. D'Angelo (✉)
Richmond School District, Richmond, BC, Canada
e-mail: kdangelo@sd38.bc.ca

G. Krivel-Zacks
Vancouver Island University, Nanaimo, BC, Canada

C. Johnson
Simon Fraser University, Burnaby, BC, Canada

through values of democracy and social justice (Shipley and Kovacs 2008, p. 216). Many characteristics of "good" governance have been identified in the literature including but not limited to: rule of law, integrity, participatory, respectful, responsive, accountable, collaborative, effective and efficient, equitable, and inclusive. While characteristics of "good" governance may differ from organization to organization, five characteristics were identified, which appear to underpin all models of "good" governance. Those characteristics are responsibility, participation, transparency, accountability, and responsiveness. Additionally, we believe "good" governance is defined by good will and collaboration between partners.

By highlighting each of these characteristics or pillars of "good" governance, this chapter explores the roles, relationships, and principles of governance that were and continue to be the underpinning of the problem based learning cohort established in 1999 in the teacher education program at the University of British Columbia.

Roles, Responsibility, and Participation

Practice teaching is an important part of any teacher education program, yet the literature identifies that there is often a weak collaboration between the school and the university (Zeichner 2010). Ulvik and Smith (2011) write that the two sites of learning often function like two different worlds:

> The different kinds of knowledge, episteme (theoretical) and techne (practical), do not interact to enhance an in-depth reflection and the development of phronesis (practical wisdom). (p. 531)

From our perspective it was important that theory and practice complement each other, and this was only possible if the Richmond School District (the school district where the PBL teacher candidates would complete their school-based practicum) was to have a significant and equal role in the governance of the PBL cohort. A number of factors underscored the Richmond School District as an ideal partner: The school district is geographically well located close to the university; there had been a history of a significant number of schools and/or teachers requesting practica students from the teacher education program at UBC; in the past, several cohorts of preservice teachers had been successfully integrated into schools in the Richmond School District for their school-based practicum; and there were seconded teachers from the district working in or for the Teacher Education Office.

In order to gauge interest in offering a unique pilot program that would build on the existing relationship with Richmond School District and UBC, an initial meeting was held between the Associate Dean of Teacher Education Charles Ungerleider, Professor Linda Seigel, and Kathyrn D'Angelo a seconded instructor and Administrator in the Richmond School District. At this meeting the philosophy of problem based learning and how such a teaching and learning pedagogy could be translated from McMaster Medical School into a pilot teacher education program was discussed. Specifically, discussion centered on establishing a cohort premised on the belief that learning is a social process and that the appropriate context for learning is in small groups. Until this time, the teacher education program at UBC had used a traditional model of teaching and learning that is premised on the instructor as the dispenser of knowledge and the student as the recipient – as opposed to the PBL approach where preservice teachers with the support of tutors are encouraged to share their understandings with both their peers and the tutors. The goal is to compare one's own way of thinking with those of others and to clarify, compare, and negotiate meanings and understanding of concepts. Within the small PBL tutorial group, learning becomes the activity, and teaching, or in this case tutoring, becomes the support for the activity of learning.

Once the basic premise for a PBL cohort in the teacher education program at UBC was hammered out, a meeting was held between the Teacher Education Office at UBC and the Executive Team of the Richmond School District. At this meeting the philosophy of problem based learning was shared as well as the possible design for a teacher education pilot program. Further discussion ensued around the joint financial contribution necessary to make this program a success for both the university and the school district. It was believed that both the university and the district invest equally in this project.

The joint funding of the PBL cohort was unique. Monies were spent to support the professional development of both the preservice teachers and practicing teachers involved in the PBL cohort. The belief of all the stakeholders was that professional development opportunities needed to be experienced by both the sponsoring teacher and the preservice teacher at the same time to model the attributes of a lifelong learner in and out of the classroom This meant that some of these funds were used to provide substitute teachers so that the sponsor teachers could be released to attend these important learning and relationship-building opportunities. Guidelines for the use of these funds were created collaboratively with the District Coordinator from PBL meeting with the school district representative and the representative from the teachers' union. The key hopes and dreams of the school district were that this type of collaboration would:

- Model lifelong learning
- Connect practicing teachers with the university
- Connect the university with the school district for their mutual benefit
- Establish a university presence in the school district to benefit both the staff and the students
- Expose district personnel to the notion of problem based learning and its methodology
- Allow student teachers to be woven into the culture of the school fabric from the beginning of the school year right through to the end of the school year

Part of the conversation also revolved around ongoing assessment of the teacher education pilot program, specifically that the teachers would be an ongoing part of the formative and summative assessment of the cases. To this end adjustments to the cases were based on teacher as well as faculty feedback.

Because the stakeholders in the PBL cohort wanted to uphold a collaborative approach, any schools interested in participating in the PBL pilot project first had to have school-wide agreement on participation in the project and then indicate their interest on an application form. The District Coordinator, district staff, and the district teacher's union president reviewed all the requests to participate and selected a number of schools to be involved. Selection was based upon the school's interest and ability to accommodate a significant number of preservice teachers. The program philosophy was to place the preservice teachers in schools in groups of six to eleven. We knew that small groups would promote promising practice and opportunities for both the preservice and the practicing teachers.

Roles and Relationships of the PBL Faculty

Teacher education programs traditionally consist of a program of studies and practica experiences. In traditional programs there is a separation between disciplines and also between the program of studies and practica experiences. The PBL teacher education program included not only changes to a program of studies but also changes to the practica. The aim of the PBL program in Teacher Education was to provide a closer connection within the study of teaching and the practice of teaching. In order to facilitate this, the typical role of professor was replaced by tutors and subject area resource specialists. The specific responsibilities of these roles are outlined below.

Roles and Responsibilities in the Field

1. *District Coordinator:* While the role of the District Coordinator was similar to a Field Coordinator, it was important that the role be defined as a District Coordinator to reflect the underlying collaborative and cooperative principles of the PBL philosophy. The District Coordinator and the PBL Coordinator worked in a collaborative manner to connect the university with the school district. As the position of Field Coordinator was a position that did not exist in either the school district or at the university, there were no existing job descriptions. This role and the expectations that went with this role were based on earlier projects that the university had conducted in lower mainland school districts. Anecdotal evidence showed that an important component for success was the ability to link the goals and objectives of the university program with the school district and its goals and objectives. Communication was also noted as being an important indicator of a successful program for both the preservice teachers and the school district. Therefore it was decided by the Associate Dean of Teacher Education Dr. Charles Ungerleider and by Dr. Linda Seigel to create a liaison position for the problem based learning cohort in the Richmond School District. It would be advantageous to both the university and the district to have an individual who

was experienced both with the university and one who had extensive experience working in the district. Dr. Ungerleider and Dr. Siegel approached Kathyrn D'Angelo to determine her interest and willingness to work in the PBL cohort and to assume this new role. Ms. D'Angelo had extensive experience working in teacher education at the university and, at that time, was working as a: school-based vice principal in Richmond. It was also noted that it would be advantageous to have an administrator in the role of Field Coordinator to handle any issues involving teachers. Since administrators (in this case a vice principal) are not members of the teacher's union, Ms D'Angelo would be able to problem solve any issues involving teachers without violating the teacher's union code of ethics. The Field Coordinator was expected to work with the school district office and the Richmond Teachers Association to coordinate funding from each of these sources to support the PBL cohort within the teacher education program, to plan for the recruitment of school sponsors, and the recruitment of a teacher coordinator at each school-based practicum site. The majority of meetings were called to discuss collaborations around the district and school involvements, to formalize the financial arrangements, and to strategize ways to recruit schools and teachers.

Another expectation of the District Coordinator was to work in collaboration with the tutors to cooperatively plan and deliver in-service opportunities that exposed the school-based personnel to the philosophy and structure of the PBL cohort. These were typically full-day sessions with the objective to understand the unique profile of problem based learning as delivered in this pilot project. It was also an expectation that the District Coordinator would connect the professional development occurring in the school district with the case study experiences of the preservice teachers at the university. Workshops were offered throughout the year for both the sponsor teachers and the preservice teachers. These co-learning opportunities were cocreated and delivered by all PBL team members: The workshops focused on three areas: assessment and evaluation, conflict resolution, and planning for instruction.

2. *School coordinator:* The role of the school coordinator was to liaise between the faculty advisor and the school advisors. Specifically, they were and are responsible for coordinating meetings at the school level. Since many schools have significant numbers of sponsor teachers, it was felt that in the interest of good communication between the school-based practicum sites and the Faculty of Education, a contact person at each school was needed.
3. *School advisor/sponsor teacher:* The school advisor or sponsor teacher was and is the classroom teachers who act as sponsors, advisors, and mentors to the preservice teachers. A unique feature of the PBL program in our teacher education program at UBC is the relationship between the faculty associate and school advisor: These two positions (one based in the school system, school advisor, and one based on the university campus, the faculty advisor) work collaboratively supervising and evaluating the practicum of the preservice teacher. This team approach is built through meetings to establish both the university expectations for preservice teacher's performance on practicum and the school advisor's expertise on classroom practice. Both the school advisors and the faculty advisors

used preservice teachers' reflections about their pedagogy as formative assessment tools.

Roles and Responsibilities on Campus

1. *PBL coordinator:* The role of the PBL coordinator is to work with the Teacher Education Office, Field Coordinator, and the tutors to guide, support, and maintain the integrity of the program.
2. *Subject area resource specialist:* The subject area resource specialists act as a "resource" during the case studies. Preservice teachers seek further clarification on case particulars during the meetings with the resource specialists. In the early years of the PBL cohort, the tutorial groups met regularly with five faculty members who were experts in the areas of social studies, mathematics, educational studies, reading, and science. Preservice teachers also attended physical education workshops on a regular basis that were led by resource specialists. The resource specialists were invited to the weekly faculty meetings where roles and responsibilities were discussed in an ongoing manner.
3. *Tutors*: The role of the tutors was and continues to be to facilitate learning: guiding preservice teachers through each case. In the early days, preservice teachers were organized in small groups of six to seven students. The groups were kept this size based on ongoing research and practice from the McMaster Medical School model. The tutorial experience needed to be open and safe in order to enhance the experiences of the students and to create an environment where ideas and problem solving could be encouraged without judgment. Each group worked with a tutor who was an experienced classroom teacher and who held a minimum of a master's degree in education. Three times per week each tutorial group met to discuss the case and to share information in a group research format. The role of the tutor was to facilitate student-led discussions through questioning techniques, Socratic dialogue, and probing questions that enabled students to connect prior knowledge and new learning to their lived experiences (Fig. 6.1).

Transparency and Responsiveness

Transparency

Transparency is a necessary aspect of good governance, and in relation to this chapter, we will be looking at transparency as closely connected to accountability, which requires the clear communication and access to up-to-date information. Transparency was and continues to be an important aspect of the governance of the PBL program

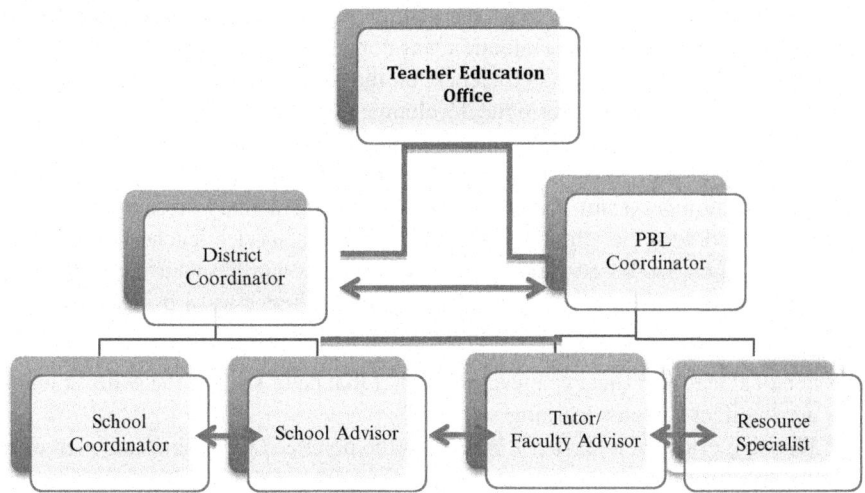

Fig. 6.1 Collaborative relationships between school district and the teacher education program at UBC

at UBC. Transparency between the school district and the university was a novel concept when the program first started. Historically there had been little connection between the campus-based course work preservice teachers were enrolled in and their school-based practica. In order for transparency between the school district and the university to be effective, it was necessary to establish communication channels to share information across the two entities. The roles of the District Coordinator and the PBL Coordinator were critical in establishing these two-way channels of information that linked the school district and the university.

In addition to the need for communication between the school district and the university, there was also the need for transparency at the university between the departments in the Faculty of Education[1] and between the departments and the PBL cohort. In her study, "Using Problem Based Learning in an Innovative Teacher Education Program," Krivel-Zacks (2001) investigated the subject area resource specialists overall satisfaction with teaching within a PBL program. Responses indicated that 100 % of the resource specialists would like to continue their role as the resource specialist for their subject area in the PBL cohort. These findings replicated previous research findings that indicate the faculty who are associated with PBL are satisfied with PBL (Krivel-Zacks 2001).

---

[1] In 1998 the Faculty of Education at the University of British Columbia was comprised of four departments: Department of Educational and Counseling Psychology and Special Education (EPSE), Department of Education Studies (EDST), Department of Curriculum and Instruction (EDCI), and the Department of Language and Literacy Education (LLED): In 2008 EDCI changed its title to the Department of Education Curriculum and Pedagogy (EDCP).

Since its inception in 1998/1999, the PBL program has been formally evaluated three times. In 1998/1999 an evaluation was conducted to provide both initial data to the faculty and the College of Teachers on the readiness to teach of PBL graduates and formative data to inform the development of the PBL program.

In 1999 a small comparative evaluation was conducted to compare the opinions and outcomes of PBL preservice teachers with preservice teachers in the regular teacher education program: The attitudes of 19 PBL elementary preservice teachers were compared with the attitudes of 12 elementary preservice teachers enrolled in the traditional course-based cohorts on their feelings regarding their perceptions of preparedness to teach (i.e., teacher efficacy) and attitudes toward inclusion. The measure of teacher efficacy was composed of two measures:

(1) Personal teacher efficacy: a teacher's belief that he or she has the skills or abilities to effect students learning
(2) Teaching efficacy: a teacher's belief that the practice of teaching can overcome the effects of negative home or family influences

All participants were group-administered measures before and after they had completed their final school-based practicum with each session taking 45 min. The results revealed that there were no significant differences between groups on their feelings of preparedness to teach. On the measures of attitudes toward inclusion, there were group differences in that traditional teacher education students were less likely to support inclusion. On the measure of teacher efficacy, there were no significant differences between groups with regard to personal efficacy. However, there was a significant group effect for teacher efficacy, indicating that PBL students believe that teaching itself can make a difference.

In 2000/2001 PBL at UBC was again the focus of a research study. The purpose of this doctoral research (Krivel-Zacks 2001) was to examine the effects of participation in a PBL teacher education program with respect to PBL preservice teachers and university- and school-based personnel. Krivel-Zacks (2001) examined changes in the PBL teacher education preservice teachers' feelings of efficacy and teacher preparedness and learning styles and strategies. She reported that the PBL preservice teachers showed significant increases in their feelings of personal teaching efficacy and teacher preparedness. The study also compared the opinions and attitudes of PBL preservice teachers with 40 non-PBL preservice teachers at the conclusion of their teacher education programs. The measures included their opinions and attitudes toward inclusion of students with special needs, feelings of satisfaction with their programs, feelings of preparedness, and ratings of self-directed learning. The results indicated that proportionally more PBL than non-PBL preservice teachers felt more positive toward having students with special needs in their classrooms, felt the time they had spent in the classroom had the greatest influence on their changes in opinions, and felt well prepared to teach in the school system.

The results of this investigation (Krivel-Zacks 2001) also revealed that the majority of university- and school-based personnel agreed that a PBL curriculum did have an effect on reasoning, interest, enthusiasm, and satisfaction of faculty and preservice teachers. The majority of participant groups were of the opinion that PBL and non-PBL curriculums provided equal knowledge of basic skills and principles and professional preparation.

Program Responsiveness

During the first 3 years of the PBL cohort, teacher education program regular meetings were held with all the stakeholders in the Richmond School District (coordinators and school advisors). At these meetings personnel from the Richmond School District and the university collaborated and reviewed the lived experiences. When the reviews indicated a need to adjust either the materials covered or the structure of the program, the university personnel conducted further conversations to determine if the change was warranted and/or possible. Three concerns in particular illustrate the cohort's responsiveness to issues raised across the cohort stakeholders:

1. Following the short 2-week practicum held in January, immediately after school resumed after the winter break, the school district faculty raised concerns that the teacher candidates did not have sufficient time to meet and plan with their school advisors in preparation for this practicum. The issue was taken forward to the Teacher Education Office, and following discussions with the Associate Dean of teacher education, the 2-week school-based practicum was extended to include a further week for planning.
2. While it was noted at the meetings that our PBL preservice teachers were growing in their ability to identify the nature and scope of problems/issues presented in the cases, concerns were raised by the school advisors, preservice teachers, and the resource specialists (subject area faculty) that teacher candidates were in need of more focused hands-on experiences with a variety of subjects including art, science, physical education, and music. A series of workshops were implemented in the areas of French as a second language, English as an additional language, classroom management, technology in the classroom, learning disabilities, Orff music, and art.
3. Meetings with on-campus resources specialists in the department of Educational Studies raised the concern that there was not enough content in the cases related to issues of social organization and social justice. The concern was addressed by having resources specialists in Educational Studies create a grid outlining issues and topics that were either represented in a case or that needed to be added to case(s).

Ensuring Organizational Responsiveness

By the academic year 2001–2002, a number of changes had been implemented. The "two-week" school experience had been changed to a 3-week school experience. Following on the lead of Educational Studies, it was noted that there was a need to coordinate cases, and to ensure that all areas were reflected in an equitable manner, a case grid was created outlining all issues in each case and connecting each issue with a subject area for resource specialists. It was also noted that the need for shared professional development for school advisors and preservice teachers was growing. Several opportunities for these teams to come together and focus on particular topics such as classroom management, supporting diverse learners in the classroom, and assessment and evaluation were provided.

Conclusions

While the problem based learning cohort remains vibrant, a number of changes have occurred both in the cohort itself and in the governance of the cohort. In 2012 a new B.Ed program was approved and implemented. At the same time the number of applications to the teacher education program dropped. In order for the PBL cohort to continue, it needed to reinvent itself and to that end two cohorts were integrated: Teaching English Language Learners through problem based learning (TELL through PBL). In Canada, children from families with linguistic minority backgrounds form a substantial and rapidly growing proportion of the school population. In the school district in the metropolitan area where our preservice teachers will work, more than 148 different language groups are represented in the schools. In some classrooms, more than a dozen different home languages are spoken; and in many classrooms, the majority of children speak a language other than English, the language of instruction, at home. The Canadian context in many ways reflects global trends. For according to UNESCO (2011), worldwide there are "214 million people now living outside their country of origin" (p. 75), and the movement of people is expected to increase. The TELL through PBL cohort has proved to be popular because it specifically prepares preservice teachers to teach in these linguistically and culturally diverse classrooms.

Over the years there have also been changes to the governance of the cohort. Specifically, with the dissolution of the District Coordinator position, administration of the cohort is now primarily concentrated in the Teacher Education Office at UBC. However, UBC and the Richmond School District still contribute financially to make the program a success for both the university and the school district. Together the university and the school district still plan and deliver in-service opportunities to expose the school-based personnel to the philosophy and structure of problem based learning and meeting the needs of all learners.

References

Gisselquist, R. (2012). *What does "good governance" mean?* Accessed at: http://unu.edu/publications/articles/what-does-good-governance-mean.html

Krivel-Zack, G. (2001). *Using problem-based learning in an innovative teacher education program.* Unpublished dissertation.

Shipley, R., & Kovacs, J. F. (2008). Good governance principles for the cultural heritage sector: Lessons from international experience. *Corporate Governance, 8*(2): 214–228. Accessed at: http://env-web2.uwaterloo.ca/hrcresearch/attachments/519fb740a129b0.53659657.pdf

Ulvik, M., & Smith, K. (2011). What characterizes a good practicum in teacher education? *Education Inquiry, 2*(3), 517–536.

UNESCO. (2011). *The state of world population.* Accessed at: http://foweb.unfpa.org/SWP2011/reports/EN-SWOP2011-FINAL.pdf

Zeichner, K. (2010). Rethinking the connections between campus courses and field experiences in college- and university-based teacher education. *Journal of Teacher Education, 6*(1–2), 89–99.

Chapter 7
Collaboration: The Heart of the School-Based Practicum

Carolyn Russo and Nicky Freeman

Introduction

Research suggests that the school-based practicum is one of the most influential components of a teacher education program and that the school advisor (cooperating teacher) exerts the greatest influence on the preservice teacher (Schussler 2006). Generally, it has been suggested that an effective school advisor *models* examples of good practice for the teacher candidate to evaluate and emulate. In addition, it is suggested the school advisor should *mentor* students to become effective practitioners and to develop as professionals in the field (Glen 2006 p. 86). In keeping with this approach, the Bachelor of Education Policy Handbook developed by our Faculty of Education for both school advisors and preservice teachers writes:

> During the initial school experience, School Advisors begin the process of acting as both mentors and models for teacher candidates. This process continues throughout the extended practicum. (p. 39)

Upon reflection, however, it seemed to us (Carolyn Russo the school advisor and Nicky Freeman the preservice teacher) that this more traditional approach to the school-based practicum was not a good match for Nicky whose teacher education programme employed a problem based learning (PBL) methodology. What seemed to us to be more appropriate for Nicky was a broader practicum experience that provided her with "opportunities for inquiry, for trying and testing new ideas within a collaborative relationship and for talking about teaching and learning in new ways" (Schultz 2005, p. 148). Such an approach, it seemed to us, was in keeping with features of a problem based learning program in teacher education, which undertakes to engage preservice teachers in critically analysing and solving real-world classroom issues and problems. Such an approach, we argue, identifies the

---

C. Russo (✉) • N. Freeman
Richmond School District, Richmond, BC, Canada
e-mail: crusso@sd38.bc.ca

school advisor and the preservice teacher as engaged problem solvers who collaborate to identify and understand issues and problems that emerge in an active and complex classroom setting and through discussion identify what the preservice teacher knows and needs to know to make an informed decision regarding every aspect of an active, working classroom.

The narrative of this chapter moves back and forth between us (Carolyn Russo, the sponsor teacher, and Nicky Freeman, the preservice teacher). It highlights our history and beliefs about our role(s) in the school-based practicum and the ways in which problem based learning provided an approach that facilitated Nicky's learning through collaboration and problem solving.

The School Advisor: Carolyn Russo

Becoming Involved

While I have always understood that practice teaching is one of the most important aspects of any teacher education program, I had never considered the possibility that I might extend my teaching practice to include preservice teachers. From my perspective, I felt that I still had much to learn before taking on the responsibility of preservice teacher supervision. However, after discussing my readiness to take on a preservice teacher with my administrator, I agreed to take a PBL preservice teacher for her school-based practicum. This decision has proved to be one of the best professional decisions I have ever made. I agree with Ochs and McDowell (2004) who write about the learning opportunities provided by being a school advisor.

> While observing a [preservice teacher] in action, I can sit on the sidelines and think about teaching and learning. I have the time to consider carefully my beliefs about education, my suitability for the profession, and what I do for my students. As I watch another person teach, I challenge myself to reflect upon my methods and my style of classroom management. I look for ways to optimize the learning that occurs in my classroom. I also take the opportunity to analyse what I enjoy about being a teacher and what concerns me about teaching. (p. 13)

Helping someone discover who they are as an educator and developing their teaching pedagogy has been very rewarding for me for various reasons, but I also feel that it is important to accept a preservice teacher into my classroom because they are future teachers and colleagues. I care about the students and who is coming into this profession, and by taking a preservice teacher, it allows me to have an impact on the future of education through a different avenue. In education we are always learning. I am a lifelong learner, and through taking PBL preservice teachers, it encourages lifelong learning and reflective teaching practices.

Each year the experience of having a preservice teacher in my classroom is very different. Numerous factors play a role, such as the preservice teacher and their level of dedication and expectations, the children and their families and the school community.

Preservice Teacher: Nicky Freeman

Nervous Beginnings

While my school-based practicum began with EDUC 315, a 1-day a week field experience during the fall term, I was aware that I would also remain in this particular classroom for not only the 1-day a week practicum but also the short 2-week practicum in the winter term (EDUC 321) and the long 10-week practicum that occurred the following April to June (EDUC 418). The placement for the school-based practicum was announced on the first day of the teacher education program, and we were informed that we would attend our practicum schools on the second day of classes and every Wednesday thereafter. As I anticipated my first school-based experience, I was both nervous and excited. I was full of questions regarding my sponsor teacher, what her expectations might be and whether I'd be able to meet the demands of a busy classroom.

Six preservice teachers from the PBL cohort were placed at the same practicum school, and for the first 6 weeks of this 1-day a week practicum, we observed the teaching style of each of the teachers who would serve as school advisors, as well as the curriculum they were responsible for teaching. We were encouraged to jump in and interact with the students and to take initiative in supporting the teacher when needed. There were also many opportunities to ask sponsor teachers questions about their teaching experiences, and I often stayed after school *to pick their brains*.

As our 6-week rotation came to a close, tensions rose regarding where each of the preservice teachers would be placed for the remaining school-based practica. Most of us already knew our preference regarding whether we wanted to teach the intermediate grades (Grades 4–7) or the primary grades (Kindergarten to Grade 3). When I found I had been placed in a Grade 1 classroom with Carolyn Russo, I was delighted to be with someone I had connected with both at a personal level and in terms of her teaching style and teaching philosophy. I felt ready and excited to begin planning my year teaching Grade 1.

However, not only did I have to consider the demands of my school advisor, Carolyn, I also had to work with a faculty advisor Monika Tarampi who ensured that I was reflecting my on-campus work at UBC in my teaching practice in the school-based practicum. Monika was seconded from her school district to teach in the teacher education program at UBC. She not only facilitated the Educational Psychology courses with preservice teachers in the PBL cohort but she was also a tutor for the PBL cohort. Monika had been seconded by UBC because she had a long history of working in the Richmond School District as a classroom teacher, as a resource teacher[1] and as a Special Education consultant. This was Monika's first year as a faculty advisor, and while I trusted her implicitly, I felt like we were learning

---

[1] Resource teachers' role is twofold: (1) To be part of the School-Based Team in the development of an IEP (e.g., autism, challenging behaviours, learning disabilities, intellectual disabilities, giftedness) and (2) to provide the classroom teacher with specialized additional support.

together. It was humbling to know that while Monika had spent many years doing the job that I was now learning, she was also taking risks in her career by changing direction and teaching at UBC. These two women were extraordinary models: Carolyn was the teacher that I wanted to be in 5 years and Monika inspired me to create distinct long-term goals. Additionally, Monika made connections to problem based learning and, in particular, how to approach my school-based practicum classroom as a case study.

Part of the on-campus expectations for my school-based practicum was the writing of weekly reflections on aspects of teaching practice and the classroom environment. Initial reflections revealed my overwhelming concern with issues of classroom management and the role of management in effective teaching practice:

What?
Afternoon chaos transformed into harmony.
After lunch, the kids had incredibly high energy. Carolyn and I think that it might have had to do with having so many (new) adults in the room including Miss Nena's 14-year-old son. They were all abuzz with excitement. Carolyn had planned a writing activity for the afternoon, which she quickly realized was *not* going to work based on their inability to concentrate when sitting on the carpet.

So what?
Teaching based on the students' needs.
Carolyn used teaching strategies to bring their energy level down to a manageable level. First, she scrapped the writing lesson all together and took them spontaneously outside for a run.
Then, when they came back inside, she put on classical music as they did an art activity that was similar to one that they had done in the past (aka it wasn't overly challenging for them). It was incredible to see the class transformed from being wild and crazy to being relaxed.

Now what?
Flexibility at its finest.
To be honest, after lunch when I saw how energetic (and somewhat unruly) the children were, I felt my stress level beginning to rise. Yet, Carolyn seemed cool as a cucumber. She read the class's mood and was flexible in the moment. She used well-thought out strategies to calm them down without yelling or losing her temper.
What I found most interesting is that Carolyn told me afterwards that she *did* feel overwhelmed during that time, but she knew that if she showed the children that, then all hell would have broken loose.
This was a great learning experience for me in the importance of being flexible as a teacher and in staying calm. She made her adaptations look so easy, yet I know they were based on a lot of experience working with this age group.

Later, as I grew more confident, I began to make more links between my work on campus and my work as a preservice teacher in the school-based practicum. For example, I decided to join a school club – Social Justice League – and began to think about how and what I had learned on campus and how Anne Zavalkoff, the Educational Studies resource specialist, might help me understand and facilitate discussion around difficult topics like race and gender.

> This Wednesday, I joined in on the Social Justice League meeting at lunchtime. It is a club that is open to Grade 6 and 7 students and it discusses/focuses on social justice issues. Two teachers who are completing their master's degrees run it and I have decided to get involved and become a part of the team. Currently, the students are planning an Art and Bake Sale to raise money to provide clean water in the Sudan.
>
> I am planning to meet with Anne Zavalkoff before my long practicum to find some ideas on how to approach the group. I would love to facilitate some discussions about racism, gender etc, but I want to do it sensitively and effectively. I also think that lunchtime clubs need to be FUN so that it doesn't feel like work for the students. Social justice issues can get heavy, and that is not my intention. James and Kelly (the teacher's who are involved) made me aware that they are open to my ideas, which is great. This is my first experience working with intermediate students and I think it will benefit me in my development. I feel nervous about not only working with a group of students that am unfamiliar with, but also collaborating with other teachers. I want to find a balance between being an observer and a being a participant.

Thus, from initial worries regarding how to manage a classroom, I moved towards thinking about ways to engage students in complex and challenging issues and how I might contribute to the school community.

Building Success: Carolyn Russo

Nicky's dedication to having a successful practicum was clear from the first time we met, but how I was going to support her and how she was going to achieve a successful practicum was something we had to discover together.

While I firmly believed part of my role was to model best practice in teaching for Nicky, I had no interest in trying to create a second Carolyn Russo. From my perspective my role as a school advisor was to support Nicky's discovery of who she was as an educator. To that end, it seemed to me that most important aspect of the preservice teacher – school advisor relationship – was and is clear, respectful communication. To that end, during my first conversations with Nicky, expectations were discussed and set. From my perspective, both the school advisor and the preservice teacher must be clear about what is expected of them. These expectations can then be referenced throughout the practicum. Therefore, having ongoing discussions and communicating on a regular basis was something I valued. As far as possible, Nicky and I met each day to debrief the day's events. These discussions ranged from short conversations on the day-to-day running of a busy classroom to long discussions on complex issues that arose.

Because Nicky's teacher education program at the University of British Columbia (UBC) used a PBL pedagogical approach, such conversations and reflections were familiar to Nicky. A major component of PBL is the use of collaborative groups to explore, analyse and solve problems presented in case form. The tutor's role is to monitor and facilitate the group's processes rather than providing content knowledge. I felt my role, like that of the tutor, was to facilitate Nicky's growth and understanding of the practice of teaching. Thus, rather than providing Nicky with answers when issues arose, I asked Nicky guiding or probing questions designed to help her build critical thinking skills. Through such exchanges Nicky took ownership of her own learning.

A second way I encouraged Nicky to communicate with me was through a two-way journal. In the journal Nicky was encouraged to write down questions, write reflections, express concerns about students and identify what worked well in a lesson, what she might do differently, ideas for teaching and plans for teaching, etc. The journal was kept in a common area where we could both write in it at any time either to contribute thoughts and ideas or to respond to each other's entries. The journal was not intended to replace our conversations; rather it was a tool to use when either I or Nicky was engaged in meetings, activities or planning that made conversation difficult. Additionally, on occasion the journal provided a space to communicate when the subject was difficult or Nicky needed time to think and reflect on an issue before we talked. Through our communication, Nicky and I were able to build deep connections and developed a strong professional relationship. I provided Nicky with the room to take risks and respectfully challenged her thinking, and, in return, Nicky provided me with a strong commitment to her role as a collaborating teacher in a highly complex classroom.

Finding My Way: Nicky Freeman

As a problem based learning preservice teacher, I had researched and presented on a number of issues and problems embedded in case studies before I started my practicum. My on-campus case-based work had provided me with many opportunities to identify and make sense of the integrated needs of teaching in a classroom. Thus, when I was placed with my school advisor Carolyn Russo in a Grade 1 classroom, I found myself naturally creating a case of this particular Grade 1 classroom:

> The Grade 1 classroom consists of 20 students from a diverse population in terms of ethnicity, language, and family support. The class consists of students with social and emotional needs, anxiety, ministry designations, and a wide range of learning needs at various developmental levels. There is a very high ESL population of students with 16 Level 1 or 2 ESL students. There are two ministry identified children, one with autism spectrum disorder and one with moderate behaviour, both working from Individual Education Plans. In addition, there is Job Action taking place in which teachers (or student teachers) cannot hold parent teacher conferences, plan fieldtrips, or write formal report cards. How can one address the needs of this diverse population?

As I began to unpack some of the issues in my *Grade 1 case*, something interesting occurred to me. Just as in the unpacking of on-campus cases, I was not alone in the school-based practicum identifying issues and making decisions regarding the needs of this community of learners: I had my school advisor Carolyn to work collaboratively with. However, while this revelation (that I would not be working alone) provided me with comfort, I knew that how the collaboration between Carolyn and me was going to work depended on how I perceived my role as a preservice teacher in someone else's classroom. Was I going to see myself as an equal partner in making the best choices for my students or was I going to defer to my school advisor no matter what my opinion was? Candidly, I was leaning towards the latter option. Yet, on the first day of my practicum, something surprising happened. Carolyn approached me with one very simple question: "What do you think, Nicky?" Without a second thought, I let down my guard and gave my opinion. At that moment, a line of communication was opened between us that we nurtured throughout the three school-based practica.

The decision was made that we would endeavour to build communication and collaboration through daily dialogue using the Socratic method. Specifically, Socratic questioning is intended to elicit ideas and support critical thinking through questions designed to:

- Clarify
- Probe assumptions
- Reveal reasons and evidence
- Reveal differing viewpoints and perspectives
- Probe implications and consequences
- Function of the question

Through such dialogue (with which my work on campus had made me very familiar), it was hoped I would be able to develop my own teaching style and identify ways of tackling teaching issues. Yet, as my teaching responsibilities began to increase, I found myself modelling Carolyn's teaching style. Not because I wanted to impress her, but simply because I *liked* her. I saw the effectiveness of her instruction and I also admired the close relationships that she had created with her students. I still don't remember whether I made a conscious choice to model her teaching style, but I soon realized that it simply wasn't going to work. I knew that Carolyn didn't require me to be a clone of her, yet it took time for me to learn this on my own. The students also didn't want another Mrs. Russo. They had formed a special relationship with their Grade 1 teacher that couldn't (and shouldn't) be imitated. As I looked at *the case* that I had created of the classroom context and reflected on my daily interactions with Carolyn, I realized that we had one very crucial common interest; we were both invested in the well-being of our students. Therefore, our commitment to their success largely influenced our commitment to be successful together. At this point, although it technically stopped being about "us", our shared intentions only served to positively influence our relationship.

Such joint understandings led Carolyn and me to sit down and create expectations for both the needs of our classroom as well our expectations for each another. As we had planned, we chatted daily to create and reassess shared goals for our students that would meet their academic, emotional and social needs. We began by tackling the British Columbia Ministry of Education's prescribed learning outcomes[2] together and then moved on to approach some of the informal (yet important) issues at hand. As we approached these issues, we created an open dialogue that welcomed inquiry and questioning in keeping with the problem based learning approach that I was familiar with and which is outlined above. It was an approach that felt both natural and fluid for us both.

Issues in a Diverse Classroom Population: Carolyn Russo and Nicky Freeman

As discussed above, the classroom in which Nicky had her 10-week-long school-based practicum was extraordinarily diverse. Responding to the diverse needs of these students required skill and sensitivity on both our parts (i.e., Carolyn, the sponsor teacher, and Nicky, the preservice teacher). While many of the issues we dealt with flowed from the needs of this particular class, some were a result of job action instigated by the British Columbia Teachers' Federation (BCTF) who, at the time of Nicky's 10-week practicum, was involved in contract negotiations with the Provincial Government of British Columbia. Through open dialogue, collaboration, Socratic questioning and mutual respect, we were able to find solutions to many of the problems and issues that arose during this practicum. The following are some examples:

Issue One: Supporting children with special needs

We both believe that all students benefit from feeling safe and secure at school and that teachers are essential to this equation. If a teacher can create a social and emotional climate of safety, then the classroom becomes a place for optimal learning. Students become inspired to learn when they are able to work in an environment without fear of failure. Therefore, good teachers gain students' trust through encouragement and positive reinforcement when combined with achievable goals and guidelines for success.

An issue that we worked through together involved a young student called Helen.[3] Helen was ministry diagnosed with behavioural issues and she had an Individual Education Program[4] (IEP). She had a great deal of anxiety around "change" and especially around going to the bathroom. As a result, she developed a strong attachment to Carolyn with whom she had developed a comfortable relation-

---

[2] The prescribed learning outcomes set the learning standards for the British Columbia provincial Kindergarten to Grade 12 education system and form the prescribed curriculum for British Colombia. They are statements of what students are expected to know and do at the end of an indicated grade or course, in this case Grade 1.

[3] Helen is a pseudonym.

[4] An IEP describes programme adaptations and/or modifications and the special services that are to be provided for a student. The IEP is reviewed regularly and updated at least annually.

ship and who she trusted to take care of her when she needed to use the toilet. No matter how hard Nicky tried, Helen would *not* go to the toilet with her. Nicky began to feel worried that when she was required to step-up and take full responsibility for the class, Helen's toileting needs would become overwhelmingly complicated. Nicky approached Carolyn about this concern and together they/we began to explore ideas about how to approach this issue. After much open discussion it was decided that Nicky needed to spend more time building a trusting relationship with Helen.

After about a month of becoming acquainted with Nicky, Helen trusted her enough to let Nicky take her to the toilets. Although this small victory was celebrated, there was still concern that Helen had not yet acquired the life skill of taking care of her own toileting needs. Thus, together we identified a common goal to support Helen independently using the toilet before entering Grade 2. After considering different solutions, we decided that when taking Helen to the toilets, we would drop her off closer and closer to the classroom, leaving a bigger distance for her to walk by herself to the toilets. Eventually, Helen was able to leave the classroom by herself and walk down the hallway alone. Our collaborative efforts on behalf of Helen had met with great success. We had wanted to create a safe environment for Helen while, at the same time, challenging her to face her fears. We also knew that if Helen were not been successful with this first strategy, we would have continued to have discussions to find alternate strategies to help her.

Issue 2: Planning/teaching

As *the case* underscores, our classroom was extremely diverse: all the students but one were identified as English language learners (ELL) with 16 students being either level-one or level-two ELL. The level-two ELL students were the largest group, making up approximately one half of the class. This large group was *pulled out* three times a week from the mainstream classroom in order to give them specialized instruction in English. Carolyn shared with Nicky that she found it difficult to plan meaningful lessons during these ELL *pullout* blocks not only because she didn't want to cover concepts that all the students needed but also because the remaining group of students consisted of both level-one ELL students and students who were fluent in English. While Nicky had been looking forward to teaching a *Fairy Tales Unit*, it was clear that any unit that Nicky planned must meet the needs of these multicultural/multilingual students. Following a discussion with Carolyn, it was decided that Nicky would plan a *Fractured Fairy Tales Unit*. Folk and fairy tales are stories passed down orally through generations and can be found in Africa, Asia, Australia and the Americas. Thus, from our perspective this unit offered opportunities to reaffirm the cultural backgrounds of our students as well as providing ample opportunities for using oral language for sharing information and storytelling. Additionally, since Nicky's background was in problem based learning, it was decided that two essential questions would drive this project-based learning unit:

1. What is a fractured fairy tale and how does it differ from a typical fairy tale?
2. What lessons can we learn from fractured fairy tales?

Together we (Carolyn and Nicky) discussed that planning must include building background knowledge of folktales. This meant building text-specific knowledge by providing students with examples of elements of folktales (e.g., stereotypical characters – wicked stepmother, talking animals; magical devices – wands, crystal ball; the rule of three and seven; and the notion that good always *trumps* evil). We also identified key vocabulary (linked to the elements of folktales) that would need to be explicitly taught. Objectives for the project-based unit included:

- *Speaking and listening to interact with others* for the purposes of making connections.
- Use the *features* of oral language to convey and derive meaning, including using most words correctly and expressing ideas clearly.
- Use *strategies* after reading and viewing to confirm and extend meaning, including retelling (p. 101).
- Use *strategies* after reading and viewing to confirm and extend meaning, including discussing with others (p. 101).
- View and demonstrate understanding that visual *texts* are sources of information.
- Create *imaginative writing* and representations, often modelled on those they have read, heard or viewed, featuring developing *word choice* by attempting to use new and descriptive words.

It was decided to begin the unit with the *Cinderella* story. Given that this folktale appears in the folklore of many cultures (over 350 versions of the story have been recorded), it seemed likely that the majority of the students would be familiar with some form of the story. We began with a discussion of what the students knew about the *Cinderella* story, specifically the European Charles Perrault retelling (2002), and we shared *The Golden Sandal: A Middle Eastern Cinderella Story* (1998) retold by Rebecca Hickox. Together we discussed the differences and similarities between the two folktales. Following this discussion students identified which version he or she preferred and shared with a partner why he or she chose that particular version. We followed this with a retelling of the European *Little Red Riding Hood* and compared it with *Pretty Salma: A Red Riding Hood Story from Africa* (2007) retold by Niki Daly and then *Yo, Hungry Wolf!: A Nursery Rap* (1995) by David Voza (also an adaptation of *Little Red Riding Hood*). Working in small groups students created small dramatic scenes from their favourite retelling of either the *Cinderella* story or the *Little Red Riding Hood* story. After a performance of a scene, the other members of the class identified which folktale the scene came from.

Following the students' explorations of these retellings of the two folktales, we discussed what *types* of characters were in each story, which was their favourite character and why and what were the particular characteristics of the character that appealed to the student. A follow-up activity required each student to draw a picture of what his or her home would look like if they were a particular character (e.g., a castle, a cottage, a hut and so on) with a description of his or her character.

At this point the focus switched to fractured fairy tales. The students viewed a video of a fractured fairytale of *Hansel and Gretel* and discussed what warning this story had for the viewer – not to trust strangers. A follow-up activity had the children draw a picture of a trusted adult in their lives, and later they developed a Venn diagram comparing and contrasting good and evil characters either within the same folktale or across texts.

After comparing and contrasting several more folktales, for example, the European retelling of *Sleeping Beauty* (2002) by Mahon F. Craft with *Waking Beauty* (2011) by Leah Wilcox, the students were able to identify three ways they could change a fairytale to create a fractured fairytale:

- Change the main character
- Have the story take place in a different location
- Have the story take place in another time

The culminating activity for the unit was the writing and sharing of the students' fractured fairy tales. Students chose from three traditional folktales (*Little Red Riding Hood, Jack and the Beanstalk* or *The Princess and the Pea*) and retold his or her folktale as a fractured folktale through changes made to the main character, the location and the time in which the story took place.

Teaching such a diverse group of students required careful research and planning to meet the students' broad range of needs. Through collaborative planning, we identified a set of goals, searched out multiple sources of information, created outlines and forms and set criteria to judge the effectiveness of the planning. We needed to consider variety and flexibility in our planning, as well as structure and routine, to take into account the students' differing developmental needs and interests.

Issue 3: Assessment (IEP)

Nicky was present for the development of Louis[5] IEP and found the process to be informing and insightful. She appreciated the energy and commitment that each member of the School-Based Team brought to providing the best possible education for Louis. Not only did she find out more about Louis' personality, she also found out how to set measurable goals when planning for and teaching students who need adaptations and/or modifications. Nicky learned that these goals are often very small because growth and development can be very slow.

Through previously completing a research package on lesson planning, Nicky knew that Louis would require adaptations rather than modifications throughout his learning. Accommodations in the form of adaptations occur when teachers differentiate instruction, assessment and materials in order to create a flexible learning environment (British Columbia Ministry of Education 2009).

It was during this time that Nicky began to reflect on her own teaching philosophy specifically with regard to the Richmond School District policy of inclusion. Carolyn and Nicky both felt privileged to be a part of a district where all students are entitled to equitable access to learning, achievement and the pursuit of excellence in all aspects of their education (Ministry of Education 2009). Students can learn from each other in the classroom, and students with disabilities who spend

---

[5] Louis is a pseudonym.

more time in regular classrooms have higher scores on achievement tests than peers who are withdrawn for instruction (Jordan et al. 2009).

Attending the IEP meeting was a great stepping-stone from which Nicky could further develop a relationship with Louis. Nicky and Carolyn used his IEP to write his report card at the end year and made a point to sit down with his Educational Assistant[6] (EA) to go back over his goals: We all relished the fact that we could write about his progress in regard to the goals that he had achieved rather than comparing him with the goals for typical children.

Issue 4: Parent-teacher meetings/conferences (job action)

All teachers in the province of British Columbia belong to the British Columbia Federation of Teachers (BCTF) which functions as a teachers' union. During Nicky's practicum, the BCTF was engaged in job action that meant that Carolyn and Nicky could not meet with and/or communicate with parents outside of the scheduled school day. This resulted in the cancellation of parent-teacher conferences, which meant Nicky was unable to take part in a critical learning experience: Planning and engaging in parent-teacher conferences. We (Carolyn and Nicky) decided to problem solve this issue. After going over our options, we chose to plan a parent-reading morning during *class time*. We were excited that we found a time where we could become more acquainted with parents. We were impressed by how many parents came to the classroom each week and were also surprised that we weren't approached about their child's development during this time. They were simply happy to be included in their child's education.

As Nicky imagined her future in the classroom (without the complications of job action), she realized that schools play a strong role in determining the level and nature of parental involvement. Invitations to parents to be involved conveys that their involvement is welcome and valued (Berthelsen and Walker 2008). We also reflected on the parents that were and *were not* able to attend the parent-reading sessions and the implications that we could draw from this. We speculated that parental participation might be motivated by the belief of parents regarding their role in their children's educational achievement i.e., parents beliefs appeared to fall into three categories: 1) parents have the primary responsibility for children's educational achievement; 2) parents and schools share responsibility for children's educational achievement; and 3) schools are responsibile for children's educational achievement. (Berthelsen and Walker 2008). Those who didn't attend either couldn't because of other obligations or may (on the rare occasion) believe that they should not take such an active role. Ultimately, we agreed that it is a part of our role as teachers to ensure that parents feel involved in their children's schooling and provide them with opportunities to be involved. We also agreed that we should leave it up to the parents of our students to decide how much or how little they would like to participate in the classroom.

---

[6] Working under the school principal, with the guidance of the School-Based Team and classroom teacher in consultation with the special programme consultants, Educational Assistants assist classroom teachers in the implementation of Individual Education Plans.

Reflecting Back: Carolyn Russo

Olsen (2008) reminds us that recent educational research suggests that teaching is not just a cognitive or technical procedure "but a complex, personal, social, often elusive, set of embedded processes and practices that concern the whole person" (p. 5). While as discussed in the introduction to this chapter many teacher educators already locate teacher preparation inside the model/mentor/apprenticeship model of learning to teach, we have located our teacher preparation (including the school-based practicum) in a problem based learning model.

Throughout the practicum we created time for ongoing communication: We conversed about all aspects of a lively, complex Grade 1 classroom; we had regular discussions not only around assessment of our students but also around Nicky's growth and educational practice – everything that was important both to the Grade 1 students' learning and to Nicky's learning was *the stuff* of our discussions. Through such discussion and communication, we developed a warm professional relationship that endures to this day.

Reflecting Back and Moving Forward: Nicky Freeman

As I reflect back upon my practicum for one last time, it feels natural to write a summative reflection using the PBL format.

What?
A relationship based on mutual respect and collaboration.
While Carolyn and I engaged in many deep and meaningful conversations, I believe the most important component of our relationship came from respectfully listening to one another. We committed to connecting daily to discuss issues in our classroom and worked together to problem-solve solutions that would benefit our students.

So what?
A strong student teacher-sponsor teacher relationship positively affects the classroom in its entirety.
Carolyn and I always had our students' best interests at heart, which I believe not only resulted in our having a strong, supportive relationship but also guaranteed that our students' best interests were always *front and centre* in our planning and teaching. While our daily discussions were predominantly about the needs of our students, they nonetheless resulted in a strong personal relationship between Carolyn and me. By creating the time and space for discussion, we put our personal relationship aside in the interest of supporting our students. Yet, our personal relationship grew stronger and closer as an indirect result of these daily, informal meetings.

Now what?
Critical thinking and collaborative learning is beneficial at every level of education.

Going forward, I plan to teach my students (no matter what the age) to use critical thinking and collaborative learning to work through their issues. Not only did I learn to become a teacher through these strategies, but I also nurtured my relationship with Carolyn and my students through using PBL methods. I now see problem solving as a lifelong learning process that requires both commitment and practice.

References

Berthelsen, D., & Walker, S. (2008). Parents' Involvement in their children's education. *Australian Institute of Family Studies, 79*, 34–41.

British Columbia Ministry of Education. (2009) *A guide to adaptations and modifications.* Available at: http://www.bced.gov.bc.ca/pubs.htm

Glenn, W. J. (2006). Model versus mentor: Defining the necessary qualities of the effective cooperating teacher. *Teacher Education Quarterly, Winter, 2006*, 85–95.

Jordan, A., Schwartz, E., & McGhie-Richmond, D. (2009). Preparing teachers for inclusive classrooms. *Teaching & Teacher Education, 26*, 259–266.

Ochs, S., & McDowell, S. (2004). *Professional growth for cooperating teachers.* Saskatoon: Dr. Stirling McDowell Foundation for Research into Teaching.

Olsen, B. (2008). Introducing teacher identity. *Teacher Education Quarterly, 35*(3), 3–6.

Schulz, R. (2005). The practicum: More than practice. *Canadian Journal of Education, 28*, 147–167.

Schussler, D. L. (2006). Defining dispositions: Wading through murky waters. *Teacher Educator, 41*(4), 251–268.

Children's Books Cited

Cinderella. (2002). *Charles Perrault* (A. Bell, Trans., L. Koopmans, Illus.). New York: Northsouth Books Inc.

Craft, M. F. (2002). *Sleeping beauty* (K. Y. Craft, Illus.). San Francisco: Chronicle Books.

Pretty Salma: A red riding hood story from Africa (2007) retold by Niki Daly. New York: Clarion Book.

The golden sandal: A Middle Eastern Cinderella story (1998) retold by Rebecca Hickox. New York: Holiday House.

Voza, D. (1995). *Yo, hungry wolf!: A nursery rap.* UK: Random House Children's Books.

Wilcox, L. (2011). *Waking beauty.* (L. Monks, Illus.). New York: Puffin.

Part III
Fostering Inquiry and Active Learning

Thinking includes ... the sense of a problem, the observation of conditions, the formation and rational elaboration of a suggested conclusion, and the active experimental testing. While all thinking results in knowledge, ultimately the value of knowledge is subordinate to its use in thinking. For we live not in a settled and finished world, but in one which is going on, and where our main task is prospective, and where retrospect—and all knowledge as distinct from thought is retrospect—is of value in the solidity, security, and fertility it affords our dealings with the future.

Once there is a clear commitment to and understanding of PBL pedagogy in place, and good governance with curricula and collaborative working relationships established, then the day-to-day enactment of a PBL program begins. In this part, an overview of the individuals and practices that foster inquiry and engage preservice teachers in active learning processes is given. Who are the individuals that facilitate the PBL process, and what are their roles as lived in the TELL/PBL program at UBC? Each chapter in this part is written by distinct members of the PBL team and acknowledges their multiple perspectives and the background knowledge that the tutors, faculty (subject resource specialists), and academic librarians bring to the PBL program. Their "lived experiences" of PBL reveal not only some of the initial feelings which teacher educators and academic librarians experience but how, through commitment and trust in the process and one another, they succeed in offering richer and deeper learning experiences for preservice teachers' learning to become teachers.

First, the experiences of the tutors are considered. An overview of their multiple and complex roles reveals that tutors play a key part in a PBL program. They guide the tutorial groups in identifying questions, tackling issues, and examining resources relevant to each case. Through dialogue and use of Socratic questioning, the tutors initiate the preservice teachers' rigorous investigations and in-depth discussions and foster their critical thinking. It is crucial for the tutors to draw upon their preservice

---

From Dewey, J. (1916). *Experience and thinking, democracy and education: An introduction to the philosophy of education.* Accessed at: http://www.gutenberg.org/files/852/852-h/852-h.htm

teachers' funds of knowledge and adeptly help identify gaps in their understandings so that they will be motivated to "find out" and learn about essential aspects of the case. The tutors facilitate the two-week inquiry cycle, handle the presentations of their information packages, and respond to their individual case syntheses.

Given that tutors are so central to the effective implementation of a PBL program, an account of the transition of an experienced teacher into this role enriches our understanding of PBL. For most teacher educators and for that matter, preservice teachers, PBL is new to them. They have not experienced PBL either as a teacher or as a learner themselves. Feelings of trepidation, anxiety, confusion, frustration, and lack of control are common. However, once they gain familiarity with PBL and experience the process by becoming active teachers and learners within it, they begin to recognize that authentic inquiries and active learning experiences outweigh the frustration, ambiguity, uncertainty, and lack of control. The messy nature of real-world learning through inquiry offers discomfort, but the resultant thinking that occurs is powerful and lasting.

PBL necessitates that preservice teachers demonstrate persistence in locating and interpreting research resources. Library collections and the ways in which academic librarians connect with preservice teachers have implications for a PBL program. During the two-week inquiry cycle, issues drawn from the case are defined, discussed, and researched. Preservice teachers compile annotated bibliographies on real teaching and learning issues using a wide variety of resources. For academic librarians, their key concerns revolve around the quality, variety, and availability of research resources, how accessible they are, and ways to ensure that preservice teachers become adept at searching and retrieving relevant information and acquire information competencies and dispositions for inquiry necessary for professional learning.

The roles of faculty (subject resource specialists) within the PBL cohort are both complicated and enriched by the fact that there are no formal classes, courses, or course reading lists—just cases. In this part, two faculty (subject resource specialists) have been selected as examples to show how faculty develop pre-teachers' subject background knowledge by taking up issues in the cases as related to social justice/ecological perspectives and mathematics education. We could easily have chosen from among any of the other subject specialists in the PBL program such as literacy, drama, art, music, physical education, and special education. However, an educational studies exemplar suggests that PBL is particularly well suited to supporting thinking through concepts of social justice. As well the mathematics education illustration shows that given the variety of worthwhile tasks for learning to teach school math and science, the process of PBL resulted in a preservice teacher's carrying inquiry into his own classroom.

This part concludes with a discussion about evaluation and assessment in the PBL program. Assessment is vitally important and includes a wide variety of measures. Continuous feedback during each case is received from tutors, faculty (subject resource specialists), and peers. Annotated bibliographies and resource packages are posted online. Presentations are given in tutorial groups where peers and tutors are expected to respond. Each preservice teacher submits a synthesis of the case summarizing their thinking and responding to questions raised by their tutors, faculty, and other members of their tutorial group. As part of the program, preservice teachers develop e-folios and engage in triple jump assessments where they are evaluated on their ability to apply content knowledge to specific classroom contexts. One of the strengths of the PBL program is the authentic nature of the assessments, their frequency, and rigor.

Chapter 8
The Multiple Roles of the Tutor in a Problem Based Learning Cohort in a Teacher Education Program

Frank Baumann, Monika Tarampi, and Lori Prodan

Introduction

It is generally understood that in problem based learning (PBL), the tutor should have expertise with group facilitation (process expertise) rather than in a subject area (content expertise) (Hmelo-Silver and Barrows 2006; Neville 1999). From our perspective as tutors in a PBL cohort in a teacher education program, this description only scratches the surface of the many roles required of us as tutors. The multiple roles and sometimes conflicting roles of challenger, motivator, consultant, manager, model, negotiator, evaluator, listener, advisor, and community builder are difficult to capture in a single phrase such as facilitator, initiator, "setting the stage," or "guide by the side." A word we think more nearly expresses our role is *provocateur*: provoking awareness, interest, and motivation to develop skills, knowledge, and understanding and apply these in the act of teaching. However, we describe our role; it is complex, complicated, and ultimately rewarding.

The three tutors in PBL at UBC are Frank, a retired administrator, Lori, a seconded classroom teacher, and Monika, a seconded district teacher. We come from three different school districts in the greater Vancouver region. We come as practitioners with knowledge of classroom teaching, working with a wide range of stu-

---

F. Baumann (✉)
North Vancouver School District, Vancouver, BC, Canada
e-mail: fbaumann@telus.net

M. Tarampi
Langley School District, Langley, BC, Canada

L. Prodan
Vancouver School District 39, Vancouver, BC, Canada

dents with diverse learning needs and with practical knowledge of staff development and/or professional development. In keeping with a PBL approach to teaching and learning, the cohort is divided into three tutorial groups of ten to twelve preservice teachers. As the tutors of these three groups of preservice teachers, we meet regularly to ensure some aspects of consistency across the groups, specifically, in the understanding of the cases, of the issues within each case, and any underlying concepts, which are critical to the preservice teachers' understandings of teaching and learning. Additionally, we meet to discuss school-based practicum placements for our preservice teachers. This is complex: matching preservice teachers with a sponsor teacher is delicate and requires an understanding of both the expectations of a particular sponsor teacher and which preservice teacher will flourish under the mentorship of a particular sponsor teacher. The following chapter outlines the multiple roles of the three tutors as these roles unfold in a problem based learning cohort in a teacher education program.

Role 1: Creating the Learning Environment

All the PBL preservice teachers have completed a 4-year degree and, while they attend an orientation on the expectations of the Teaching English Language Learners through Problem based Learning (TELL/PBL) cohort and the expectations of problem based learning, the background of these particular students reflects a typically traditional university experience of working independently, and with a competitive orientation. Thus, many of our preservice teachers express confusion and concern, not knowing or understanding (fully) the expectations of the PBL program. We assure them that after only one or two case cycles, they will become more comfortable with the process. In previous years, more information regarding problem based learning was front-loaded, but this had the negative outcome of creating more stress than was necessary in this new and unfamiliar program. Consequently, a decision was made to *take things slowly* during the first week of the program and to provide information only as it is needed to complete tasks. We reassure the preservice teachers that once they have completed the first case, the PBL pedagogical approach to learning will become clear.

We also introduce Socratic questioning in our tutorial groups during the first days of the program. The expectation was and is that teacher candidates will contribute to discussions, that other members of the group will extend an idea, pose questions, summarize, and ask for explanations and clarification, and that preconceived notions and assumptions will be examined. We also show the teacher candidates a short PowerPoint presentation entitled *Dialogue versus Debate*, that is, how to discuss and converse about sometimes difficult issues without attacking others and to embrace multiple perspectives.

Thus, during the first few cases, we underscore the need for a safe, respectful space for everyone to be able to have their voice heard.

Table 8.1 Dialogue versus debate

Dialogue is	Debate is
Searching for strength in the other's position	Searching for flaws and weaknesses in the other's position
Finding common ground	Winning
Reflecting on one's own beliefs	Critiquing the other's beliefs
Care and concern for the other's beliefs	Without concern for the other's feelings
Temporarily suspending one's own beliefs	Defending one's beliefs
Trying to reach an agreement	Trying to prove the other side is wrong
Having an open mind including being wrong	Having a closed mind, trying to prove the other wrong
Looking for basic agreements	Finding and highlighting major differences
Collaborative, seeking common ground	Oppositional, seeking to prove the other side is wrong
The number one difference between dialogue and debate	
Dialogue is learning from each other	Debate is defeating the other at any costs

Power Point adapted from Shelley Berman (1996) Dialogue Group of the Boston Chapter of Educators for Social Responsibility

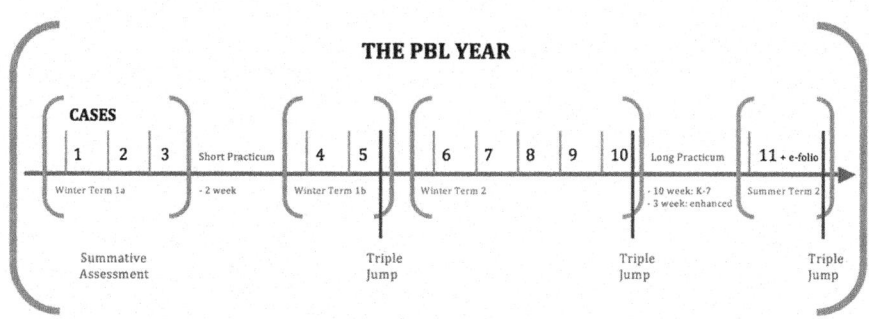

Fig. 8.1 The problem based learning academic year

Role 2: Faculty Advisor

The PBL year in the teacher education program is organized around eleven cases (see Fig. 8.1), three school-based field practica, and a community practicum. As tutors we are involved in every aspect of the preservice teachers' program, which includes not only our role as on-campus tutors but also as field-based faculty advisors. Preservice teachers attend a weekly 1-day school-based practicum (EDUC 315) from the first week of their program until the start of their long practicum. The weekly 1-day practicum is intended to introduce preservice teachers to classroom practice and have them reflect on any interactions, activities, or lessons they may be involved with. Preservice teachers are required to produce weekly reflections on their observations and involvement in teaching. The short 2-week school-based practicum (EDUC 321) occurs at the end of October in the first term of the teacher education program. The intent of this practicum is for the preservice teachers to become integrated into the school classroom community, to conduct observations of classroom teaching and learning, and to identify and generate questions or issues arising from observations and participation in the elementary school classroom. These questions and issues form the content of the case following the short practicum (Case 4). The final long school-based practicum is 10 weeks in length (EDUC 418) starting in April and ending in June. During this practicum the preservice teachers are required to address issues of classroom management and classroom discourse, to engage in evaluation and reporting practices associated with pupil learning as well as take on increasing curriculum and teaching responsibilities throughout the learning experience of the practicum. This culminates in 4 weeks of assuming responsibility for at least 80 % of the teaching. Following successful completion of the long practicum, the preservice teachers complete a 3-week field experience that occurs outside schools (EDUC 430). This practicum is informed by research that underscores that teachers develop a broader, more holistic view of education when the school practica are balanced with community teaching and learning (e.g., early childhood education settings, community services, museum and cultural education, rural education, sustainability/environmental education). Again, experiences and questions arising from these two practica are *grist for the mill* in the final case that occurs when preservice teachers return to campus to reflect on their work in the schools and community.

As faculty advisors, we work to prepare our preservice teachers by helping them with the crucial communication building that must underpin their professional relationship with their school advisors. We encourage them to get to know their school advisor's personality type, deeply held beliefs about education, and their school advisor's style. We try to help the preservice teachers understand that there is a continuum of sponsor teacher *styles* from "the absentee landlord" to the "collegial partnership" to the "boss." However, we also underscore that whether they are predominantly on their own or constantly planning and communicating with their school advisor or working to please *the boss*, each style has its benefits and drawbacks and that they need to adapt as much as possible and appreciate the opportunities their particular classroom and sponsor teacher offer in learning their craft.

As faculty advisors, we meet regularly with the school advisor and her/his preservice teacher to ensure everyone hears the same information and sets similar goals, in short, doing our best to achieve a level of communication, which is clear, consistent, and predictable. Achieving a positive rapport between the school advisor and the teacher candidate is essential. When the practicum does not go well, it is our task as faculty advisors to intervene, have the difficult conversation, and cooperatively set goals to "right the ship." When this is not possible, moving the teacher candidate to another placement may be required.

In addition to our role of working directly with the preservice teacher and the school advisor, we need to have a presence in the school community. We strive to build a positive rapport with the teaching staff, the support staff, and administration and become part of the school community. We need to be at the school at recess, lunchtime, and before and after school during the course of the year. From time to time, we attend school community events such as assemblies, concerts, and student/teacher lunch hour games as well as sports days and other school community celebrations.

We view our faculty advising as critically important. Our goal is to support our preservice teachers in becoming as emotionally fit as possible for the practicum by offering an ongoing one-on-one relationship. We also provide them with regular, specific feedback based on our observations of their teaching practice. In addition, we support them through the planning process, providing frameworks and advice, and suggesting resources. On a weekly basis, we reply to teacher candidates' written reflections (see Box 8.1) giving us insights into their perceptions and concerns. At times, we calm them down from panic attacks and reassure them that they can do it. As well, we need to have difficult conversations with some of our preservice teachers when it is not going well for them in the classroom. We help them stay energized and motivated to deal with their steep learning curve. Infrequently, a counseling role becomes necessary with our school advisors as well who often blame themselves when a teacher candidate is not successful.

Box 8.1: Example of Weekly Reflection
This week in my practicum classroom, I taught my second French lesson, which I believe was received with moderate success. In this lesson I introduced concepts of "Il y a" and "Il n'y a pas" (There is/There is not) as well as thirty vocabulary words specific to the approaching holiday season. In preparation for the lesson, I created a handout for the students with a list of winter and Christmas-themed vocabulary (e.g., winter, gift, Yule log) in French along with an image of the object or idea. During the lesson I used SMART notebook to create a file where I rolled dice with the vocabulary images on them and as a group the students would state "Il y a [object in French]." After the group dice activity, I had an image of a Christmas tree with different objects on it, and each student then individually had to state in French both something that was and was not on the tree "Il y a une cloche sur l'arbre. Il n'y a pas une dindon sur l'arbre."

Though both activities had their merits, I feel that they were somewhat problematic. First I think I spent far too much time on the group activity going over the vocabulary and not enough time on the individual practice. The students likely would have benefited more from the individual work, since they were both listening to their peers and thinking about what they were going to say. Unfortunately we only did one round and I think I should have done at least three or four rounds. In my lesson plan I planned to do only one individual round but I did not expect the group activity to lag as much as it did. It is in this situation where I need to learn how to be more flexible and alter my

(continued)

Box 8.1 (continued)

plan as I go in order to better suit the class. Hopefully I'll gain that flexibility the longer I teach.

Another problematic aspect of the activity that I did not address in my preparation is the homogenous nature of the vocabulary. Both my SA and I want to do Christmas-themed activities in French; however, not all of our students celebrate Christmas. Thinking back to Anne Zavalkoff's seminars, I now fully realize that oppression can be seen subtly in this kind of homogenous activity. Ultimately I know I want to incorporate as many cultures as possible in our French classes, though I am uncertain on how to approach the situation. I am tempted to recreate my vocabulary list with both Christmas and Hanukkah vocabulary (since I do know of at least two students in the class that celebrate Hanukkah), but what about the students who celebrate neither?

Despite the work done in our classes and seminars, I find it truly difficult to implement the understanding and sensitivity to cultures that are not my own. However I am (partially) glad to be making these mistakes now so that I have a better reference and understanding of these problems that I know I will encounter in the future. If I do not make the mistakes, then how can I possibly learn from them? Either way I know I have a vocabulary list that needs to be revamped.

Role 3: Promoting Learning: The Two-Week Cycle

While the school-based practica can be thought of as the cornerstone of the teacher education program in that they provide preservice teachers with supervised experiences and help in understanding the full scope of the teacher's role(s), it is the cases that are the foundation supporting preservice teachers' problem-solving and decision-making skills within the framework of teaching and learning. Specifically, problem based curricula provides preservice teachers with guided experience in learning through solving complex, real-world problems. In the PBL teacher education cohort at the University of British Columbia, the first seven cases are organized by grade level (i.e., K/Grade 1, primary grades, Grade 4/5, Grade 5/6, and Grade 7): Case 4 (as mentioned above) reflects the questions and issues identified by the preservice teachers while on their short school-based practicum. The remaining cases are designed around the following issues: teaching in a resource-based, coastal community with a large Haisla First Nations community (Grade 3/4), planning for instruction, bullying, technology in the elementary classroom, and special needs education. Figure 8.1 provides an overview of the way in which the practica and cases are scheduled throughout the academic years.

Our preservice teachers' schedule is very different from the traditional weekly schedule that requires students to attend individual courses that are offered on a weekly basis – some of which might be offered through engagement with cases.

Each case in our PBL program follows a 2-week inquiry cycle. Figure 8.2 outlines week one of this two-week cycle.

On the first Monday of each two-week cycle, the tutors introduce a case such as the one below (Fig. 8.1). After introducing the case, the tutors facilitate the first task of the teacher candidates, which is to clarify terms and vocabulary within the case (Box 8.2).

The following is an example of problems and issues identified in Case 3 (above) (Box 8.3):

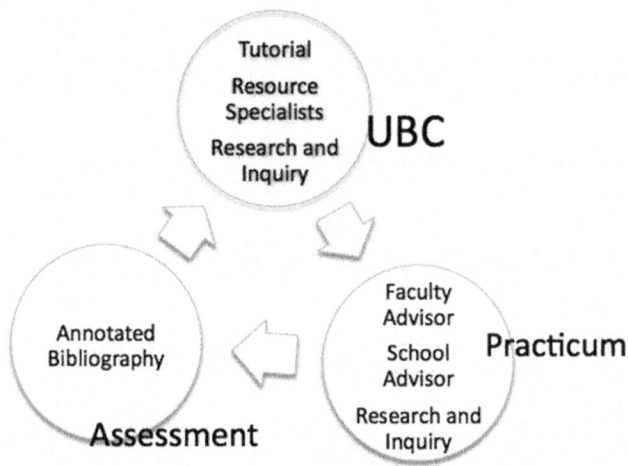

Fig. 8.2 Inquiry cycle week one

Box 8.2: Case 3
The cries of seagulls and scent of ocean air greet you as you drive off the ferry at Oceanridge, a resource-based coastal community where you will teach a grade 3/4 class this year. Oceanridge is located near an old growth forest that has been the focus of several environmental protests. As you take the main road through town, you pass the school and wonder how the coming year will compare to your previous teaching experiences at two schools in a bustling urban area.

Thinking back, you feel happy about the many "fun" activities you provided for your classes. Last year's group really loved that penguin unit and the baking sessions! Still, you remember wondering what your students actually learned.

You attended a professional development presentation in the summer on balanced literacy and have been planning a balanced literacy program that reflects all the language arts and the classroom environment. You are confident that this approach will provide opportunities to access and build on students' funds of knowledge.

(continued)

Box 8.2 (continued)

Approximately half of your 22 new students are of Haisla First Nation ancestry and you are looking forward to creating a classroom that honors their heritage. You've been told that many of these students have been designated "ESD" and you are wondering exactly what that means. When you were interviewed for this job, you spoke of integrating First Nations content into math, literacy, and all the subject areas. Now you're wondering how to do this in a way that acknowledges Haisla knowledge, culture, language/dialects, traditions, and approaches to learning. You are considering the ways in which Indigenous knowledge and approaches can be integrated across the curriculum.

Box 8.3: Example of Case 3 Issues

Place-Based Learning

- Environmental education
- Rural school vs. urban school
- Resource-based coastal community
- What does environment education entail?

Integration of Indigenous Knowledge

- How to speak to students about Indigenous issues?
- What resources are available to support teaching and learning Indigenous knowledge?
- How to integrate Indigenous knowledge across the curriculum?

Social and Ecological Justice Issues

- How can we engage sensitively in social and ecological issues in a classroom?
- How can we bring awareness of sensitive issues to students?
- How can I, as a teacher from the city, learn about a rural community's issues?

English as a Second Dialect (ESD)

- What is ESD?
- What are the language needs of ESD students?

Professional Development/Literacy Program

- What is a balanced literacy program?
- What is meant by balanced literacy?
- How can we support diverse learners?
- How can we build lifelong learning into professional development?

Following the tutorial meeting to identify and clarify the issues, the preservice teachers are required to research and develop an annotated bibliography of 2–3 sources per identified issue, to be shared and discussed at the next tutorial session. These materials are posted on a learning management system (LMS) that provides a platform for the delivery of educational materials and discussion space using the Internet as a delivery system. In this way preservice teacher candidates' work is made available to each other, the tutors, and the subject area resource specialists. If important citations are lacking for any of the issues, the tutors and subject area resource specialists are responsible for contacting the preservice teacher(s) with the additional citations.

The following is an excerpt from a bibliography developed for Case 3 (Box 8.4).

At the second tutorial meeting, which occurs on the Friday of the first week of the two-week cycle, preservice teachers under the guidance of the tutors revisit the issues and problems identified at the beginning of the cycle: These issues and problems are reframed and/or honed in light of learning from independent inquiry, meetings with subject area resource specialists, observations during the weekly school-based practicum, and workshop experiences. Following discussion and re-articulation of issues, learning tasks are formulated and agreement on the distribution of tasks is planned. For example, following the second tutorial of Case 3, the

---

Box 8.4: Example of Case 3 Bibliography

First Nations: How can we integrate and honor the heritage within the classroom in a way that acknowledges Haisla knowledge, culture, language/dialects, traditions, and approaches to learning (Haisla First Nation: Retrieved from http://haisla.ca/)?

This website is a great resource to educate ourselves about the Haisla nation. It describes who they are as a people including language, history, location, and band. It also has links to the council of Haisla who is responsible for setting and managing the Nation's budget and for representing the Haisla people for dealings with Canada. It also includes economic development and current events surrounding the Haisla nation.

Kundoque, J.G. (2008). Reclaiming Haisla ways: Remembering oolichan fishing. *Canadian Journal of Native Education, 31*(1), 11–23.

The author of this article draws on personal experiences of being part of the Haisla culture and its importance to her in finding herself. It discusses oolichan fishing and describes it as the core of Haisla culture and also discusses other aspects of the Haisla culture. It discusses what Gyawaglaab (best practices through teachings of oolichan fishing) is and how it is practiced in the culture through fishing. Lastly it discusses how, through the stories of elders, Indigenous peoples are reminded of their resilience.

following learning tasks were identified by the preservice teachers: English as a Second Dialect (ESD), Integrating Indigenous Education, Honoring Haisla Heritage and Knowledge in Education, Balanced Literacy, Place-based Learning, Environmental Learning, and Authentic Assessment.

Generally, two preservice teachers work together to create a resource package on one of the identified issues. This package, informed by research in academic journals, teacher-created materials, Ministry of Education documents, and their own in-school practice and observations, is a key element of the case cycle. Each resource package is 15–20 "pages" in length, including graphic organizers, illustrations, and diagrams. It becomes a learning tool for the other members of the tutorial group, who are researching a different issue. The specific criteria for the research packages are as follows:

- Provides multiple perspectives of the issue.
- Includes relevant and reliable research.
- Identifies issues of language and how they intersect with the issues of the case.
- Research is drawn from a variety of sources.
- All material is properly cited.
- Information has been framed in ways relevant to the case.
- Material from outside sources is presented with relevant commentary.
- Package contains a table of contents, introduction and conclusion, glossary, and annotated bibliography.
- Visuals and graphic organizers are used to enhance understanding.

Each package is uploaded onto the learning management system, to be viewed by other members of the tutorial group, as well as the subject specialists (instructors) and members of the other tutorial groups. The preservice teachers are encouraged to view this package as both their responsibility and their opportunity to teach their colleagues about an important issue of the case.

Based on this research package, each pair of preservice teachers prepares and delivers a 15-min presentation to the tutorial group on the final Friday tutorial of the case cycle. During these presentations, preservice teachers are encouraged to engage their colleagues in active participation, dialogue, and professional reflection. Sometimes the presentations take the form of a *PowerPoint* presentation outlining the highlights of the research package; other presentations include a sample lesson and ask colleagues to participate as though they were elementary students; still others involve debate, role play, and science experiments – creativity is encouraged. The specific criteria for these presentations are as follows:

- Clear, focused, and interesting
- Includes an activity/discussion considering a key issue from the research package
- Enhanced with handouts/visuals
- Clear and expressive delivery

- Eye contact and engaging body language
- Effective use of time (15 min)

In much the same way that in-service teachers are encouraged to see themselves as teaching their colleagues through their research packages, the presentations allow them repeated opportunities to practice their oral teaching skills, as well as to situate themselves within an ongoing professional dialogue about important educational issues.

During week 2 of the case cycle, preservice teachers continue to acquire knowledge in relation to their learning task/expert area. Preservice teachers continue to attend classes with subject area resource specialists, attend the 1-day a week, school-based practicum while continuing to prepare their research package and their presentation for the case. Tutorial members are responsible for providing feedback on the presentations through peer evaluations. Additionally, all research packages are posted online for the subject area resource specialists to provide feedback.

Following the presentations, preservice teachers collect the research packages from their tutorial group members (i.e., in Case 3 as outlined above, research packages were English as a Second Dialect (ESD), Integrating Indigenous Education, Honoring Haisla Heritage and Knowledge in Education, Balanced Literacy, Place-Based Learning, Environmental Learning, and Authentic Assessment) and over the weekend (Saturday and Sunday) are responsible for responding to any questions raised by their tutor and other members of their tutorial group and in reading and developing a synthesis of the issues raised and addressed by members of the tutorial group in their research packages. The syntheses can be written/represented in any form and in the past have included such formats as an iMovie of an interview between a reporter and teacher on issues arising from the case (the roles of reporter and teacher were played by the preservice teacher), a journal/diary written from the perspective of the *new* teacher in Case 3, a newspaper article, and a correspondence between the *new* teacher and a mentor.

The synthesis of learning, peer evaluations, and responses to the tutor's questions regarding the research package and presentation are submitted to the tutor on the Monday. Following a discussion/wrap-up of the case, the new case is introduced and the two-week case cycle begins again. However, while the new case integrates new issues and problems, it is iterative in that issues and problems may reoccur but in different educational contexts. For example, while Case 3 focuses on a grade 3/4 class with a large population of Haisla First Nations students in a resource-based coastal community, Case 1 focuses on aboriginal students in a kindergarten class in an urban, inner-city school. The issues in Case 1 are intended to engage preservice teachers with the diversity among aboriginal people in Canada and British Columbia, the relationship of aboriginal people to Canada, and the Indigenous pedagogies. Case 3 builds on the preservice teachers learning in Case 1 by having them revisit many of the issues but in greater depth and in the context of a First Nations rural community.

Role 4: Evaluating Preservice Teacher Candidates

While the assessment of preservice teachers performance on campus (bibliographies and resource packages) is generally a team responsibility shared with the subject area resource specialists, the tutors take full responsibility for two areas of assessment and evaluation: (1) the synthesis and (2) the preservice teachers' performance in the school-based practicum

Synthesis

As discussed above, at the end of the two-week inquiry cycle, the preservice teachers are required to produce a synthesis of his or her learning over the 2 weeks of the case study. The synthesis is submitted on the Monday of the beginning of the new 2-week inquiry cycle to the tutor for feedback and evaluation. The following is an example of a synthesis (written as a letter to a friend) and the tutor feedback (written as underlined) (Box 8.5):

> **Box 8.5: Synthesis with Tutor Feedback**
> Dear Wendy,
>   This summer just flew by, and I believe I completely forgot to tell you that I took a job in Oceanridge this year, teaching a grade 3/4 class. I am so thankful that I did some research before I arrived in this beautiful but small coastal resource-based town; I am going to have to do some serious navigating through some complex relationships that exist in this community. A community that relies on extracting natural resources for their economic livelihood in this day and age is dealing with job loss, unreliable external markets, government limits, and moratoriums, to name a few. There is an old growth forest right next door, which I'm sure is the topic for some heated environmental discussions as well. However, I am hopeful that because of hard work and the building of meaningful relationships between the students, the families and the community, the school has the potential to be the heart of the community. My goal is to contribute to the growth of my class and help create a positive identity for these kids within Oceanridge.
>   I have had to rethink my "fun" activities that I did with my students in Richmond. I believe that there are an unlimited number of opportunities to make my units more meaningful to the children here, aboriginal or not, by basing them on the children's surroundings. I want to help create a tangible connection between my students and their personal experiences and the health of their community, and I believe I can do that across the curriculum.

(continued)

Box 8.5 (continued)
Integrating First Nation content into math, and language arts, will also include field trips to visit old growth trees and to the ocean for a lesson on fishing, and hopefully many opportunities for storytelling with vital members of the community. <u>These are good examples – how might you assess what the students have learned? How might this relate to the curriculum (or not)?</u> I truly believe that there is so much excitement to be had connecting students with their "place" and subsequently create a feeling of stewardship for the nature that is all around them.

This meaningful connection I hope to foster will rely on a number of factors. It is my responsibility to motivate my students through my clear instruction and meaningful activities, so that my assessment can be authentic one. I believe that a student can be assessed on many different levels and in many different ways, and using real-world applications to solve local problems, it creates a very motivated learner. If my students can apply what they've learned, then I think the benefit will go beyond just getting a letter grade on their report card. <u>A specific example of what this might look like in your classroom would be helpful</u>.

I researched the creation story of the Haisla nation, which I thought would be a good place to start because the school is situated on traditional Haisla territory. With permission from the elders of the community, this story I believe will provide me with an anchor point, which we can always return to. It will ground the class in a sense of *place*. <u>Interesting idea – would you also welcome other creation stories into the class? What might you do when/if the stories don't align? How might Grade 3/4 students react? What might be your role as a teacher?</u> This strategy of storytelling plus the integration of relevant literature will involve reading aloud to the students, which ultimately increases their reading comprehension, as well as allow all of the students to participate and engage in their community's history. The balanced literacy strategy I see now will permeate throughout my entire curriculum. We will be listening to these stories, researching for ourselves the history of the area together, posing careful questions to the community members in a respectful way to further our understanding of the area, and reflect on experiences we have had ourselves. However, it will also be important to discuss how the community has evolved and changed and what the current issues are concerning the fishing and forest industry. For example, what will happen to the traditional cedar canoes if all of the cedar trees big enough to carve are gone?

I would like to take my class outside as often as I can, and I believe a lot of subjects can be learned through experiencing and questioning what is going on outside the walls of the school. Math is an excellent example of a subject that should be more versatile and based in the practical versus abstract world. I am looking into integrating the math objectives for grades 3 and 4 into everyday life, looking at patterns in nature for example. A section of a cedar

(continued)

Box 8.5 (continued)

leaf will show a pattern and symmetry. We might compare leaves of different trees and their symmetry. Weaving is another strategy to explain pattern, symmetry, and geometry and offers opportunities to gain an understanding of measurement. <u>How does weaving relate to nature?</u> The more humans connect with nature, the more they feel a sense of responsibility and stewardship towards it as well. I also love the idea of using a cedar tree to understand circumference and measurement. Using the dugout cedar bark canoe, you can talk about history, tradition, trades, artistry, circumference, measurement, geometry, and science. Everything is connected. Physically seeing and potentially lying inside a canoe will give the students a grasp of the size needed, which will translate to the width of the cedar needed to be able to carve out the canoe. Finally, a trip to a cedar forest will allow for exploration and finding the perfect-sized cedar tree for a dugout canoe. <u>Great details – I can really picture what might be happening in your class. This demonstrates a great ability to translate the ideas you have learned into potential action.</u>

Half of my students are Haisla First Nation and I've been told that many of them are "designated" ESD. Perhaps a few weeks into the school year, I will have a discussion with all of the family members, together or separate; I have not decided yet, to get a read on what they feel about their child being designated or not designated. I know that if there are any new children with parents who are comfortable with the designation, I will need to submit their names before October to acquire extra funding. I will make a note to get in touch with the ELL/D specialist as well as who should be involved in this process. However, I have researched this area of teaching, and I hope that the ELL/D and I are on the same page. I think a bidialectal approach is the way to go because it teaches Standard English in addition to the students' own dialect. I feel this strategy does not diminish the value of the students' home dialect especially because it is tied with identity. Showing these students how to code switch between dialects I think will be beneficial so they know when to use which dialect, which will depend on the topic or situation.

The excitement I feel starting off the year in Oceanridge is coupled with a feeling of responsibility to do right by these students, to respect the history of the area, and not over-romanticize this coastal community and be stuck in elements of the past that are not relevant anymore. Learning the value and morals through stories and through that past will guide these students into the future and hopefully create a strong sense of identity through seamlessly integrating provincial learning objectives with real life. Empowering my class to realize their place in their community and their value to the community is incredibly important. If they feel like learning is relevant and helpful to their present and their future, then it will be a very self-motivated class.

<u>Great work, Evan! This document clearly demonstrates your understanding of these complex issues. You have done an effective job of showing how the issues are interrelated as well. However, I don't see a lot of ideas/information here about the issues of balanced literacy and assessment. What have you learned about those topics that you would incorporate into your teaching?</u>

Field-Based Practicum

Specifically, supervision and evaluation of the three school-based practica (EDUC 315, EDUC 321 and EDUC 418) includes:

- Engaging in regular, appropriate, systematic use of the observation/feedback cycle
- Providing formal written feedback on a regular basis
- Monitoring and assisting preservice teacher candidates with planning
- Guiding teacher candidates in self-assessment and reflection
- Meeting with preservice teachers and school advisors to review performance
- Use data from observations and conferences to compile a final report and final performance checklist for each preservice teacher

On-going documentation of the preservice teachers' progress is provided in two ways through an open-ended anecdotal form for written comments and a performance checklist that includes:

- Professional qualities (e.g., communicates effectively with students parents, is respectful, and cooperative with advisors and other professionals)
- Inquiry and reflective practice (e.g., uses effective cycle of questioning, reflection, and action and links education research to classroom practice)
- Curriculum, pedagogy, and assessment (e.g., preparing detailed unit/lesson plans designed to support identified goals and objectives; uses diverse and pedagogically sound teaching strategies; uses subject-appropriate assessment, evaluation, and reporting strategies; demonstrates understanding of subject content)
- Language, literacies, and cultures (e.g., communicates curriculum content clearly and accessibly and demonstrates understanding and skill in using a variety of modes to communicate)
- Classroom climate (e.g., organizes the physical environment for learning, establishes appropriate/safe classroom procedures, and reinforces classroom expectations)

Observations recorded on both the anecdotal form and performance checklist are shared with the school advisors and preservice teachers.

At the end of the practicum, school and faculty advisors prepare two kinds of documentation of the teachers' performance: the final performance checklist and the final report. These documents summarize the preservice teacher's performance as demonstrated throughout their long, 10-week practicum and form the basis for assigning the final standing and reflects the following:

- A detailed description of the context in which the practicum took place
- General description of units/themes and lesson planning prepared by the preservice teacher
- The workload of the preservice teacher including any involvement with clubs, coaching, committee work, or workshops
- General observations supported by examples from each item on the performance checklist (Box 8.6)

Box 8.6: Example of a Final Report
Introductory Comments

Ms. Kwok completed her extended practicum at a very high level of achievement in a Grade 3 primary-level classroom. This was a class of twenty-four students with ten girls and fourteen boys. The majority of students were ELL and there were two special needs students in the class. Ms. Kwok was able to identify student needs with strong assessment tools before, during and after learning. She frequently would adjust assignments to match the learner's abilities, knowledge levels, and interests. Ms. Kwok was under the supervision of two sponsor teachers. She taught all subjects.

Professional Qualities

Ms. Kwok has a sincere, positive outlook, and most capably embraced classroom and school life. With her strong work ethic, she could be counted on to take the initiative at all times and get things done. She thoughtfully created a classroom community that allows each student to be an individual and work to his/her own potential. She is a skillful classroom practitioner with clear values, knowing where she is going and why. Ms. Kwok interacts extremely well with her students and thoroughly enjoys working with young people. She is able through creating interest, surprise, entertainment, and many "a-ha" moments to fully engage her students, constantly finding ways to draw them into fully participating in the curriculum. Ms. Kwok's philosophy of education is guided by imaginative education and cooperative learning where engagement and intrinsic motivation provide the foundation of importance for her teaching practices. She loves learning and leads by example.

Ms. Kwok's interactions with students, parents, and staff were most professional and respectful. She has demonstrated an appreciation and understanding of the importance of being a part of the school community by beautifying the school library with her artistic talents. She volunteered time to work with the sports day committee. She connected with as many students outside of her classroom as possible and worked closely with resource teachers and administration.

Ms. Kwok's commitment to lifelong learning is evident in the professional development activities she undertook, implemented and reflected upon during her practicum. She attended workshops on starting up one's own class and the *Mind Up* workshop to promote mindfulness. Along with her cohort, she attended four after-school workshops organized by the UBC staff during the time of her practicum. She sought suggestions and advice with sincerity and regularly incorporated these suggestions into her lessons.

Instructional Planning

Ms. Kwok has demonstrated appropriate use of the ministry guidelines as described in the BC Ministry of Education Integrated Resource Packages

(continued)

Box 8.6 (continued)
(IRPs) and Prescribed Learning Outcomes (PLOs). Goals and objectives for units and individual lesson plans were very clearly laid out and were logically organized. All planning was completed well in advance. Sequence of lessons was well thought out so that each lesson built on prior knowledge. Lessons were designed to meet diverse student needs. She consistently demonstrated an expert knowledge of all subjects taught.

She planned so that students felt excited, curious, and intent on learning. She frequently provided opportunities for students' emotions to become part of their learning as well. For example, she planned to celebrate the conclusion of her *Pioneer unit* by holding a pioneer day. For this day she has created crafts and activity stations throughout the morning. A special pioneer lunch was served and students watched a pioneer movie. In her planning, she made sure that pupils discussed important ideas among themselves, using vocabulary and concepts introduced by her to accomplish learning tasks. Ms. Kwok enjoyed the complexity of unit and lesson planning and displayed a special talent for challenging students with rich concept learning using ideas and language students readily understood.

Instructional Implementation

Ms. Kwok used whole class, small group, and individual instruction to foster both cooperative learning and independent learning. She was skillful in what she did in the class. Her teaching strategies and the curriculum materials she used were always appropriate to her educational goals. She was able to describe what students were doing and why they were doing it in a clear and educationally sound way. She generated feelings of confidence in what was happening in her classroom and became skillful in setting up all students for success.

Expectations, assessment, and evaluation procedures were fully explained and exercises were marked and returned promptly. She learned to use a variety of forms of assessment (rubrics, peer review, criteria rubrics, self-assessment, and anecdotal) and evaluation to obtain data to promote further learning. As well, she was able to give her students constant feedback on their performances during the lessons. Ms. Kwok fully participated in the reporting to parent's process.

Ms. Kwok's classroom, both as a physical space and as a social environment, was well organized, and always communicated relevant features of what was being studied at the time. All students had roles and jobs and made positive contributions to having a pleasing, well-organized and cared-for room. Rules, timetables, reward systems, and activities were all appropriately displayed in the classroom. She was able to provide for individual choice excellent pacing of lessons and cooperative learning in all activities. Her class was an inviting, relaxed environment for learning.

(continued)

Box 8.6 (continued)

Ms. Kwok inspired her students with her love of reading, writing, art, music, and drama. She is a gifted artist and storyteller and often told stories at the beginning of a lesson to create a context for the lesson and invite students to "bond" with the subject matter. She was able to create in her students a sense of awe and wonder. A good example of this is when students built the strongest and sturdiest bridge out of straws and tape. Her outstanding Pioneer unit taught students about Canada's history of immigrants colonizing a new land, their methods of survival, and their interactions with the First Nations peoples with many visuals and display of artifacts, as well; Ms. Kwok created her own activity booklet for the unit. This unit culminated in Ms. Kwok planning a field trip to the Burnaby Heritage Museum.

Classroom Management

Ms. Kwok is very competent in interpreting and dealing successfully with pupil's behavior in a consistent manner. She responded to students with genuine concern for their well-being. When confronted with pupils' difficult behavior, she responded effectively without being defensive. Her reactions were honest and open at all times. Her pupils' abilities to make positive contributions to their class community steadily increased under her leadership. Ms. Kwok fully nurtured the social and emotional aspects of her students and ignited each student's desire to learn.

Communication

In her interactions with students, Ms. Kwok's facial expressions, her tone of voice, and language gave explicit evidence of warmth, praise, and encouragement. The class enjoyed her sense of humor and dramatic flair when she read out loud to them. She used the art of reflective responses that enabled pupils to become clearer in their own thinking, work out their ideas, and assume responsibility for their own ideas. Questions she chose to ask pupils were often concerned with the higher cognitive skills of interpreting data, problem-solving, and applying principles, along with questions recalling factual information. She gave students time to think. She made it clear that she was interested in many possible explanations and answers. She invited students to think for themselves. Ms. Kwok always gave timely, clear, and concise directions.

Assigned Standing

Ms. Kwok has completed the requirements of her EDUC 418 extended practicum in an outstanding way. She is a most talented teacher and brings a highly professional approach to her role in the classroom. She has demonstrated her dedication, drive, and sincere enjoyment in working with children.

Conclusions

This chapter has provided an overview of the multiple and complex roles of the tutors in a PBL cohort in a teacher education program. Specifically, during the two-week case inquiry cycle (which includes the 1-day a week, the 2-week, and 10-week school-based practica) with the support, facilitation, and provocation of the tutors, the preservice teachers are engaged in

- Clarifying terms and concepts
- Defining case problems
- Generating case issues to be researched
- Prioritizing the learning needs of the group and identifying which task(s) tutorial members will take responsibility for
- Engaging in independent research
- Effectively sharing new knowledge with group members
- Integrating new knowledge shared by group members in a comprehensive synthesis
- Bridging what is learned on campus with learning experiences in the school-based practicum
- Reflecting on both what was learned and the process of learning
- Supervising and evaluating preservice teachers' school-based practicum experiences

References

Berman, S. (1996). *A comparison of dialogue and debate*. Distributed by the Dialogue Group of the Boston Chapter of Educators for Social Responsibility.
Hmelo-Silver, C. E., & Barrows, H. S. (2006). Goals and strategies of a problem- based learning facilitator. *Interdisciplinary Journal of Problem-based Learning, 1*(1). Available at: http://dx.doi.org?10.7771/1541-5015.1004
Kundoque, J.G. (2008). Reclaiming Haisla ways: Remembering oolichan fishing. *Canadian Journal of Native Education, 31*(1), 11–23.
Neville, A. J. (1999). The problem-based learning tutor: Teacher? Facilitator? Evaluator? *Medical Teacher, 21*(4), 393–401.

Chapter 9
"I'm Not Allowed to Tell You": What Does It Mean to Be a Problem Based Learning Tutor?

Lori Prodan

Introduction

You are an experienced elementary teacher and teacher educator who will be taking on the role of Problem Based Learning Tutor in the coming year. You will be working with a group of thirteen Preservice Teachers, meeting with them twice a week to help guide them through the cycle of learning through cases. It is now the third week of August and you're wondering how to transition to this new role. You will be working with experienced PBL Tutors who have offered their support and advice, but you are still wondering how to face the students on that first day understanding so little about how PBL actually works and about what you are actually supposed to be doing. What aspects of being a tutor will be consistent with your understanding of being an instructor? What aspects will be different? How will you adapt to the new role?

This was the *case* as I lived it. The issues that arise in the transition between instructor and PBL tutor are multifaceted and come to the heart of what it means to be an educator. As a teacher in an elementary school and as an instructor in a traditional teacher education cohort, the role of instructor/teacher is linked to the curriculum guidelines, supported by prescribed texts, a syllabus, and other external structures. When one becomes a tutor, most of this apparatus of teaching is stripped away. What is left are the students, the cases, and the case cycle. Hendry et al. (1999) calls tutor performance a "key function" of the success of a PBL program (p. 366): a tutor in PBL functions as a moderator of student learning. The role of the tutor, therefore, is as a custodian of the group process (Neame 1984) rather than a source of knowledge. For an instructor who used to work in traditional courses within a teacher education program, where the instructor is seen as holding expert knowledge, the switch to the role of a tutor in a PBL cohort can be a complicated and destabilizing journey.

L. Prodan (✉)
Vancouver School District 39, Vancouver, BC, Canada
e-mail: lori.prodan@ubc.ca

Walsh (2005) writes:

> The switch from disseminator of information to facilitator of learning can be challenging for those new to tutoring. Those unfamiliar with the PBL process often express uncertainty about the function of the tutor. How directive should the tutor be within the group? What are the necessary facilitation skills for effective group functioning? (p. 10)

This chapter outlines *my case* in adapting to the transition from instructor to tutor and specifically the questions I posed about my own practice and role as a teacher educator throughout the experience. At the end of my first year as tutor, 11 of the students in my tutorial group volunteered to speak with me about their experience with PBL and about how they saw the role of the tutor and the tutorial sessions. Throughout the chapter their important insights and perspectives will be compared and contrasted with my own. Amador et al. (2006) describes problem based learning as moving through a series of questions as one works through a case: What do I know? What do I need to know? How will I learn it? Thinking about the transition between instructor and PBL tutor as a case, what are then are the issues?

Issue One: What Background Knowledge and Experience Do I Bring to the Role of a Problem Based Learning Tutor?

I initially welcomed the opportunity to work with the problem based learning approach because I thought it more effectively embodied my own understanding of the role of an elementary teacher. I came to the university as an adjunct professor after having taught kindergarten to grade five, primarily in schools that had been designated "inner city" due to the high level of various social and economic needs of the students. Partly as a response to teaching in this inspiring and challenging environment, I have come to see the role of teacher as inherently multidimensional and highly complex. The discrete courses that make up traditional teacher education programs do not fit with this reality. As a teacher, I do not think about educational psychology at one point in the day, curriculum and pedagogy at another point, nor do I switch between being a math teacher and being a language arts teacher any more than I think about teaching English as an additional language as an add-on to a lesson plan. An effective elementary teacher thinks about all these things at once. The discrete nature of traditional course work can limit preservice teachers' understanding of how the various aspects of a teacher's role must constantly work together. The holistic nature of PBL, wherein preservice teachers are asked to think about the relationships between pedagogy and social justice, between mathematics and place-based learning, and between special needs education and language arts *on the very first day*, is more in keeping with the thinking they will necessarily do as teachers. Rather than spend an academic year gathering puzzle pieces and then frantically putting them together during the teaching practicum, I was intrigued by the idea that I could help PBL preservice teachers see the whole puzzle at once.

Having taught and been a faculty advisor in the regular program for 1 year at the same institution where I became a PBL tutor, as well as for 2 years in an education program at the Awassa College of Teacher Education in Southern Ethiopia, I had some familiarity with the traditional structures of course work, syllabi, assigned readings, and assignments. In addition to the holistic nature of PBL, the concept of working with only 13 students throughout two terms appealed to my deeply held beliefs about the importance of caring communities in education. As an instructor in the traditional model, creating safe environments in which all preservice teachers could engage in the risk taking necessary for true learning had proven to be very challenging as I generally worked with a group of 36 with whom I spent 4 hour a week. I felt frustrated by my inability to get to know each of them in meaningful ways and was therefore only very superficially able, if at all, to respond to their individual learning needs. Furthermore, a syllabus that must be published and distributed before one meets the preservice teachers seems to make any attempts at *student-centered* learning minimal at best.

Issue Two: Establishing Trust

Clearly I came to PBL predisposed to value many of its core tenets. As Pourshafie and Murray-Harvey (2013) note:

> [F]or teacher educators, the appeal of this approach lies in the potential of PBL pedagogy to meet desired learning outcomes for preservice teachers to become self-directed learners who are competent problem-solvers, able to work effectively with others and to reflect on their own practice. (p 1690)

And yet, the role of tutor remained unclear to me. If I wasn't instructing my preservice teachers, what was I supposed to be doing with them? There was a conundrum for me: On the one hand, it seemed that the role of tutor, as opposed to instructor, required me to withhold my knowledge and experience as a teacher educator; on the other hand, the role of tutor within the PBL model was completely outside my area of experience and knowledge. I felt at once too knowledgeable and too ignorant. I had too much content knowledge and experience and no process knowledge or experience, leading me to two central questions: to what extent would I be able to withhold my knowledge and experience from my preservice teachers? How could I guide them through the two-week case cycle when I lacked that very experience as a teacher or as a learner myself?

Much has been written about preservice teachers' initial response to being in a PBL program, often focusing on their sense of frustration and disorientation (Silén, 2004; Amador et al. 2006; Neville 1999; Hung et al. 2003). When asked to think back to their feelings during their first few weeks in the program, my own preservice teachers responded with words like "unsettling" and "frustrating" and reported feeling "confused," "apprehensive," "a little skeptical," "worried if I was doing it right," "perturbed by it," and not being "a happy camper." One recalled thinking, "Oh, what did I get myself into? I'm responsible for all of my learning. And that's what it was, it felt like a big responsibility." As a new tutor, I also felt unsettled, confused, certainly frustrated at times, and, in spite of the alignment between the PBL pedagogy and my own educational beliefs, somewhat skeptical. It is one thing to believe in student-centered, constructivist learning but be constrained by the institutional requirements of a standard syllabus, assigned readings, and assignments with assessment criteria which must be set before one has even met the students. When these constraints were largely, although not wholly, as I will discuss later, removed, and the learners are indeed in control of their own learning, it was destabilizing.

Deborah Britzman (2003) explains that the story of learning to teach is inherently contradictory because:

> [T]eaching and learning have multiple and conflicting meanings that shift with our lived lives, with the theories produced and encountered, with the deep convictions and desires brought to and created in education, with the practices we negotiate, and with the identities we construct. (p. 32)

In some ways I had constructed an identity for myself as a teacher educator invested in student-centered learning when it was safe to do so because I was unable to fully practice it. Now, as a PBL tutor I had to trust my preservice teachers, trust their ability to pose the right questions and to organize their own learning – in short, to be enough. Pourshafie and Murray-Harvey (2013) research into PBL in a teacher education program suggesting "that the complex skills of 'holding back' and 'creating space' are particularly challenging as they also rely on the facilitator's attitude, characterized by trust in students to direct their own learning" (p. 176). At the outset, the case cycle that the preservice teachers would be going through seemed less robust to me than regular course work. Perhaps because the preservice teachers were given minimal guidance on what a research package should contain, it resulted in the quality of the first packages varying broadly. Some seemed very superficial and disorganized, while others were more thorough. I had many moments of panic, certain that they would not in fact be able to learn the skills and content knowledge necessary to become competent teachers by the end of the year. In PBL, the need for trust is explicit and valued. As Amador et al. (2006) note, "we need to trust that our planning, our problems, and our procedures will facilitate preservice teacher learning with only a little direction and encouragement from us" (p. 93).

So, I had to trust the preservice teachers. Interestingly for several of my preservice teachers, responding near the end of their academic year, they viewed my role as one of creating trust among the group. As one said, "I think you played a really big role in getting us bonding and comfortable with each other in order to have these huge discussions and deep discussions" (2013). Walsh (2005) puts "climate setting – creating a safe, conducive environment for self-directed learning" (p. 11) first on the list of tasks for the PBL tutor. Hendry et al. (1999) contend that the "fundamental role of the tutor is to promote a relaxed atmosphere and allow discussion to proceed" (p. 367). I would argue that an atmosphere conducive to learning and shifts in core beliefs is not simply a "relaxed" one, but rather one in which each learner feels respected, safe, and listened to. From the outset of the year, I saw this as a challenging and important part of my role. When asked about the role of the tutor, one preservice teacher noted, "people have come with all different experiences and so finding a balance…to kind of have everybody: Okay, we're all learning this together, [the tutor has] to know how to manage all the personalities and people" (2013). A third agreed, adding the tutor "brought us together…at the start of the year I wasn't someone who would speak, but [the tutor] made it so comfortable for me to express myself" (2013). As a tutor who is also a learner, I worked to build a community of safety and trust that was necessarily reciprocal. While this was essentially what I had believed education to be about, in the PBL program, I had to go farther, to trust more, to more consciously build trust. In many ways, the whole year's learning for each of my preservice teachers depended on this community trust in a manner that is much more explicit and obvious than in the regular program.

Issue Three: Tutor as Expert

While not an expert in the academic research sense, I came to the role of a PBL tutor with years of elementary teaching and as an experienced teacher educator. I was therefore relatively comfortable with the idea of answering preservice teachers' questions about various aspects of teaching and learning. What was I to do with this expertise as a tutor? I have a clear memory of my very first tutorial, introducing *case one*. The preservice teachers, as noted above, were nervous, anxious, and uncertain about the process. I was as well. After we had read through the case silently, I then asked them to find a partner and discuss what they had noticed. When I felt the discussion wane in the room, I asked the partners to join with another set of two, forming groups of four, and compare what they had discovered about the case. We then came together as a group. One preservice teacher raised her hand and posed a question about the case. It was an interesting question, relevant and rich with potential for exploration. In response, I blurted out, "I'm not allowed to tell you." In my first half hour as a PBL tutor, I had panicked. Fearful of the *PBL police* I suppose, I externalized my withholding of information and went no further. It was not an auspicious beginning. I was deeply uncomfortable withholding information. My instinct was to answer the question. I felt constrained by the PBL pedagogy and made that painfully obvious.

In their study of a PBL program in teacher education, Pourshafie and Murray-Harvey (2013) discuss the issue of tutor expertise:

> PBL tutoring demands a radical shift from teacher as the all-knowing subject content expert to a co-constructor of knowledge within a community of learners (Hmelo-Silver and Barrows 2006; Lekakala-Mokgele 2010; Roberts 2010; Rotgans and Schmidt 2011). Assuming such a humble posture is not an immediately comfortable position (in power relationship terms) for many teachers and students alike in their early experience of PBL. (p. 170)

Other people have discussed the challenge tutors may face in giving up power to their students (Amador et al. 2006). Although I may have been dealing with these feelings unknowingly, the much more overt frustration I had was almost the opposite. I felt a certain dishonesty in observing my students pose questions that I had the ability to help them with, but was choosing not to. I sensed frustration on their part, not that they felt I was powerless or unknowing, but that I had the power, through my experience to help them, but was choosing not to. The power to deny assistance, as one preservice teacher recalled 10 months later, "…here it was like, so what do you want to know? And I was like, I don't know, shouldn't you tell me? Shouldn't you tell me what I should know? That was my biggest doubt at the beginning. Am I really going to learn anything?" (2013) After a few case cycles of insisting that I could tell them nothing, I began to gradually provide guidance when I felt it warranted. I also learned to pose better questions in order to promote their learning from each other and to encourage them to deepen their own thinking, most often through questioning assumptions they had made. After seeing the preservice teachers go through a few case cycles, I could feel myself relaxing into the PBL pedagogy, believing in it more and therefore internalizing its tenets. Instead of always refusing to answer my preservice teachers' questions, while I most often responded with a question of my own, I did choose to answer some questions based on my own experiences.

When asked about the role of the tutor in terms of the program itself and of their own growth as learners, my preservice teachers provided considered and sometimes vivid descriptions. One said, "I feel like you kind of hinted at us where to go sometimes. You didn't directly tell us where to go but you were like, 'ah'!" Another felt emphatically that the tutor's expertise was very important, saying, "I don't think that an effective tutor would be someone who had no experience with education." A third used a metaphor to express her ideas:

> …If we went on a hike, you'd be at the back and then you'd kind of be watching out for us, so if we went too close to the edge, or if we were kind of like on the edge, you would guide us back in, and you would motivate us to keep going, but not so much leading us, but you would kind of be at the back.

While I felt more comfortable with the role I had created as *tutor* being someone who occasionally answers questions and does provide guiding opinions from time to time, I did wonder if I was simply manipulating the PBL pedagogy to suit my own interests, to replicate what I knew and was comfortable with. Was I unintentionally turning *tutor* into *instructor*? A preservice teacher also questioned this: "You knew what some of those big ideas that we needed to be looking at and you hinted at us sometimes and we needed that…I wonder, if that was pure PBL then or not?" (2013). Perhaps the idealized notion of PBL, the preservice teachers as a band of independent knowledge creators is something both this student and I were objecting to, both through words and actions. However, PBL pedagogy does not call for an educational free-for-all wherein the learners are set free on the Internet and in the library to research what they like. As Savery (2006) notes in an overview of PBL:

> [T]he reality is that learners who are new to PBL require significant instructional scaffolding to support the development of problem-solving skills, self-directed learning skills, and teamwork/collaboration skills to a level of self-sufficiency where the scaffolds can be removed. (p. 15)

Taking the concept of the tutor as someone who helps provide instructional scaffolding when required, providing direction and even answering questions does not seem removed from the pedagogical approach, but rather an integral part of it.

Issue Four: Tutor as Facilitator

Many discussions of the role of tutor highlight the facilitation aspect of the function (Savery 2006; Amador et al. 2006; Savin-Baden and Wilkie 2004; Walsh 2005; Hmelo-Silver and Barrows 2006). Before the term started, my job was most often described to me as someone who leads discussions. I could picture myself sitting around a circular table, calling on various preservice teachers to speak, responding to what they had said, and moving on to the next preservice teacher. In some respects, this is what a tutorial session might have looked like to an outside observer. We did sit in a roughly circular arrangement, one person at a time spoke, and most often I was the person who determined who would speak. Rather than facilitation, however, which conjures up ideas of helping a group arrive at a common decision, I came to see my role as more disruptive. Within the boundaries of a trusting community of learners, I sought to disrupt the preservice teachers' assumptions, to encourage them to disagree with each other. The group's discussion often opened with a simple consensus about a seemingly straightforward aspect of education, and I actively tried to elicit dissent, multiple perspectives and ways of thinking that challenged assumptions. In describing the ideal tutor, Mayo et al. (1995) reject the term facilitator, in favor of activator, explaining, "to facilitate is to help, to make something easy or easier … In contrast, the activator *causes* students to engage in activity" (p. 127). While I would argue that I couldn't *cause* students to do anything, I do think that I attempted to engage them in critique and dissent rather than facilitate consensus.

In the interests of allowing the preservice teachers to own the process as much as possible, after the first two case cycles, I experimented with asking a preservice teacher to volunteer to lead the discussion. This seemed consistent with the PBL aims of student-centered learning, as well as with the program's goals of helping create active, professional teachers. However, after watching this play out during two or three tutorial sessions, I became aware of two things: the first being that what I had been doing was clearly not "facilitation" as one would do in a meeting – that is, to simply call on the next speaker and move through a list of agenda items – and the second being that running a PBL discussion seemed to require skills that most of my preservice teachers simply didn't yet have. Indeed, it doesn't seem reasonable to expect that they would, particularly when simultaneously being engaged in the learning process the case required. In their study of PBL facilitation, based on careful observation and analysis of two tutorial sessions, Hmelo-Silver and Barrows (2006) conclude that an expert facilitator employs a variety of strategies, often switching between them in rapid succession:

> Barrows [the tutor] used modeling, scaffolding and fading progressively as the students grew more responsible for their own learning and began questioning each other. He modeled the questions students should be asking themselves until they appropriated these questioning strategies themselves. (p. 37)

While I am not at all an expert facilitator, I was using many of these strategies while leading tutorial discussions in ways that my students, acting as "guest facilitators," were unable to do. Rather than allowing the discussion to suffer, I took back control of this aspect of the group process. As with answering and posing questions, it would seem that I became less student centered in doing so. However, I would argue that student-centered learning involves not simply letting preservice teachers explore but also means responding to their learning needs in ways that further their journey. Commenting on the tutorial discussions, one recalled, "I think it still worked in the end and we were able to learn from one another and learn what are these different views. So you were a facilitator" (2013).

Issue Five: Tutor as Evaluator

As a PBL tutor, I was a discussion leader, engaged in disrupting assumptions, a facilitator of community building, and an experienced member of the larger professional community my preservice teachers sought to join. I was also an evaluator of student progress. Throughout the program, including during my students' school-based practica, I assessed and evaluated the preservice teachers' skills and knowledge. As an instructor, the evaluative aspect of my role was clear, explicit, and a large focus of my energies. In the pass/fail program, the criteria and learning outcomes for student assignments are provided, along with deadlines. I then decide if the preservice teachers' submissions meet or do not meet the set criteria and provide written feedback. Although even as an instructor the evaluative process is itself much more messy than what I've described here, I found the evaluative aspect of PBL tutor to be very complex. I provided written and oral feedback based on specific criteria at each phase of the case cycle – annotated bibliography (after three case cycles, I stopped providing this feedback), research packages, presentations, and synthesis. All of this feedback was privately given to the relevant student authors. Thus, there was a continual one-way stream of assessment and pass/fail evaluation from me as tutor to the students. The sheer volume of feedback per student as well as its cyclical nature was very different from being an instructor. Additionally, there was and is an intimacy to the tutorials and the community we had created which sometimes emotionally complicated my feedback. Furthermore, within PBL pedagogy, the tutor is clearly *not* an authority. Indeed, Mayo et al. (1995) state that "the tutor must surrender the seat of authority" (126) and that "tutors must become partners in the PBL group without losing their identity" (129). As one shifts from the "sage on the stage to the guide on the side," what becomes of the powers of assessment and evaluation? Can one be a partner in inquiry with someone one has the power to deny progress in the program?

The term *tutor* itself seems to minimize the evaluative aspect of the role. Instead of *instructor* or *teacher*, terms that are imbued with conceptions of evaluation and often gate-keeping, the title *tutor* connotes a more familiar, supportive role. It traditionally refers to a one-on-one situation wherein a student is receiving extra support. Many years earlier, as a graduate student, I had been a tutorial assistant, working under the supervision of a professor. As it seemed like a reversion to a younger, less experienced and knowledgeable version of myself, I was reluctant to take on this job title once again. So in many ways, the title of *tutor* did not sit comfortably with me. Indeed, throughout my first year as a PBL tutor, I rarely used the term. Yet in our PBL program, as in others, tutors have considerable power in whether or how the students proceed through the program. At the end of the list of tasks for a PBL tutor, Walsh (2005) includes "evaluating learning outcomes – include formative feedback as well as summative evaluation" (p. 11). Rather than making the power dynamic explicit, as it is with the instructor/student relationship, the term *tutor* and some functions of the role seem to obscure or camouflage the tutor's power.

In terms of providing feedback, I found the cyclical nature of the cases to be a very satisfying structure. In the traditional program, preservice teachers completed each type of assignment, such as an autobiography or a group presentation once in the course. The feedback I provide is then not going to be used to help improve that specific product or process in the future. With PBL, I felt that my feedback might be used in future responses: that is, constructive feedback on a particular case synthesis might be used by the preservice teacher in the writing of the next case synthesis. However, when I asked my preservice teachers an open-ended question about how they viewed the role of the tutor, in their extensive and considered responses, no one mentioned anything about feedback, assessment, or evaluation. For whatever reasons, this aspect of the role was not central to their conception of tutor.

Synthesis

As I continue to make the transition from instructor to PBL tutor, I return to Amodar's (2006) three questions:

- What do I know?
- What do I need to know?
- How will I learn it?

To pose these questions in the past tense:

What did I think I knew?

I thought I knew very little about the PBL process. I thought that being a tutor meant that I could not answer questions and not provide advice or guidance. I thought my role was primarily to facilitate discussion and make sure everyone was an active participant. I did know very little about the PBL process, but was able to use what I did know about questioning, group dynamics, creating trusting communities, and providing feedback from my other teaching experiences to guide me through the process.

What did I need to know?

An explanation of the terminology of PBL would have been very helpful. Perhaps because it is a pedagogy founded on principles of constructivism where there are no assigned readings, I found it difficult to learn the language of PBL. The specific use of terms within the PBL community – case, tutor, and synthesis, to name a few – had the effect of making me feel like an outsider rather than a participant until I had been through many case cycles.

How did I learn it?

I learned primarily from my students. I listened to their struggles, observed their progress, and came to believe more strongly in the method we were using together. Of course I learned a great deal from my colleagues who usually answered my many questions but occasionally responded with another question in the PBL way.

I began the year by acting as though being a tutor was a radical departure from being an instructor, when in many ways it wasn't. I still used my expertise and experience, and I still responded to student needs to the best of my abilities. Over the course of the year, I became more and more myself as PBL tutor. Teaching is a continual becoming; one is always in the process of constructing an identity. My identity as PBL tutor continues to feel tentative and emergent.

References

Amador, J. A., Miles, L., & Peters, C. B. (2006). *The practice of problem-based learning: A guide to implementing PBL in the college classroom.* Bolton: Anker Publishing Company, Inc.

Britzman, D. P. (2003). *Practice makes practice: A critical study of learning to teach.* Albany: State University of New York Press.

Hendry, G. D., Frommer, M., & Walker, R. A. (1999). Constructivism and problem-based learning. *Journal of Further and Higher Education, 23*(3), 369–371.

Hmelo-Silver, C. E., & Barrows, H. S. (2006). Goals and strategies of a problem-based learning facilitator. *Interdisciplinary Journal of Problem-Based Learning, 1*(1), 21–39.

Hung, W., Bailey, J. H., & Jonassen, D. H. (2003). Exploring the tensions of problem- based learning: Insights from research. *New Directions in Teaching and Learning, 95*, 13–24.

Mayo, W. P., Donnelly, M. B., & Schwartz, R. W. (1995). Characteristics of the ideal problem-based learning tutor in clinical medicine. *Evaluation & the Health Professions, 18*(2), 124–136. doi:10.1177/016327879501800202.

Neame, R. L. B. (1984). Problem-centred learning in medical education: The role of context in the development of process skills. In H. G. Schmidt & M. L. de Volder (Eds.), *Tutorials in problem-based learning: A new direction in teaching the health professions* (pp. 33–47). Assen/Maastricht: van Gorcum.

Neville, A. J. (1999). The problem-based learning tutor: Teacher? Facilitator? Evaluator? *Medical Teacher, 21*(4), 393–401. doi:10.1080/01421599979338.

Pourshafie, T., & Murray-Harvey, R. (2013). Facilitating problem- based learning in teacher education: Getting the challenge right. *Journal of Education for Teaching: International Research and Pedagogy, 39*(2), 169–180.

Roberts, G. W. (2010). *Creative tuition: The experience of tutors in problem based learning.* Unpublished dissertation. Retrieved from http://search.proquest.com.ezproxy.library.ubc.ca/docview/899759850?accountid=14656

Rotgans, J. I., & Schmidt, H. G. (2011). Cognitive engagement in the problem-based learning classroom. *Advances in Health Sciences Education, 16*(4), 465–479. doi:10.1007/s10459-011-9272-9.

Savery, J. R. (2006). Overview of problem-based learning: Definitions and distinctions. *Interdisciplinary Journal of Problem-based Learning, 1*(1), 9–20.

Savin-Baden, M., & Wilkie, K. (2004). *Challenging research in problem-based learning.* New York: Open University Press.

Silén, C. (2004). Chapter 11: Does problem-based learning make students 'go meta'?. In M. Savin-Baden, K. Wilkie, & Society for Research into Higher Education (Eds.), *Challenging research in problem-based learning.* New York/Maidenhead: Society for Research into Higher Education & Open University Press.

Walsh, A. (2005) *The tutor in PBL: A novice's guide.* Hamilton: McMaster University. http://fhs.mcmaster.ca/facdev/documents/tutorPBL.pdf

Chapter 10
Investigating Cases: Problem-Based Learning and the Library

Jo-Anne Naslund

Introduction

Academic librarians are well positioned to assume significant roles in problem-based education ranging from resource consultants to collection developers, curriculum designers to course collaborators, and information literacy coaches to problem-based learning (PBL) resource persons/tutors. In this chapter, I examine how the underlying pedagogies of PBL fundamental for student engagement and case-based learning align with and complement the academic mission of libraries, librarians, and information literacy programs in higher education.

My role is that of an academic librarian serving elementary and secondary pre-service teachers in the Education Library at the University of British Columbia. The TELL through PBL cohort is an elementary cohort of special significance to me, as it not only embraces the "process of inquiry" and "learning how to learn" but embodies it. My positive experiences with this cohort are shared through a semi-sequential narrative about our library services, collections, and instruction. As these evolve and change, the fundamental role of the library remains constant, which is to provide the necessary resources, technologies, and information literacy supports. I hope this discussion of PBL and the academic library will benefit those embarking upon a PBL program or to those thinking about reshaping their programs within networked learning environments.

J. Naslund (✉)
Education Library, University of British Columbia, Vancouver, BC, Canada
e-mail: joanne.naslund@ubc.ca

Problem Based Learning and the UBC Education Library

In 1998, Dr. Linda Siegel announced the first problem based learning cohort in the Faculty of Education at the University of British Columbia. The move was an innovative direction for the Faculty and was applauded by those who championed student-centered learning and inquiry-based teaching methods. One of the direct beneficiaries of this announcement was the UBC Education Library and its librarians. Imagine the possibilities for librarians – to work with teacher education cohorts where information skills, library resources and critical inquiry would be central to their program. As a teacher and academic librarian, I was excited by this emphasis on information gathering and lifelong learning. These were values and ideals to which I had espoused throughout my career, and for nearly two decades had been articulated by others in the field (Fitzgerald 1996; Rankin 1996). The time had come to position the library as a true partner in PBL.

So to be a true partner, how would the UBC Education Library best serve the PBL program? At faculty meetings, I learned more about the PBL philosophy and how the cohort would be organized around a series of cases based on authentic teaching scenarios. No formal courses, just cases – this PBL approach was different. I wanted to be involved so I consulted with individual faculty to determine what resources and services would be required of the library. I offered to produce bibliographies for the individual cases. These resource lists, although helpful, were not exactly what was needed and they were challenging to produce. I relied upon faculty recommendations of key books, articles, and websites, and soon realized I was trying to create what would have been traditionally a "course reading list". This was not really part of the PBL paradigm.

Now I had more questions. How was the library supposed to serve this program which in many ways seemed nebulous, confusing and hard to pin down? Should we start by placing books and articles in a special reserve section where they could be organized according to the specific cases? If so, how long should the loan periods be? Depending on how the case issues were interpreted, not all these materials would really need to be put on reserve and we would have expended staff time for naught. Perhaps we should create a PBL web page with links to suggested resources covering a range of anticipated queries for each case. This may help save preservice teachers' time as they conduct their research. However, would they actually look at them?

Once the program was underway, we tried many of these strategies. Some were not sustainable and others did not really save preservice teachers' time or make their access to resources easier, rather it seemed to complicate the process. In addition, they did not fit with the PBL philosophy of independent research and learning to "find out." Perhaps, preservice teachers should simply investigate and search for information on their own. In that case, what role would I play and how would I ensure that the preservice teachers possessed the necessary information skills to investigate their cases?

The PBL cohort would require library instruction. Should it be offered by means of a single workshop or through specific tutorial sessions about key resources, education databases and effective search strategies? Where would we start – with their first case? Maybe brief instruction sessions over several cases would be more effective. Or, perhaps librarians should offer individualized tutorials to assist preservice teachers on a need-to-know basis as they complete their investigations. In the end, we scheduled a three-hour library workshop for the PBL cohort (for all three tutorial groups) designed around the first case and added special library instruction sessions regarding specific cases as needed.

With case descriptions in hand, I realized that many of the search questions potentially arising out of a single case were far too complex for librarians to adeptly answer at a busy information desk. These queries were *authentic and messy*, and there was no guarantee of finding key resources with all the required answers. I felt out of my depth and poorly equipped to know enough about the specific cases to actually offer effective reference help. Without participating in the tutorial groups and their discussions, how could I as a librarian understand and be able to answer preservice teachers' questions, especially without knowing the contexts of their cases? How would it be feasible for me to find the time to attend all their tutorials, and even if I did attend, would it really help? I was uncertain that I could provide the "expert" assistance they required. Scheduling time for this cohort was daunting, given that this was one of the fifteen elementary and secondary cohorts with whom I worked. In addition I couldn't make sense of the PBL schedule – their tutorials were not weekly, they alternated, and sometimes they did not meet in the same classrooms.

During this time I remained enthusiastic, although I must admit my confidence was low and I felt rather discombobulated. I wasn't sure if my role was to help preservice teachers find resources to answer their specific questions or if I should simply focus on imparting those skills necessary for them to find answers on their own. Each case could be interpreted in innumerable ways, and even though my background experiences as a practicing teacher helped in contextualizing the questions, I was troubled by the fact that there really were no specific answers. How could I assist them with their investigations to locate the most useful and relevant information for each case? More importantly, I wondered if preservice teachers would locate and use *quality* resources for these cases or would they settle with what they could find most easily and accept less than reliable resources.

In these early stages, I wanted to find out how other libraries had dealt with problem-based learning. Through a review of the library literature, I obtained an overview of the experiences of other academic librarians in serving PBL programs. Once this was complete, it became clear that while a move to PBL would challenge us, the library was well equipped to support our preservice teachers. This was going to be part of an evolving program that wouldn't change us overnight. Moreover, the benefits to the library through involvement in PBL would be considerable and measurable. I was excited to consider how this newer, closer relationship with preservice teachers, tutors and faculty would play out and develop.

Academic Libraries and Problem-Based Learning: Some Findings

Problem-based learning aligns itself well with the academic mission of the university library. The first academic libraries, studied in regard to PBL programs and their effect on collections and services, were those primarily serving medical, nursing, pharmaceutical, dental, and health sciences programs (Eldredge 1993; Fitzgerald 1996; Fitzgerald et al. 1999; Rankin 1996). At McMaster University, where PBL was first introduced in 1969, the academic library was viewed as critical for PBL students in their research and served the academic mission to "produce graduates with demonstrated ability to identify, analyse and manage [clinical] problems in order to provide effective, efficient and [humane patient] care" (Fitzgerald 1996, p. 15).

An immediate impact of PBL programs resulted in a major increase in the use of academic libraries' resources and services. At the University of Toronto and Queen's University in Ontario, the emphasis on self-directed learning increased library use (Fitzgerald 1996, p. 20). Similarly, at the University of Calgary, major increases were noted in overall library use, especially in the use of scholarly journals, both in-house and through interlibrary loans, and there was also a rise in the use of networked databases such as Medline (Fitzgerald 1996). What these studies confirmed is "that PBL students use the library for longer periods of time; use a wider variety of resources to support their learning and require additional instruction in their information seeking skills" (Oker-Blom 1998; Dodd 2007, p. 208).

Whether increased library use can be attributed to the demands of PBL programs or to the very nature of the students enrolled in them is open to question. PBL students are described as "highly motivated, independent people, often working on a second career" (Fitzgerald 1996, p. 16). At Dalhousie University, most students arrived knowing how to use the online catalogue and various online databases. PBL students used the library more frequently and selected information sources, such as online databases and journal literature, more typical of independent learners (Rankin 1996). In addition, they acquired information-seeking skills earlier in the term, asked complex questions at the reference desk, and demonstrated greater ease in locating information than their traditional curriculum counterparts (Dodd 2007, p. 208).

At some institutions, PBL programs presented huge service and resource challenges, as librarians tried to balance the needs of PBL students and those in other non-PBL programs. Often, the expectations and requirements of PBL faculty and students meant they spent more time in the library and took up more time with the librarians. Initially, many libraries provided extensive reserve collections (short term) and incorporated special systems requirements. This placed a strain on the libraries' service desks and budgets, especially where multiple copies of heavily used items were in high demand. In some cases, these high-demand reserve collections were moved to buildings outside the library and were operated independently of the library. This proved problematic especially in trying to meet the resource needs of both PBL and non-PBL users.

Another impact of PBL for the library, as experienced at Queen's University, was the need to prepare students for self-directed learning. Information literacy programs for PBL required a greater allotment of librarian time for instruction, and PBL students needed to gain awareness of the library's resources as soon as possible (Chen et al. 2011; Ispahany et al 2007). Academic librarians offered orientations and in-depth training sessions for PBL students to meet their program demands, especially with respect to using health statistics, databases and information management.

At McMaster University Library, the academic librarians offered faculty and tutor training sessions in order to augment faculty and tutor competencies with respect to their use of library resources and services. This was seen to be "a worthwhile approach to promoting information management and health informatics skills" (Fitzgerald 1996, p. 18). At the University of Western Ontario, the PBL program had its own Learning Resources Centre (LRC) separate from the library and located in a medical building. There, librarians offered special training classes not to students but to the LRC staff (Fitzgerald 1996, p. 22).

Graduates from PBL programs seem to have a better knowledge and retention of the curricula. Dodd found that PBL students in a veterinary program spent longer time in the library because PBL required more research and the learning involved was more intensive and drew upon a wider variety of sources (2007, p. 207). PBL students self-selected materials, verified their sources, and were more discerning regarding the information. They displayed higher levels of information literacy and used recommended resources less often than students in non-PBL programs. They were more likely to use the Internet and were more discerning. They required additional instruction in information seeking, and they were better at integrating information effectively.

Through these experiences, as described by academic librarians from several libraries, I gained a unique view of how academic libraries could serve PBL programs, and I took note of the recommendations that had surfaced:

1. Academic librarians should be involved in PBL curriculum planning, receive PBL training, and be part of the PBL learning community.
2. Academic librarians need to be flexible in adapting to changes as the curriculum unfolds and comfortable with ambiguity and uncertainty.
3. Academic librarians should provide ongoing training for faculty, tutors, and pre-service teachers on information seeking and information management.
4. Academic library budgets are required for collections, technology, and licensed resources to meet PBL program requirements.

The Role of Librarians in the PBL Learning Community

Resource Consultant to Collection Developer

The role of the academic librarian as resource consultant and collection developer is important to the PBL environment where library and information services and a wider range of resources are used more often and for longer periods of time (Eaton and Richardson 1993; Rankin 1996). Our experiences in the UBC Education Library show that PBL preservice teachers use the Education Library extensively in conducting their research. An analysis of their case bibliographies and resource packages in 2012 demonstrated that on average 70–82 % of the materials they used for each case came from the UBC library; 16 % were open source resources, and only 2–5 % of the time did the library not have the resources they needed for their cases. Moreover, preservice teachers indicated via an online survey (with full participation by all members of the cohort) that 90 % of them rated the library as essential for their PBL studies. This result was striking. Similarly, 80 % of the faculty and tutors rated the library as essential and very important for their studies.

A rich collection of learning resources should mimic as closely as possible the types of professional and information gathering resources/processes utilized by practicing teachers (Barrows and Tamblyn 1980). This means having available theoretical and practical resources, Canadian and locally developed content resources from the British Columbia Ministry of Education and British Columbia Teachers' Federation, as well as materials for children and youth commonly found in school and public libraries. Preservice teachers use a wide range of resources when investigating their cases; and upon analyses of their research bibliographies (2012), it was evident that they consulted scholarly journals, books, BC Ministry documents, BCTF resources, YouTube videos, web resources and curriculum resources. The frequency with which they used these resources varied in accord with the contexts of their cases. Preservice teachers valued peer support in locating information sources, and they liked sharing their annotated bibliographies within the course content management system and also via Twitter – tweeting good resources to members of their tutorial group.

Sometimes it is not feasible for a library collection to sustain the breadth of resources required for PBL cases and to simultaneously meet the immediate demand for resources (a definite consideration for small libraries). According to Blumberg (1992), even the presence of faculty-generated learning objectives doesn't eliminate students' independent selection of learning materials. It is therefore critical for a library to establish fair and reasonable collection development policies. Standards of equitable access are important, especially regarding access to resources in school districts or through professional associations and government sources. Partnerships with school districts can help provide resources that are too expensive or just not appropriate for university library collections. Preservice teachers depend upon the university library for professional and research resources that inform their theoretical understandings of teaching and during their practice teaching look to their school libraries and school districts for teacher resources and curriculum materials.

Initially, our library materials for the PBL cohort were selected in collaboration with faculty and tutors and funded in part by new program funding. Nonetheless, the library's policy of purchasing only one copy of a book was not changed. The goal was to purchase as wide a variety of monographs, journals, and carefully selected examples of curriculum resources (including textbooks, juvenile books, big books, kits, DVDs, etc.). In addition we linked to online policies, government documents, and school district resources whenever possible.

Our current collection policy places a high priority on selecting e-books over print titles, and we try to balance the number of theoretical works to those practical titles purchased. A benefit of electronic resources is that preservice teachers have multiuser access to them, both on and off campus. Based on discussions with preservice teachers, online resources are preferred, and they are reluctant to carry home too many books. They choose practical titles over theoretical ones and especially value resources that offer teaching ideas and tips applicable to classroom practice.

Our collection of scholarly books and journals in the UBC Education Library may not reflect the reality of information access typically available to practicing teachers; however, it does reflect the current landscape of teaching, learning, and research. For the past 2 years, our library has piloted "patron-driven" collection development, which for a cohort such as PBL is beneficial. As preservice teachers explore resources for their cases, they generate orders for materials based directly on their case inquiries.

Database searching remains an extremely important part of our collection and services. We license many databases including *Ebsco Databases* such as ERIC (Ebsco), Education Source, PsycINFO, Communication & Mass Media Complete, Academic Search Complete, GreenFILE, and Professional Development Collection; *ProQuest Databases* such as CBCA Complete, Language and Linguistic Behavior Abstracts, and ProQuest Dissertations and Theses; EdITLib; First Nations Index; Web of Science; and JSTOR. Our goal is to strengthen and deepen our back runs of electronic journals and whenever possible subscribe to new electronic journals – especially those with Canadian coverage.

The search engines used to locate and record citation information include our library's discovery tool, *Summon*, together with Google Scholar, Google, Google Blogs, and Microsoft Academic Search. One goal of our library instruction is to be sure that preservice teachers are aware of these electronic resources and what is available to them through our library portal.

Curriculum Designer to Course Collaborator

With an understanding of scholarly inquiry and the research process, academic librarians play a role in curriculum design by personalizing curricula and selecting a wide variety of resources in multiple formats (Eaton and Richardson 1993; Rankin

1996). For example, as PBL cases are planned, I alert faculty and tutors as to some of the difficulties preservice teachers may encounter when conducting their research. Moreover, I locate and purchase resources relevant for a current case and make links to library resources within the course management system.

However, to really be part of the curriculum design process in PBL, it means making time to regularly attend the biweekly faculty/tutor meetings where cases are planned, revised, and discussed. For many years, I simply gleaned information from these meetings via emails (after the fact) without actually attending and being part of the discussions. I now realize it is critical to be actively connected with the PBL case planners and curricula, as it changes and evolves (Cheney 2004; Miller 2001). To be "present" in the PBL community means giving over time to it. Even though my role remains largely "indistinguishable," the result could be described as "seamless immersion within the curriculum" and is well worth it (Eldredge 2004, p. 58).

Seamless immersion is enhanced when academic librarians understand and are conversant with the knowledge bases of teacher education and how professional learning occurs. However, even if librarians initially possess only a partial understanding, it is critical that they be included as part of the PBL community of learning. When librarians learn of upcoming cases and take part in crafting and revising the authentic scenarios, they forge personal connections with tutors and faculty. The library space, collections, and programs as a consequence may be accorded more prominence as preservice teachers investigate their PBL cases and issues.

Information Literacy Coach to PBL Resource Person/Tutor

"Using libraries has played a large role in my learning this year" (Preservice teacher comment). Academic librarians working in PBL curricula have an opportunity to impact the information-seeking behavior and information literacy skills of preservice teachers. I know that some academic librarians especially those in medical programs often serve as information literacy coaches and as tutors embedded within the PBL program (Eldredge 2004). My role, however, started as a keen instruction librarian offering library orientation workshops at the beginning of each term for the PBL preservice teachers. Our first workshop, a hands-on computer workshop, provided an overview of our library, education databases, together with possible search strategies for finding journal articles, Ministry of Education documents, policy documents, and other resources related to a specific case (Case 1).

After this orientation, then what's up? At times I feel my role with PBL is "See you in September and then it's over!" My direct involvement fluctuates according to my available time and personal commitment to the program. The PBL cohort is one of many elementary and secondary cohorts I serve, as well as several hundred graduate students in education. In rare instances are academic librarians given the opportunity to assume full-time positions as information literacy coaches within PBL programs. However, the UBC Faculty of Medicine has funded a full-time librarian to fulfill this specialist role as part of their program. In the meantime, I consult with the PBL team, at least once per term, follow up on their suggestions for resources, attend at least two faculty/tutor meetings a year, and sit in on at least one tutorial group during the course of the school year to observe and learn more about the PBL cases and processes.

For the first 5 years of the PBL program, I really was on the periphery. My excuse was that I did not have enough time. However, I have come to realize that the real reason could be attributed to my lack of understanding of PBL pedagogy. For any academic librarian involved with a newly established PBL program, it is essential to become involved. Invite yourself to a PBL tutorial group, observe, listen and learn from their discussions. When you begin to *personally* understand PBL pedagogy, it will transform your practice.

Initially, I did invite myself to sit in on two tutorial groups. In most instances I was warmly received, but at other times especially with new tutors or faculty, they did not readily understand why a librarian would want to be part of the community. I also attended two PBL e-portfolio presentations. These experiences did affect me. I came away convinced that through inquiry, preservice teachers' understandings of educational research and teaching were not only deepened but situated in authentic contexts. I was inspired by their questions and discussions about teaching. My personal observations suggested that their understandings were far more complex and definitely different than those exhibited by preservice teachers in the regular B.Ed. program. I definitely wanted to become more deeply involved, and I could see my role shifting from information literacy coach to becoming a resource person/co-tutor.

Some PBL librarians hold faculty appointments and serve as tutors or even co-tutors taking on various tasks in curriculum planning and in other administrative areas (Rankin 1996). According to Eldredge, when the librarian serves as tutor, he/she has the chance to really experience the PBL curricula and acquire an understanding as to how it actually functions. What's more, the librarian may form wonderful relationships with students, tutors and faculty. This contributes to the creation of an atmosphere of collegial cooperation and collaboration where everyone respects one another (2004).

Help seeking can be expedited by librarians in their role as tutors and by providing coaching assistance. The librarian offers procedural guidance and assists in determining subtasks. He/she uses prompts, questions, clarifications and hints, coaching the preservice teachers through the process of finding information. This coaching is more about offering feedback on results and giving explanations when errors occur than providing answers to questions.

Reshaping Our Library Services and Instruction

Reshaping our UBC Education Library services and instruction is ongoing. One of the major benefits that academic librarians can bring to PBL programs is their planning for effective library and information literacy instruction. The type of library instruction can be as simple as a short information session to more "classic" library orientations, show-and-tell workshops, or two-way consultations with preservice teachers online or face to face. There are several options for how library instruction may be structured and implemented within PBL and may be a combination of online and in person, synchronous and asynchronous.

To reshape this instruction involves critical reflection (Mackey and Jacobsen 2011). For some time, I have been critical of the skills-based approach to library instruction and find the Association of College and Research Library (2000) information standards limited. Learners are denied "the rich potential that may be gained from broader attention to different ways of experiencing information use in the disciplines, the professions, and community" (Bruce 2008, p. 5). Further Bruce states "that the notion of 'informed learning', also referred to as 'using information to learn', can bring 'learner centered, experiential, and reflective approaches' to the information literacy agenda" (2008, p. 5). For me this is exactly what has happened as a consequence of my working with the PBL cohort.

As preservice teachers begin to investigate cases, they use different lenses to see or approach a concept, problem or practice (Diekema and Olsen 2011). Specifically, our library instruction program can become a situated and distributed activity, learned in specific contexts; information is more important than the mechanics of finding and organizing it (Lipponen 2010; Montiel-Overall 2007, p. 59).

So how are library services and instruction being reshaped? As a first step, I consider those "knowledge bases" associated with professional learning and specifically for teacher learning that have implications for library services and instruction. Then the second step is to examine how connectivity and information technologies are central to our library services and instructional programs. We need to employ technologies to aid preservice teachers as they organize and share information via e-mail, social media and social bookmarking. As educators, they will become content curators with their own personal/professional libraries of resources. And as a final step, I will reflect on the nature of inquiry and problem-based learning and what this means for our library instruction programs.

Understanding Professional Learning and Knowledge Bases

For academic librarians (in teacher education, undergraduate medicine, business or other disciplines), it is important to understand professional learning and how sources are made available, especially for novice professionals. With this information and increased understanding, librarians will be in a better position to offer *relevant* library services and instruction.

In *Professional Learning and the Knowledge Society*, a chapter on "Professional training and Knowledge Sources," Klette and Smeby explore the professional learning expressly of novice nurses and novice teachers (2012). Based on their study, the key characteristics of knowledge used by novice teachers are helpful in gauging what types of experiences seem to be the most useful in equipping them for real-world practice. This may also contribute to their developing habits for lifelong professional learning (a goal of the PBL program).

Professional learning involves negotiating meaning as a lived experience. In essence, the lived practice is where meaning resides. Professional knowledge includes a culture of practice and places learning within a community, where its use of information and artifacts come to represent accepted knowledge (Lave and Wenger 1991; Klette and Smeby 2012). It is community driven where learning begins and is ultimately applied in situ (where the work is done).

So how do preservice teachers connect to different sources of professional knowledge? One major knowledge source consulted most often by novice teaching professionals is the knowledgeable colleague (i.e., "colleagues and other professionals working nearby") and experts further afield. "Communication with colleagues takes place most often on an ad hoc basis and concerns practical matters related to specific concrete tasks, exchange of materials and conversations about individual pupils" (Klette and Smeby 2012, p. 151). In reshaping our library services and programs, librarians need to observe and talk with teachers in the field and become informed about their current teaching practices and resources.

Teachers use multiple knowledge sources to perform their jobs and in their search are faced with a lack of accessible and applicable sources available at their local work sites. Often teachers expend energy and time spent on making materials and things from scratch. Characteristics of novice teachers' knowledge base and their information-seeking behaviors drawn from the work of Klette and Smebey (2012) include the following:

1. A high percentage of teachers use the Internet; they locate resources at home to acquire information in content areas and other information relevant for instructional activities.
2. Teachers spend considerable time reading professional journals and articles (paper and web) and specialist literature such as books and works of reference and professional information on the Internet.
3. Knowledge in teaching is both a means and a goal (Klette and Smebey 2012, p 150).
4. Teachers' broad and rather general questions and problems combined with a continuous quest for content knowledge applicable to their teaching purposes result in their using the Internet, Google and similar tools as reference works. Their questions tend to be framed in terms that are about general themes. This in fact is more time-consuming when it comes to finding relevant information.

There are several implications of these information-seeking behaviors for our library services and information literacy instruction. First, given the high percentage of novice teachers who use Internet resources, it would be ideal if preservice teachers acquired sophisticated and effective Internet search strategies. Secondly, because reading professional journals is important, then preservice teachers should be aware of these journals. Often, we have focused primarily on scholarly journals, ignoring practical teacher magazines with articles about curricular and teaching topics. One wonders if some of these magazines have now been replaced by teacher blogs. And finally, a third implication is to figure out how to enhance preservice teachers' reasoning and analysis so that they employ effective search strategies. At Columbia University Library, for example, they introduced an online library toolkit (Ispahany et al. 2007) for the express purpose of helping their dental medical students become more efficient users of the resources available to them. The toolkit consists of a series of algorithmic templates, to help students recognize the types of questions govern their choice of search strategies and most appropriate library resources to use. Would such a toolkit be beneficial in teacher education and help preservice teachers become better at finding relevant and appropriate information sources quickly and effectively?

Connectivity and Information Management in a Networked Environment

One principle of the digital age is that of connectivity. It is all important. If I am connected, I have a world of knowledge at my fingertips. Connectivity is a large part of the changing landscape for libraries and consummate academic librarians (that I know and admire) are connected through social media, blogs and devices. They offer virtual reference, create visual guides on the fly and are experienced content curators. My goal is to find ways to be connected in this networked environment wherever preservice teachers study or need help.

The PBL emphasis "on enabling the student to become an independent self-directed learner generates an environment that is particularly receptive to technology as a means to facilitate learning" (Rankin 1996 p. 36). And technology applications most useful in augmenting the PBL process include course management systems, e-mail, blogs, Facebook, Twitter, Delicious, Dropbox, Google Drive, etc. The PBL information gathering becomes a shared learning activity. As part of the PBL cohort, I have been able to access our UBC course management system, and in reshaping our program, I want to use it more fully to share resources, information and instruction.

An area where I can help preservice teachers is in managing and organizing their information. I will continue to provide instruction on the use of the following: citation management software (such as RefWorks, Zotero, Mendeley) (Steeleworthy and Dewan 2013), presentation programs (such as Prezi, Animoto, wiki, blogs, etc.), curriculum planning and project management tools (such as Inspiration, CMap, and other Mindmapping tools), cloud devices (such as Google Drive, Dropbox), and crowdsourcing devices (such as bookmarking and social media networks such as Delicious, Good Reads, Pinterest, Facebook, Twitter). Increasingly preservice teachers will curate and manage their own professional libraries of digital teaching and learning resources as efficiently as possible.

Impact of Inquiry- and Problem-Based Learning on Library Instruction

Fortunately for me, my positive experiences of PBL coincided with a faculty review of our teacher education program. Inquiry was identified as one of the four foundational pillars of the revised teacher education program. When this was announced, I immediately proposed a study leave designed to learn more about PBL, the nature of inquiry, dispositions for inquiry, and how PBL preservice teachers find, select, obtain, and use resources. I was interested to learn more about the PBL tutorial cycle; I also wanted to shadow with a tutor to observe the preservice teachers during their practice teaching – "the ultimate place of practice".

These experiences have helped shape my library instruction, which has transitioned from information literacy workshops to coaching sessions. I know that providing the "answers" as we might at an information desk is not realistic when examining PBL case issues. I have learned to live with ambiguity and uncertainty, and this means messy, constructivist class work and sessions where preservice teachers have the opportunity to explore and search with me. At first I felt embarrassed when their searches produced better results than mine or when they knew of a source that I didn't. Over time I grew more confident in "not knowing" and appreciated our sharing openly and honestly together.

I would describe the shape of this library instruction, as individual conferencing sessions conducted during cohort tutorials or class time. My conferencing occurs with students, working individually or in pairs. Primarily, the instruction is "a conversation," and through our talk, I find out more about their thinking. I use prompts to clarify or expand upon their search questions, identifying potentially relevant and synonymous terms. Moreover, I provoke a critical lens when they evaluate their resources. However, at other times I try to find out in advance what aspect of the case they are researching and identify for them search terms, potential databases, and two to four relevant resources – journal articles or books.

The messiness of these sessions and the back and forth nature of the learning that occurs is not that of the librarian as "expert searcher"; it is as an equal co-investigator. These sessions are the most "authentic part" of my professional work and have afforded me the opportunity to build relationships (which I believe are central to teaching and learning) with faculty, tutors and preservice teachers. Through inquiry and problem-based learning, information literacy is embedded within a meaningful context – within a case or an inquiry. As the preservice teachers engage in the inquiry process, they use information skills and they share what they have learned with their peers. This is definitely information literacy in action (Dodd 2007).

I have been realizing that my role as information literacy coach is actually morphing into that of digital literacy coach, and as a digital literate citizen, I should "know[s] how to create and publish video and images, create and run a blog, share links to meaningful and innovative content, edit multimedia files and documents, build profiles appropriately on social networking sites and adapt and incorporate new communications technologies into daily life" (Digital Literacy in Canada 2010). To advance my knowledge in this area, I have collaborated this year with a seconded elementary teacher who has been hired to work with faculty and preservice teachers to integrate technology into their teaching. I have resolved that in the next year I want to connect with the PBL tutorial groups in digitally meaningful ways.

Given that there are three tutorial groups that meet at the same time weekly, I could not meet with them all at once. I decided to focus on one tutorial group every two week cycle and arranged to be part of their tutorial group at the point where they had just completed their preliminary bibliographies. I could look at their bibliographies prior to the tutorial session where they decide what aspect of the case they want to investigate more fully. This way I could establish a personal connection with them as part of their tutorial group at least for one case. At the biweekly meetings of faculty and tutors, I became familiar with the cases and was able to schedule with the tutor the meeting times for their tutorial group.

So far this has been an invaluable way to connect to the preservice teachers and has resulted in my suggesting resources for them and in offering some valuable search tips about their research work. I have also realized it would be possible to offer specialized workshops for the entire cohort about topics such as citation management, content curation, and digital literacy. Another workshop topic could focus on how to read and understand research literature in education. Based on a survey (2012) of the PBL preservice teachers, they identified reading and understanding educational research as an area where they needed more help. It may also be possible to build critical reading of educational research into the design of one of the PBL cases. As I move forward I will incorporate many of these ideas into next year's program.

Conclusion

PBL offers authentic opportunities for librarians to connect with students and is a reminder of the critical role libraries and librarians play in fostering lifelong professional learning. If the effective and efficient deployment of academic library resources within self-directed and peer-based learning programs is to occur, then collaborative planning and teaching with faculty and academic librarians will ensure that the necessary resources, technologies, and information literacy supports are in place. Academic librarians are dedicated to scholarship and know intimately that learning how to learn is critical for twenty-first-century professionals. As preservice teachers investigate their problems, cases drawn from professional practice, they identify what they know and what they need to learn and then determine where they need to find the information and as one preservice teacher commented – we just PBL it!

References

Association of College and Research Libraries. (2000) *Information literacy competency standards for higher education*. Retrieved from http://www.ala.org/arcl/ilcomstan.html

Barrows, H. S., & Tamblyn, R. M. (1980). *Problem-based learning: An approach to medical education*. New York: Springer.

Blumberg, P., & Michael, J. A. (1992). Development of self-directed learning behaviors in a partially teacher-directed problem-based learning curriculum. *Teaching and Learning in Medicine: An International Journal, 4*(1), 3–8.

Bruce, C. (2008). *Informed learning*. Chicago: Association of College and Research Libraries.

Chen, K., Lin, P., & Chang, S. (2011). Integrating library instruction into a problem-based learning curriculum. *Aslib Proceedings: New Information Perspectives, 63*(5), 517–532. doi:10.1108/00012531111164996.

Cheney, D. (2004). Problem based learning: Librarians as collaborators and consultants. *Portal: Libraries and the Academy, 4*(4), 495–508.

Diekema, A. R., & Olsen, M. W. (2011). Personal information management practices of teachers. *Proceedings of the American Society for Information Science and Technology, 48*(1), 1–10.

Digital Literacy in Canada. (2010). *From inclusion to transformation, submission to the digital economy strategy consultation, media awareness network*. Retrieved March 3, 2014, from http://mediasmarts.ca/sites/default/files/pdfs/publication-report/full/digitalliteracypaper.pdf

Dodd, L. (2007). The Impact of problem-based learning on the information behavior and literacy of veterinary medicine students at the University College Dublin. *The Journal of Academic Librarianship, 33*(3), 206–216.

Eaton, E. K., & Richardson, E. (1993). Strategies for libraries serving problem-based learning programs. In P. A. J. Bouhuijs, H. G. Schmidt, & H. J. M. Van Berkel (Eds.), *Problem-based learning as and educational strategy*. Maastricht: Network Publications.

Eldredge, J. D. (1993). A problem-based learning curriculum in transition: The emerging role of the library. *Bulletin of the Medical Library Association, 81*(3), 310–315.

Eldredge, J. D. (2004). The librarian as tutor/facilitator in a problem-based learning (PBL) curriculum. *Reference Services Review, 32*(1), 54–59. doi:10.1108/00907320410519414.

Fitzgerald, D. (1996). Problem based learning and libraries: A Canadian perspective. *Health Libraries Review, 13*, 13–32.

Fitzgerald, D., Flemming, T., & Bayley, L. (1999). Problem-based learning and libraries: The McMaster experience. In J. A. Rankin (Ed.), *Handbook on problem based learning* (pp. 2325–2341). New York: Medical Library Association Forbes Custom Publishing.

Ispahany, N., Torraca, K., Chilov, M., Zimbler, E. R., Matsoukas, K., & Allen, T. Y. (2007). Library support for problem-based learning: An algorithmic approach. *Medical Reference Services Quarterly, 26*(4), 45–63. doi:10.1300/J115v26n04_04.

Klette, K., & Smeby, J. (2012). Professional training and knowledge sources. In K. Jensen, L. C. Lahn & M. Nerland (Eds.), *Professional learning in the knowledge society* (pp. 143–162). New York: Sense Publishers [Imprint]. doi:10.1007/978-94-6091-994-7.

Lave, J., & Wenger, E. (1991). *Situated learning: Legitimate peripheral participation*. Cambridge: Cambridge University Press.

Lipponen, L. (2010). Information literacy as situated and distributed activity. In A. Lloyd & S. Talja (Eds.), *Practising information literacy: Bringing theories of learning, practice and information literacy together* (pp. 51–64). Wagga Wagga: Center for Information Studies/Charles Sturt University.

Mackey, T. P., & Jacobson, T. E. (2011). Reframing information literacy as a metaliteracy. *College & Research Libraries, 72*(1), 62–78.

Miller, J. (2001). A framework for the multiple roles of librarians in problem-based learning. *Medical Reference Services Quarterly, 20*(3), 23–30. doi:10.1300/J115v20n03_03.

Montiel-Overall, P. (2007). Information literacy: Toward a cultural model. *Canadian Journal of Information and Library Science, 31*(1), 43–68.

Oker-blom, T. (1998). *Integration of information skills in problem based curricula*. Paper presented at the 64th IFLA general conference, Amsterdam, The Netherlands, August 16–21, 1994. pp. 1–8.

Rankin, J. A. (1996). Problem-based learning and libraries a survey of the literature. *Health Libraries Review, 13*, 33–42.

Steeleworthy, M., & Dewan, P. (2013). Web-based citation management systems: Which one is best? *Partnership: The Canadian Journal of Library and Information Practice and Research, 8*(1), 1–8.

Chapter 11
Investigating Social Justice Education Through Problem Based Learning: A Subject Area Resource Specialist's Perspective

Anne Zavalkoff

Introduction

Social justice and anti-oppression education are foundational components of many teacher education programs.[1] However, many educators encounter resistance when helping preservice teachers to investigate what these concepts mean, why they are important, and how they might be pursued (Solomon et al. 2005; Kumashiro 2000; Kelly and Minnes Brandes 2001; Kelly and Brooks 2009). As the Department of Educational Studies' (EDST) representative to the TELL through PBL (Teaching English Language Learners through Problem Based Learning) cohort, I am responsible for helping our preservice teachers think through what these themes mean for their teaching and their identities. In the 8 years that I have been working with the PBL[2] cohort as a subject area resource specialist, I have come to appreciate the many ways in which the PBL pedagogy is exceptionally well suited to supporting these ends. In this chapter, I demonstrate PBL's strengths in teaching for social justice. First, I explore the role of the subject area resource specialist within TELL through PBL. I then articulate the conceptions of social justice and anti-oppression that underpin my teaching and discuss why PBL is an excellent model for facilitating preservice teachers' explorations of these concepts. Finally, I demonstrate what my work exploring privilege and oppression with preservice teachers looks like.

---

[1] The newly revised UBC program also has social justice education as one of its foundational themes.

[2] When I joined the PBL cohort in 2006, it was a standalone cohort that focused on the principles and practices of PBL pedagogy. The PBL cohort merged with the TELL cohort as part of UBC's B.Ed. restructuring in the 2012–2013 academic year, becoming the TELL through PBL cohort

A. Zavalkoff (✉)
Department of Educational Studies, University of British Columbia, Vancouver, BC, Canada
e-mail: anne.zavalkoff@ubc.ca

My Role as a PBL Subject Area Resource Specialist

I have been working with the University British Columbia (UBC) Bachelor of Education (B.Ed.) PBL cohort as a subject area resource specialist since 2006. I fell into teaching with the PBL cohort, as many other first timers do, quite by accident. After a number of years teaching social justice education and philosophy of education courses[3] in the UBC's B.Ed. program, my department offered me the opportunity to continue this work within the PBL cohort.

When I accepted this invitation, I did not know much about PBL pedagogy. What I soon discovered was that teaching and learning in PBL was unlike any schooling I had been involved with as either a student or as a teacher. Very few of the conventional teaching tools I had come to expect were used. No formal course outlines. No assigned readings. No course-specific papers or projects. Instead, I would meet with my students face to face once every two-week case cycle. I would have ongoing opportunities to engage with them through my resource recommendations and my feedback on exit slips, annotated bibliographies, and research packages, as well as during the end of term triple-jump examinations. I would work closely with a team of PBL tutors, coordinators, and other subject area resource specialists. Our joint planning would be anchored by biweekly meetings where we could check in with each other about student progress, refine upcoming cases, better educate each other about emerging case issues, and inquire into our cohort's varied assessment practices. While I now deeply appreciate the student-centered, dialectical, and team-based learning that the PBL model enables, when I first came to the cohort, it did take some time for me to come to understand my role within the overarching cohort structure.[4]

The tutors are the first of the instructors to meet with the preservice teachers in each case cycle. They help spark initial curiosity about the case and its embedded issues, generating with the preservice teachers a list of questions for them to research. As a subject area resource specialist, I then review the identified case issues. I plan my teaching around the case questions, both asked and unasked. When it all works well, the tutors and subject area resource specialists help the preservice teachers to trouble assumptions made so as to deepen the complexity of the process and products of their inquiry. This collaborative, team-based approach invites an ongoing reframing of case questions, a layering of perspectives, and an enriching of the meanings constructed.

As the EDST representative to the TELL through PBL cohort, I engage primarily with the themes of social justice and anti-oppression education, the purposes of

---

[3] From 2002 to 2006, I taught many sections of EDST 314: Social Issues in Education and EDST 427: Philosophy of Education for UBC's Department of Educational Studies.

[4] I am indebted to Margot Filipenko and the rest of the PBL team for helping me develop my understanding of how to better use the PBL structure to support student learning, particularly in that first year.

schooling, and ethical educational practice.[5] Of course, these themes are not strictly my purview. In fact, social justice education is one of the foundational strands in the revised UBC's B.Ed. program that began in 2012–2013; this strand is intended to be woven into all cohorts and courses.

There are many avenues through which the PBL team attempts to support the preservice teachers' inquiries into social justice education. We have worked through multiple case rewrites, planting hooks intended to capture the preservice teachers' curiosity about the evolving contexts in which privilege and oppression play out in schools and society. We have designed guiding questions to be used by the tutors and other subject area resource specialists in helping the preservice teachers unpack each case with a social justice lens in mind. The team's preparatory work with each case is an essential part of our ongoing curriculum development, as the preservice teachers' "content learning" emerges directly from the inquiries that each case sparks.

I further support the preservice teachers' inquiries into the institutional and cultural dimensions of privilege and oppression by sending them case-specific recommendations for anti-oppression education. Each case cycle, I send out my own annotated list of academic, policy, and classroom resources. I try to assemble this list in ways that make clear how my recommendations respond to the preservice teachers' stated interests, so they are more likely to filter through to their Week 1 annotated bibliographies and Week 2 research packages. Preservice teachers working in pairs produce these packages at the end of each two-week cycle. The research packages provide them with an opportunity to delve more deeply into one of the case issues. They also form the basis for their peers' further learning around the chosen theme. At the end of each case cycle, I give the preservice teachers feedback on what I see as the strengths, gaps, and framings of the social justice dimensions of their packages. As I will detail in more depth below, I also meet with the preservice teachers once during each two-week case cycle to help them inquire more deeply and reflexively into the direction, content, and implementation of their inquiries into social justice education.

It is also my goal to help support the tutors and other subject area resource specialists in thinking about how their areas of specialization intersect with the institutional and cultural dimensions of privilege and oppression. Similarly it is their responsibility to help me better understand how their areas of specialization complicate the process of social justice education. These conversations arise naturally at our biweekly instructor meetings, but we have talked about implementing a more regular, explicit process where 20 minutes would be set aside in our instructor meetings for mini-infusions of professional development. The suggestion is that on every Monday before the next case, each of the resource specialists and tutors would

---

[5] While the specific framing and content of my courses has shifted in the revised B.Ed. program that began in 2012–2013, these general themes have remained consistent across programs.

speak briefly about how we understand the upcoming case issues, perhaps focusing on one foundational concept or question that we hope the preservice teachers will take away from the case. When tutors and faculty resource persons understand each other's areas of specialization better, there is greater likelihood of teaching in interdisciplinary ways. By bringing greater structure and intention to our ongoing conversations across disciplines and perspectives, our instructional team can help to better integrate learning across all TELL through PBL coursework and the entire cohort experience.

Social Justice and Anti-oppression Education in Teacher Education

Before moving onto a closer look at why PBL is so well suited to doing social justice work with preservice teachers, as well as to what my work as the primary social justice education resource person looks like, I will say a few words about the conceptions of social justice, anti-oppression, and multicultural education that I bring with me to my role as a resource person. These concepts have evolved into buzzwords that are used differently across and within academic and professional contexts, both reflecting and contributing to disagreements about whether and how they ought to impact life in schools. I understand anti-oppression and multicultural education as two different approaches to the broader umbrella of social justice work.[6] Building from the official Canadian policy of multiculturalism,[7] multicultural education tends to take a celebratory approach to difference, recognizing diversity and welcoming it as a form of cultural enrichment. It tends to lend itself toward singular, isolated celebrations or one-off events that keep an analysis of oppression at the level of the individual. As such, it has been critiqued as inviting a "tourist approach" (Derman Sparks 1995) to social justice education that allows dominant discourses and cultural privileges to remain invisible and intact.[8]

By contrast, anti-oppression education draws attention to structural and lived inequities that play out across and within cultural differences. It examines privilege as well as oppression. It rejects the idea that oppression is caused solely or predominantly by individuals who intentionally do mean things to other individuals. Instead,

---

[6] In BC schools, "social responsibility" is another purposefully nonconfrontational term used in classrooms and in policy documents to refer to a particular strand of social justice education.

[7] Pierre Elliott Trudeau began the discussion of multiculturalism as Canada's official state policy in 1971. This policy evolved into the Multiculturalism Act of 1988 (United Nations Association of Canada, 2002). In some ways, this policy has worked directly counter to social justice concerns by contributing to the national identity of Canada as a tolerant and multicultural mosaic of cultural and other diversities.

[8] Multicultural education is sometimes theorized as critical multiculturalism. This form of social justice education is far closer to the anti-oppression education described below.

it looks to "the everyday practices of a well-intentioned liberal society" (Young 1990, p. 41) as they manifest across institutional arrangements, systems of communication, and opportunities for social participation. Recognizing that oppression and privilege play out systemically, it advocates for a systemic, ongoing, and integrated approach to social justice education. A multicultural celebration of difference might be a hopeful and strategic starting point for this approach, but only if supplemented by an exploration of the meanings, histories, complexities, and structural inequities associated with those differences. Anti-oppression education also underlines the necessity of working actively and ethically toward social justice across intersecting forms of oppression; it is concerned with process as well as product (Kelly 2012). Finally, it understands reflexivity to be a necessary component of effective social justice work, as existing beliefs, identities, and investments are the lens through which we experience and interpret our worlds. If we are to better understand their impact on what we know and how we act, we must labor to surface, and possibly alter, them (Kumashiro 2000; Kelly 2012; Kelly and Brooks 2009; Raby 2004; Kelly and Minnes Brandes 2001).

My work with the preservice teachers explores these differences between anti-oppression and multicultural approaches to social justice education. At the same time, I tend to slide easily and strategically between my use of the terms "social justice" and "anti-oppression education." I do not want what we call this work to get in the way of engaging with its ideas and practices. The very mention of big, scary concepts like "oppression" and "privilege" can raise defenses and forestall open-minded inquiry. With this in mind, I tend to use the softer, fuzzier language of "social justice" with the preservice teachers to work through and around our potential resistances, especially at the outset of our conversations.

> The 'problem' that anti-oppressive education needs to address is not merely a lack of knowledge, but a resistance to knowledge (Luhmann 1998 as cited in Kumashiro), and in particular, a resistance to any knowledge that disrupts what one already 'knows.' (Kumashiro 2000, p. 43)

I also use the language of "anti-oppression" with the preservice teachers to signal that I believe all social justice education ought to involve an exploration of historical and contemporary social contexts, a real grappling with the concepts and impacts of oppression and privilege, as well as an honest look inward. I am explicit in my beliefs that we all ought to explore how social structure, as well as our own lived experiences of privilege and oppression, shape how we make sense of the world. I argue that we must all attempt to investigate how who we have come to be as people impacts what we see and do not see and, therefore, who we are and can be in the classroom. I also recognize that genuinely opening up to such reflexive explorations can be threatening to identity, so I try to allow in-class space and time for working through any reactions that might arise.

By keeping the language of both social justice and anti-oppression alive in the classroom, I hope that the preservice teachers will come to see anti-oppression education as an essential part of the social justice work that they will want to do throughout their careers. At the very least, I explain to them that whichever approach to social justice education they choose to take up, they should be clear both about the differences between multicultural and anti-oppression education and their reasons for choosing one approach over the other in any given context.

PBL as a Model for Facilitating Explorations of Social Justice and Anti-oppression Education

The PBL structure offers many advantages for exploring social justice and anti-oppression education. One strength is that my conversations with the preservice teachers are not limited to our assigned, face-to-face meeting times. My interactions with them begin when they post the case issues that they have identified with the tutors to our online learning platform. These issues act as a pre-assessment tool, helping me to better understand what they already know, see, and feel about the case. In highlighting the preservice teachers' interests and assumptions, they also help me to get to know the preservice teachers a little bit better. My interactions with the preservice teachers continue when I post my own annotated bibliography of potential case resources near the beginning of each case cycle. Although the pedagogy of PBL does not require the preservice teachers to follow up on these specific resources in their research, I attempt to influence their evolving explorations by framing my annotations in ways that respond to their identified interests. I also try to link explicitly to these resources during our classroom time, so that the preservice teachers are more likely to understand their relevance to the case. Sometimes, our conversations about social justice also continue in one-to-one interactions via email and Skype. Always, they culminate with the feedback I give them on their completed research packages. I send them notes about the strengths and weaknesses of their packages. I also pose a few questions in an attempt to extend the thinking that they have already done. As the arc described above demonstrates, my classroom interactions with the preservice teachers are only one of the ways that the PBL structure supports me in uncovering and complicating the preservice teachers' existing knowledge and beliefs.

The interdicisplinarity of our cohort is another strength of PBL for pursuing social justice education; I am not the only instructor who explicitly takes up these themes. All too often in teacher education programs such themes are quarantined in singular courses, disconnected from other learning in the program. In PBL, the preservice teachers' investigations into anti-oppression education are supported and extended both through the learning they do with me and their other subject area resource specialists and through the Socratic dialogue of their 10–12-person tutorial group meetings. These smaller meetings take place three times over the course of each case[9] and provide support for their thinking around privilege, oppression, and schooling. Having this shared dialogue is important, because the very real themes of social inequity and

---

[9] Originally, the tutors and preservice teachers met four times each case. Since the 2013–2014 year, they now meet three times per case.

justice cannot be easily "put back in the box," particularly once the preservice teachers begin to question their own position within these social relationships. I know that we are truly making progress in our investigations when the tutors tell me that our class conversations have spilled over into their ongoing tutorial discussions. Because preservice teachers have opportunities to explore social inequities across all of their TELL through PBL inquiries, they are more likely to come to see social justice education as an essential and routine part of their work as teachers.

Another advantage of the PBL structure for exploring social justice themes is that the end of each case does not bring an end to our conversations. While each case has its own distinct foci and set of case issues, PBL conversations are never closed. By design, our themes, conversations, and questions loop back on each other. As the cases progress throughout the year, they intentionally move to more challenging themes.[10] In doing so, the PBL structure enacts Bruner's (1960) arguments about the spiral curriculum: "a curriculum as it develops should revisit basic ideas repeatedly, building upon them until the student has grasped the full formal apparatus that goes with them" (p. 13). I elaborate upon this progression in my description of the relationship between Case 2 and Case 9 below, where the PBL structure offers the preservice teachers the opportunity to build from what they know so that they can gradually deepen their questioning and understanding over time.

The structures that support the development of strong cohort relationships are another advantage of teaching social justice education within TELL through PBL. Throughout the course of the year, the preservice teachers work within their own contained cohort of roughly 33 people, both as a whole group and in the important, relationship-building small-group tutorials. As Daniel (2009) argues, a "cohort facilitates a degree of familiarity and support amongst the teacher candidates" (p. 175). Connections grow, not only because of the sheer amount of time they spend together, but also because of the degree to which their learning is enmeshing with the learning and research of their peers. Our Orientation Week[11] programming has also evolved to provide varied opportunities for the preservice teachers to become familiar not only with the PBL pedagogy but also with each other. For example, in the 2013–2014 year, we introduced a very successful full-day exercise in multimodal, place-based autobiography to help the preservice teachers, subject area resource specialists, and tutors foster our connections as human beings outside of our institutional roles. Often the exploration of social justice themes can be identity threatening; therefore, it is important that institutional supports be in place to encourage the development of trusting bonds among preservice teachers and their instructors.

The unique opportunity I have to work with the same group of preservice teachers throughout the entire year only enhances these bonds and their benefits for social

---

[10] I make this claim recognizing that, especially with respect to social justice themes, every person will have different experiences, resistances, and trigger points.

[11] Because PBL's 2-week case cycle makes its scheduling mostly independent of the rest of the B.Ed. program, we have the opportunity to schedule in an orientation week where other cohorts generally do not.

justice education. Typically, instructors teaching EDST course offerings in the B.Ed. program stay with the same group of students for no more than one term. As the social justice resource person for PBL, I am hired across Winter Terms 1 and 2, a period spanning 8 months.[12] This means that the themes of the multiple courses offered by EDST can be woven throughout the PBL cases in ways that serve the complexity of the case narratives rather than the somewhat artificial boundaries imposed by the standard B.Ed. timetable. This ongoing and integrated approach invites a deepening, substantive inquiry.

Explorations of Privilege and Oppression

Generally, I meet face to face with the preservice teachers for 3 hours once each two-week case cycle. Occasionally, I also meet with them in the special timeslots reserved for our TELL through PBL Workshop Series. During these meetings, my central task is to build from the case and the preservice teachers' identified case issues in ways that help them to deepen their research and self-reflection. I do very little in the way of straight content delivery; instead, I attempt to craft in-class activities that help to spark curiosity, refine the scope of the preservice teachers' research questions, and surface our deep-seated assumptions about oppression, privilege, and identity. While part of my task is to help lay the conceptual foundations upon which rest further queries into social justice and anti-oppression education, sometimes laying these foundations first involves destabilizing old knowledge systems (Kumashiro 2000). I know I am on a productive track when preservice teachers remark that their "brains hurt" after my class. Ultimately, while my explicit intent is to advocate for a specific conception of social justice education, my more fundamental, and also explicit, concern is that the preservice teachers develop good reasons to support their chosen professional principles and practices.

So what does my course work with the preservice teachers actually look like? How do I use in-class activities to help deepen thinking about the concepts and practices central to social justice education, as well as how we are all situated in relation to them? I will provide two examples of this work by examining two cases: Case 2, the affectionately known *Stinky Lunch*, and Case 9, otherwise known as *Day of Pink*. *Stinky Lunch* attempts to make real the subtle, systemic workings of privilege and oppression, broadly conceived. *Day of Pink* focuses more narrowly on privilege and oppression in the context of gender identities, performances, and discourses. *Stinky Lunch* departs from a simple, seemingly inconsequential phrase; *Day of Pink* unfolds robustly over the course of the entire opening paragraph, setting the context for the whole case. While these two cases use very different strategies in their attempt to hook the curiosity of the preservice teachers and spark an

---

[12] Moreover, the same person usually also has the opportunity to work with the preservice teachers after they return from their long practicum placements for the duration of the summer term, extending these relationships and conversations across the entirety of their programs.

exploration of specific foundational concepts and questions, both are the result of our teams' work in trying to puzzle through how best to build a narrative that accomplishes these pedagogical goals.

Case 2: **The Stinky Lunch**

In Case 1, the first case of the year, we introduce the preservice teachers to the importance, opportunities, and challenges of building a classroom community amid ethnic, economic, linguistic, cultural, and other diversities. For the most part, conversations and research at this point tend to take a multiculturalist approach to social justice education, focusing on how to use diversity as a resource. By Case 2, our goal is to complicate these initial explorations with a more anti-oppressive lens, bringing the concepts of privilege and oppression into the mix. However, many preservice teachers find engaging with these themes conceptually and emotionally difficult. As Solomon et al. (2005) note, it is difficult to admit that we are each implicated in systems of oppression. "It could also be argued that we unconsciously desire to learn only that which affirms our sense that we are good people" (Kumashiro 2000, p. 43). Perhaps even more difficult is the idea that our varied social locations bring us unearned privileges, making us complicit in the oppression of others (McIntosh 1990). One of my central challenges then is to help minimize preservice teachers' resistance and defensiveness, so that we can consider our responsibilities toward social change, both as teachers and as people.

The framing and language of Case 2 has evolved over time in an attempt to evoke a thoughtful exploration of privilege and oppression without using these potentially triggering words themselves. It references the concept of classroom community introduced in Case 1, but begins to subtly integrate the idea of conflict into the classroom. The relevant part of the case reads:

> Although most of the children [in your primary class] have adjusted to the routines of the classroom and seem to be happy at school, a few have not yet settled into being part of the classroom community. When you mentioned this to their parents at the conferences, some seemed genuinely surprised. For instance, when you told Drew's parents that he seems quiet and withdrawn in class, they said, "At home he's always on the go and talking a mile a minute!" *When you explained to Kayla's mother that her daughter has been teasing her classmate, Nikesh, about his "stinky lunches," she told you that Kayla is so "caring" at home, "always helping with her two younger brothers."* It made you wonder: are we talking about the same child? [Emphasis added]

As case issues, preservice teachers typically identify "differences in home life and school life" or "differences in parent and teacher perception of students." Often, they also take up the problem of bullying, trying to determine the seriousness of Kayla's "teasing." Once or twice, the question of whether a 6-/7-year-old can be racist has been raised. Never have the ideas of privilege and oppression been foregrounded in the initial case unpacking. Given our emphasis on constructing a soft entry into these concepts, it is just as well.

When I meet with the preservice teachers for Case 2, I use an in-class activity to bring these concepts to the fore. After briefly reviewing their case issues and questions with them, I invite them to play with the question of whether food can be separated from culture and, if not, with what implications. How should the cultural contexts of the so-called stinky lunches, as well as the cultural backgrounds of Kayla and Nikesh, impact how we interpret and respond to the case?

I divide the room up into four stations that the preservice teachers then rotate through in groups. They have 10 minutes at each station to interact with one or two concealed, unnamed, strongly aromatic food(s). Each station also brings a set of questions. To pique curiosity and establish routine, each station opens the same way: What food is at your station? With which culture/social group/country do you associate it?[13] The ensuing questions then vary by station so as to highlight different dimensions that ought to be thought through in working toward a response to the case.

At Station 1, I place a tea egg and chopped egg salad. Both items are highly aromatic variations of the same food, but are strongly linked to different cultural backgrounds. Most, if not all, of the preservice teachers are familiar with the egg salad of White/Western culture; many have never seen the beautifully marbled tea egg common in China, Taiwan, Indonesia, and other countries in Asia. I leave two additional sets of questions at this station: (1) Are the cultural backgrounds of the children or food relevant to the case? Why? How? (2) Are the concepts of "privilege" and "oppression" relevant? What do they mean? So begins an exploration into the subtleties of these concepts. The preservice teachers are generally quite divided about their answers to these questions which makes the discussions animated, engaging, and meaningful.

It always fascinates me to see how the composition of each group of preservice teachers tends to impact their conversations. When most members of the small group have had previous exposure to tea eggs, they generally talk about their positive memories of interacting with the food and then get onto the business of the questions. When most of the group has no prior experience with tea eggs, there is often a good deal of wrinkled noses, recoiling heads, and high-pitched exclamations. These initial visceral reactions are usually balanced somewhat by an emerging curiosity. Still, all too often what this looks like is a group of predominantly White students sending subtle (and not so subtle) messages about a food or experience associated with the current or ancestral culture of some of the Asian students in the class. The irony is that in our opening exploration of privilege and oppression, these racially[14] and ethnically privileged students often do not realize that they are replicating the same systems that have allowed them to "remain oblivious of the

---

[13] I place the name and cultural origin of the foods underneath the food containers, so that the bulk of the time at each station can be spent on the analysis associated with the ensuing questions. I also ask the preservice teachers to keep their discussion of the foods themselves to a maximum of 3 minutes, which sometimes works and sometimes does not.

[14] There is a healthy debate about the usefulness of perpetuating the "myth of realness" of the concept of race through its continued use. I would argue that although "race" is a social construct that mostly serves to reinforce systems of oppression, its structural and lived effects are ongoing. As such, we cannot simply abandon the term.

language and customs of persons of color who constitute the world's majority without feeling in [their] culture any penalty for such oblivion" (McIntosh 1990, p. 3). Of course, they intend no harm, but as Young (1990) argues, oppression operates most perniciously and effectively in the "everyday practices of a well-intention liberal society" (p. 41).

For me, the egg salad represents and reveals the invisible, normalized, and naturalized workings of privilege. In North America, people know what egg salad is, precisely because of its dominant, widespread representation. You can buy it in the deli cases of major grocery chains and in the sandwiches sold at airports, vending machines, and 7/11 convenience stores. While it might be hard to peg egg salad to a particular cultural group, its vague pervasiveness is exactly the point: the advantage of privilege is unearned, unsought, and unseen by those who have it (McIntosh 1990).

By contrast, for me the tea egg represents and reveals the workings of the symbiotic flipside of privilege: oppression. While egg salad is ubiquitous, I can not purchase a tea egg for this activity outside of a specialized Asian market,[15] not even in the city of Vancouver where up to 40 % of the population speaks some variation of Chinese as their first language.[16] This cultural marginalization is woven into the very social and structural fabric of Western culture from the level of individuals who internalize these norms (Schmidt 2005) to the level of "systematic institutional processes" and "institutionalized social processes" (Young 1990, p. 38).

Luckily, I don't have to try to make this argument to the preservice teachers from high on the teacher's pulpit. Because of the collaborative, inquiry model of PBL, I enter their evolving conversations only during our post-station rotation debrief. By then, the preservice teachers have had the opportunity to open up (to) these concepts. They have listened to each other's varied experiences and perspectives, learning from and questioning each other. Not only can their dialogue work to lessen their resistance to these challenging concepts (Daniel 2009), its dialectic often makes the argument far more convincingly than I alone ever could. While preservice teachers' exit slips reveal a very real and deep split in class opinion about the extent to which the *Stinky Lunch* is implicated in systems of privilege and oppression, their evolving reasons for their judgments are a far more important outcome than the specific content of their conclusions.

For me, the *Egg Station* is the most central and foundational of the four stations that the preservice teachers visit, but the remaining three also each bring forth a different piece of the puzzle. At Station 2, the preservice teachers might encounter a fragrant curry from Northern India as they are asked to imagine the concrete consequences of the so-called teasing.[17] How might Nikesh experience it? How might

---

[15] Instead, I've downloaded a recipe for the tea eggs and cook them at home at the same time as I make the hard-boiled eggs.

[16] http://www.cbc.ca/news/canada/british-columbia/punjabi-and-chinese-top-immigrant-languages-in-vancouver-1.1213824

[17] Over the years, I have used many different foods at the remaining stations, including durian, chopped liver, kimchi, spoilt milk, stinky tofu, and shrimp paste.

he feel? How might it impact his understanding of himself and his culture, as well as his social location or his behaviors at school?

This station brings the preservice teachers firmly back to the context of schools, helping them to explore how privilege and oppression might play out in their professional lives. It also provides a springboard into the academic literature, specifically Young's *Five Faces of Oppression*: exploitation, marginalization, powerlessness, cultural imperialism, and violence (1990). The preservice teachers have speculated that Nikesh might bring something else for lunch to school (cultural imperialism), that he might eat by himself or feign sickness so that he need not come to school at all (marginalization), that he might become anxious or distraught or physically ill (powerlessness), or that the teasing might escalate to physical bullying (violence).[18] Their concrete examples not only help to make real and accessible the *Fives Faces of Oppression*, they begin to underline the heterogeneity and situatedness of oppression that Young describes. From this point, there is a clear opening for us to discuss Young's idea that social justice can be understood as freedom from oppression. I also always point out that there are many different ways of conceptualizing social justice that the preservice teachers might pursue in their annotated bibliographies and research packages.

Station 3 might bring a pickled herring and *chrane* (horseradish) duo that are familiar to Jews of Eastern Europe ancestry.[19] This station places the preservice teachers squarely in the role of teacher, asking them to imagine what they might do in response: Would you respond directly or indirectly or not at all? How does the age of your students impact your decision? Who would your response involve: Nikesh, Kayla, your class, and/or the school? (How) would you discuss cultural and student diversity, as well as social inequities?

Bringing our discussion back to the richness of professional practice and judgment is important, because it helps to make learning relevant, authentic, and meaningful to the preservice teachers. Moreover, for them to become comfortable with the idea of working toward social justice in schools, preservice teachers must be given opportunities to imagine what that could look like, especially with young children. As Kelly and Brooks (2009) note, preservice teachers often shy away from addressing social inequities, because they feel that their students are too young to handle these conversations or too innocent to be implicated in systems of oppression. This station also allows us to link to Kelly's (2012) elaboration of what Young's *Five Faces* model of anti-oppression education might look like in schools.

At the final station, the opaque container holds a big question mark and the phrase "your lunch." Enacting Styles' (1988) metaphor of curriculum as windows

---

[18]The preservice teachers generally do not generate examples that illuminate the face of exploitation.

[19]I like to include a food that links to Jewish culture, as it is my heritage. This link provides a springboard both for educating the preservice teachers about Jewish culture and for continuing the process of getting to know each other that we begin in the orientation week and Case 1.

and mirrors, this station encourages ongoing community building, cross-cultural learning, and reflexive analysis within the cohort. After discussing their own experiences with so-called stinky lunches, the station questions nudge their self-reflections further by asking: were you ever teased, marginalized, or simply made to feel different, because of your cultural foods, beliefs, or practices? What happened? The other set of questions at the station moves from experience to belief, attempting to draw out preservice teachers' existing knowledge about teasing and bullying: how is bullying based on identity (e.g., language, ancestry, skin color, class, gender, sexuality, etc.) different from or similar to generic bullying (e.g., your pencils)? Can you make a list of the similarities and differences? The question of where to draw the line between good-natured bonding and harmful, systemic practices that require the intervention of teachers is a perennial concern. The dual trajectories of this station's questions are designed to help the preservice teachers surface their own experiences and beliefs, so that they can begin to consider how who they are impacts who are they becoming as teachers.

At the end of our class, I ask the preservice teachers to respond in a brief exit slip about what they think is happening when Kayla teases Nikesh about his "stinky lunch" and what (if anything) they should do. Even though there is always wide variability in the extent to which the preservice teachers think the concepts of privilege, oppression, and social justice are relevant to this case, their exit slips give me a glimpse into how they are beginning to make sense of these concepts more generally. In 2012, some of their comments included:

- "It is interesting to me to think about this as more than just celebrating the diversity in the classroom, but rather thinking of ways of being 'anti-oppressive'" (Preservice teacher A, Sept 25, 2012).
- "I had never thought of how oppression could be well intended practices or done without the intention of harm" (Preservice teacher B, Sept 25, 2012).
- "To understand justice, it's important to look at injustice too" (Preservice teacher C, Sept 25, 2012).
- "Privilege can be invisible, especially for those who have it" (Preservice teacher D, Sept 25, 2012).

These comments demonstrate the kind of deep theoretical engagement that can be evoked when the preservice teachers are invited to ponder the school-based contexts in which social inequities can play out. The exit slip responses also give me immediate feedback about how concepts are landing and for whom. Particularly within the case cycle structure of PBL, where I typically do not see the preservice teachers again for two full weeks, finding ways to initiate ongoing assessment loops is an essential part of my role as a subject area resource specialist.

The exit slips also reveal how disruptive social justice education, and the PBL process itself, can be. Our work together is meant to open questions and avoid easy answers. It is meant to surface what the preservice teachers believe, sometimes bringing affirmation, but often also bringing confusion, challenge, and the "brain hurting" phenomenon to which I refer above.

- "I think I have a better understanding of [oppression] now but still lots I don't know and need to think about. I still feel a bit confused about everything and will need some time to process it" (Preservice teacher B, Sept 25, 2012).
- "I feel like I've been left with far too many questions than answers. After today, I'm anxious and really unsure about how to deal with these issues in a concrete manner. I felt I have learned a lot but I need more information" (Preservice teacher E, Sept 25, 2012).
- "It takes me time to process new information so, at this point, I don't see how it all goes together – but it will come together eventually…The whole concept of privilege is not new to me – but recognizing what impact this has and the responsibility it brings is rather huge. Ummm…does that make sense? Did I even answer the question?! Still processing" (Preservice teacher F, Sept 25, 2012).

From my perspective as a social justice resource person who is hoping to spark an analysis of social structure and self, these responses are encouraging. Our work together requires time to process; it does not end when our meeting time does. Learning to live with grace amid uncertainty as conversations extend across time and place is central to the PBL process and the kind of work I hope to do with the preservice teachers.

The research packages produced in each tutorial group also give me a deeper picture of the ways the preservice teachers are engaging with the concepts of privilege, oppression, and social justice. In 2012, research themes of just one tutorial group included: The 5 W's (what, why, who, when, and where) of cultural diversity; multiculturalism; social justice; barriers and strategies; self-examination; range of teaching methods; classroom atmosphere and learning environment; cultural awareness, assessment, and collaboration; culturally responsive classroom management; strategies for addressing diversity and social justice; incorporating diversity and social justice into the curriculum; communicating with culturally diverse parents; perceived barriers to teaching ELL students; and linguistic needs and register (Preservice teachers B and F, Oct 5, 2012).

Not only are the preservice teachers responsible for engaging with the research packages produced in their own tutorial groups, they are also responsible for those produced in the other two tutorials. This requirement serves to diversify even further the range of perspectives that are engaged with on each case issue. Other inquiries into *Stinky Lunch* offered in 2012 include: how bullying relates to Case 2; types of bullying; alternative views on bullying; preventing bullying (for teachers and parents); definition of racism; can a 6-year old be racist?; anti-racism education; teaching for diversity and anti-racism; making space: teaching for diversity and social justice throughout the K–12 curriculum; social responsibility performance standards for kindergarten to Grade 3; and lesson plans for diversity in the BC curriculum.

These lists of topics give a sense of the breadth of the research packages that the preservice teachers produce, but their work often also goes deep. The preservice teachers are meant not only to compile the work of others, but also to comment on what lessons they believe are to be drawn from the work they have chosen to include in their final packages. For the 2012 Case 2 packages, such explanations included:

- "Doing a self examination allows teachers to assess how they address diversity and social justice within their own teaching practices...Other methods of self examination help teachers to realize their own assumptions and biases towards cultures and allows them to reflect and change their practices" (Preservice teachers B and F, Oct 5, 2012).
- "Boyd (1998; in Raby 2004) defines racism as 'any action or institutional practice - backed by institutional power - that subordinates people because of their colour or ethnicity' (p. 368). While many of us think of racism in more direct, concrete terms – i.e., acts of physical or verbal aggression on behalf of one or a group of people towards another person or group of people on the basis of race – Boyd is asserting that racism also includes institutional ideas or practices that act to marginalize individuals or groups indirectly, or subtly, on the basis of race. Thus, racism and indirect bullying are inextricably linked" (Preservice teachers G and H, Oct 5, 2012).
- "Raby (2004) in her article *'There's no racism at my school, it's just joking around'*: *ramifications for anti-racist education* presents the concept of anti-racism education as a more effective way of teaching for diversity than multiculturalism education...anti-racism education 'shifts talk away from tolerance of diversity to the notion of difference and power' (Dei and Calliste 2000, p. 21, as quoted in Raby 2004, p. 379). Anti-racism education emphasizes the inclusion of systematic, structural, unequal relations of power in the definition of racism. It is based on the premise that racism exists, and that as teachers we should encourage students to identify and explore the concepts of racism and power and oppression, and how these concepts are interrelated" (Preservice teachers G and H, Oct. 5, 2012).

As these samples of student work show, the PBL process supports the asking of some very rich questions. It is true that it takes many of the preservice teachers multiple case cycles to more fully develop their confidence in the PBL process and their ability to learn successfully through it. At the same time, the dialectical repetition of our eleven cases gives the preservice teachers ongoing opportunities to cultivate their abilities and dispositions toward open-minded inquiry about social justice themes and many other elements central to good teaching.

Case 9: **Day of Pink**

By the time the preservice teachers encounter Case 9, *Day of Pink*, they are at a very different point on their journeys. The case arc and research routine have become second nature for most of them.[20] Case 9 capitalizes on this difference in capacity

---

[20] In fact, many preservice teachers object vocally when the occasional Term 2 teacher who is new to the PBL cohort and pedagogy attempts to teach them in a more traditional style.

and disposition by asking them to reconsider the theme of bullying first broached in *Stinky Lunch*. It also invites the preservice teachers to stretch their learning in new ways by weaving this thread with that of gender variance. This potential for preservice teachers to loop back dialectically to prior learning, across contexts, and over time is one of PBL's fundamental strengths.

Case 9 is a special case for many of us that form the PBL instructional team, as its narrative evolved out of our own learning some years ago. While all of our cases build from and satisfy the curricular objectives of UBC's Teacher Education Program, this case is also a direct response to our own lived experiences of not being able to better support a past PBL preservice teacher who identified as transgender.[21] James'[22] experiences both on and off campus highlighted how we lacked sufficient conceptual understandings and classroom strategies to teach for and about those with fluid gender identities and expressions. This preservice teacher's visible and vocal presence in our group also helped us to see how our own case structure framed gender, and the resulting preservice teacher research, in problematic ways. While our cases have long offered preservice teachers an opportunity to explore the ways in which gender does and does not matter to teaching and learning, they had unconsciously assumed and reinforced an understanding of gender as a binary. James' difficult journey through our program,[23] along with our growing awareness of our complicity in it, prompted us to more clearly see the subtle workings of oppression in our case structure, pedagogical choices, and thinking. Around the same time, our team also began to encounter an increasing discussion of gender variance and gender nonconformity in academic literatures and practical classroom resources.[24] We committed to reworking the framing of gender within our cases and thus evolved *Day of Pink*. It opens:

> It's the Grade 7 lead up to "The Day of Pink" and everyone in your school is busy preparing for the big event: assemblies are planned, the hallways are plastered with posters, and your class is choreographing an anti-bullying flash mob. At the same time, you've noticed that Jamie's gender non-conformity is increasingly being targeted. When you have intervened,

---

[21] The following is a self-description offered by this former preservice teacher as we corresponded throughout the writing of this chapter: "since Teacher Ed, I've been identifying more as gender queer than male. My preferred pronoun is they. I decided to keep the name [*removed for privacy*] because after being on hormone therapy, I now get read as male and my "feminine" name complicates that (in a good way). Transgender or trans is also still a good word to describe me."

[22] The former preservice teacher's chosen pseudonym.

[23] This successful preservice teacher was one of the brightest, most capable students I have ever had the honor to know. Unfortunately, much of this preservice teacher's energy was directed toward repeated attempts to educate cohort members, instructors, school advisors, and others in the broader school community. An excellent, but problematic, example of Young's (1990) description of exploitation: where social groups with privilege profit from the uncompensated labor of others.

[24] The Gender Spectrum: What Educators Need to Know (Pride Education Network of BC 2011) is a comprehensive, local example produced by Pride Education Network BC (formerly GALE BC). Questions and Answers: Gender Identity in Schools (Public Health Agency of Canada 2010) and Bending the Mold: An Action Kit for Transgender Youth (Lambda Legal and the National Youth Advocacy Coalition 2008) are just two more of many others.

everyone, including Jamie, has said they were "just kidding around." Still, you can't help but wonder how well your school's anti-bullying efforts are succeeding. Is Jamie being bullied? What should you do in response?

From my perspective as a social justice resource person, *Day of Pink* is notable as a PBL case study for a number of reasons. First, as described above, it demonstrates the flexibility of our cohort. We are forever reshaping the cases in response to identified needs. In fact, we have completely rewritten our cases twice in the 8 years that I have been with the program. For me, this flexibility is incredibly exciting. The knowledge that the team will alter cases when good reasons are offered invites ongoing reflection, both on the case groundings and on our own casework with the preservice teachers. How might a phrase be tweaked to better capture imagination, invoke deeper reflection, or shape the likely direction of interest and research? How might we build from preservice teachers' beliefs and experiences, as expressed through the case issues they identify, to guide them toward perspectives and resources they otherwise might not have considered? The flexibility inherent in our model and realized through the predominantly collegial work of our instructor meetings keeps us learning and the cases alive.

Day of Pink is also notable from my perspective as a social justice resource person, because it exemplifies our emphasis on constructing authentic narratives grounded in real but messy contexts. We are constantly asking ourselves what broad concepts currently look like in the everyday lives of schools. When our cases link to the dynamics and events that the preservice teachers see unfolding in their concurrent practicum placements, they immediately understand the case issues as relevant to their careers as teachers. This connection made, it is far easier to engage their curiosity and care. Getting students on board with their own learning is a foundational challenge for any teacher, but especially so for one who is centrally concerned with the difficult and often dismissed task of anti-oppression education.

When it became clear that we needed to develop a new case that would foreground gender variance and bullying, we asked ourselves how they are expressed in schools, both productively and problematically. *Day of Pink* provides a current, complex entry point into these themes. Its narrative centers on the ever-growing annual event of the same name,[25] with real-life origins in the fall of 2007. In a high school in Halifax, a male Grade 9 student was bullied for wearing a pink shirt to school. In response, two Grade 12 students bought 50 pink T-shirts and started a chain of texts asking students to wear pink to school. The texts went viral. A "sea of pink" flooded the school.[26] Since then, Day of Pink has evolved into an international anti-bullying day that celebrates the power of the collective to stop bullying, with particular emphasis on expressions of bullying linked to gender and sexual oppression.

The real-life origin story of *Day of Pink* varies slightly in the different retellings publicly consumable, which makes it an even better grounding for a PBL case.

---

[25] The Day of Pink annual event is also known as Pink Shirt Day. See: http://www.pinkshirtday.ca and http://www.dayofpink.org and http://www.bctf.ca/DayOfPink/

[26] http://www.cbc.ca/news/canada/nova-scotia/story/2007/09/18/pink-tshirts-students.html

There is discrepancy in reporting as to whether the Grade 9 student who was originally bullied identified as gay,[27] was perceived as gay,[28] or identified as straight but simply failed to perform his gender according to dominant, normalized expectations. Some reports make links to the sexual identity of the Grade 9 student; others do not.[29] Some reports suggest that the bullying took the form of homophobic slurs.[30] Some reports suggest that the two Grade 12 students who organized the pink shirt response identified as straight.[31] For the purposes of our PBL case, the uncertainty of these details is an asset. It begs the preservice teachers to consider what difference these variables might make to how they understand and resolve the case. It invites them to consider the myriad ways in which the matrices of gender and sexuality are, and are not, intertwined.

The wonderful real-life messiness of this case is amplified by its reference to anti-bullying flash mobs. In Vancouver, they have become an increasingly common way for schools to take part in the Day of Pink anti-bullying campaign. In 2011, synchronous with the rising popularity of the musical TV show GLEE, two local schools joined forces to perform a flash mob in a local shopping mall.[32] By 2013, many PBL preservice teachers reported that they and their practicum schools were taking part in an ever-expanding range of anti-bullying flash mob events. One such event was a flash mob at a home game of the Western Hockey League's Vancouver Giants, where 17 schools throughout the Lower Mainland performed together and the hockey team wore pink laces to help show their support of the schools' efforts.[33]

Just like the Day of Pink itself, these anti-bullying flash mobs present a productive yet problematic launching point for inquiry. Are the flash mobs and pink T-shirts a bracketed, one-day event? What kind of learning precedes and follows them? Are they part of ongoing efforts across curriculum areas to explore bullying and normalized expectations of gender? Are they a foray into the humanist or multicultural social justice work described above that foregrounds a feel-good celebration of difference, but sidesteps difficult conversations about social inequities and discrimination? Do they open the pointed inquiries of anti-oppression frameworks, considering structural and historical expressions of oppression and privilege as it is lived across multiple contexts and facets of identity? To what extent are flash mobs and pink shirts an integration or extension of district, school, and classroom policies and practices throughout the entire year? As the case text itself begs: why, amid pink shirts, assemblies, and flash mobs, is Jamie's gender nonconformity increasingly being targeted? Because the narrative of the *Day of Pink* is set firmly in the com-

---

[27] http://www.dayofpink.org/en/info; http://www.bctf.ca/DayOfPink/

[28] http://www.thegalleryofheroes.com/david-shepherd-and-travis-price/

[29] http://novascotia.ca/news/release/?id=20070925006

[30] http://www.theglobeandmail.com/news/national/students-give-world-a-lesson-in-courage/article1092569/

[31] http://www.dayofpink.org/en/info; http://www.bctf.ca/DayOfPink/

[32] To see the performance of David Lloyd George Elementary and Churchill Secondary at Oakridge shopping center, visit: http://vimeo.com/19310370.

[33] http://www.youtube.com/watch?v=IT4qzVWGU8w

plex, messy world of schools, not only are the questions generated powerful, they are also perceived as meaningful by the preservice teachers. This authenticity is precisely the advantage of the PBL case study, both from my perspective as a social justice resource person and, more generally, when considered as a pedagogical approach.

Day of Pink is also notable from my perspective as a social justice resource person, because it allows such natural links for learning across subject areas. The sound and movement inherent in flash mobs can provide easy entries for music and physical education curriculum specialists.[34] Social studies might consider how to choose a song or analyze lyrics and other expressions of pop culture. Visual art specialists might pick up on the *Day of Pink* posters that plaster the hallways. The breadth of the case narrative allows each resource person a unique but connected entry point into the case, inviting an increasingly complex and situated consideration of its issues from multiple perspectives. Moreover, it provides good modeling for the preservice teachers, as an interdisciplinary approach is central to good teaching and learning in elementary schools.

This case's natural links across subject areas also can work to counter the unwarranted perception that teaching for social justice presents an additional, onerous burden for teachers in an already packed school curriculum. It suggests that teachers can and should work across the curriculum to achieve multiple course objectives simultaneously. Instead of being seen as curriculum add-ons that teachers might choose to take up or disregard, concerns for social justice can and should be infused into every planning decision. Teaching for social justice is mandated by the British Columbia (BC) Ministry of Education (British Columbia Ministry of Education 2008). Moreover, as I argue throughout my year with the preservice teachers, it is the moral responsibility of all good teachers. The interdisciplinarity of *Day of Pink* helps the preservice teachers to attend to the strategic question of how teachers might satisfy their multiple roles and responsibilities in the BC public school system. It also it provides yet another opportunity for us to enter into conversation about the (moral) purposes of public schools and the place of social justice education within them.

Finally, *Day of Pink* is notable as a PBL case study from my perspective as a social justice resource person, because of its relationship to the PBL Workshop Series. Offered once a week, this series is built into the PBL case cycle structure as a way to extend the supported learning opportunities available to the preservice teachers. While not all workshops are tied directly to the investigations of the current case, we do often use workshop time to offer enriched, case-specific programming. This programming takes many forms, including: direct instruction designed to build foundational knowledge of a particular academic discipline or framework, visits by specialized guest speakers designed to bring alternate perspectives or experiences into view, field trips designed to take advantage of serendipitous opportuni-

---

[34] The idea to include flash mobs in this reworked case stems in part from the multiple flash mob final assignments that have been performed throughout UBC's education building by physical education students in recent years.

ties for learning, and any other programming important to the preservice teachers' professional development that does not fit naturally within the case arc.

Day of Pink is an excellent example of the possible synergy between the Workshop Series and the preservice teachers' deepening case investigations, where experts can be brought in from the field to help them gain a better understanding of emerging case issues. During this case, we currently offer a workshop entitled, *Queer and Trans Issues in Education* in partnership with UBC's Positive Space Campaign.[35] We first offered this workshop in James' year. Attendance this first year was not mandatory. Still, we hoped it would help to cultivate an inclusive climate and respectful dialogue within the cohort. We also hoped to offer a space where James might find allies among those who opted to participate. Since then, we have continued to offer the workshop during the *Day of Pink* case cycle as a way to help the preservice teachers unravel the myriad ways that diverse gender and sexual identities and expressions might (and might not) intersect, so that they can better think through how these intersections impact teaching and learning in elementary schools. Given the complexity of the concepts, relationships, and languages involved, the opportunity to extend our discussions beyond our typical, singular 3 hour resource specialist meeting is particularly welcome.

The workshop itself is part practical and part theoretical. It opens with the preservice teachers trying to puzzle through some foundational terminology relevant to gender, sex, and sexuality. In this activity, each small group receives two or three terms, with past examples including: trans, cisgender, women, man, lesbian, gay, homosexual, heterosexual, straight, intersex, and closeted. The groups are then given time to work through four guiding questions: (1) What do these words mean (consider denotations and connotations)? (2) What is their relationship to gender, sex, and sexuality? (3) What is the history of these words? (4) How would you explain these words to your elementary students? While the preservice teachers work through these questions, we post the terms "gender," "sex," and "sexuality" in a triangle on a board at the front of the room. During the debrief, each group places their terms somewhere inside or outside of the triangle to visually display a preliminary understanding of the terms' relationships to gender, sex, and/or sexuality.

This first exercise begins to clarify the ever-evolving meanings of key terms, while still keeping them firmly rooted in world of schools. It works to demystify language and relationships, so that the preservice teachers fear less that they might inadvertently use a term that offends. At the same time, we try to underline that given the complex histories of the terms, and that people's experiences with them are heterogeneous and situated, there is no such thing as safe, universally accepted language. One of the fundamental lessons of this day is that language is continually evolving. Another is that we ought to reflect back to people the language that they choose to describe themselves and represent their identities.

The second half of the workshop turns attention fully to "what would you do?" scenarios, because these very practical explorations are always the central concern of the preservice teachers. In this exercise, each group receives a different scenario.

---

[35] http://positivespace.ubc.ca

We ask the groups to develop a response and supporting rationales and then present them back to the class. The scenarios vary from year to year, depending on the kinds of conversations that have already taken place in the cohort, but always try to present authentic, school-based moments where gender, sex, and/or sexuality emerge problematically. The following four scenarios are the ones we explored in 2013:

Scenario 1: Your grade 1 class is talking about their families. One of the students is telling about her two moms and some of the kids start to giggle. How do you respond? Why? How might you work proactively to incorporate strategies that create a safer space for all students?

Scenario 2: You live in a small community where news travels. The parent of one of your grade 4 students is in the process of transitioning. How can you support your student?

Scenario 3: You are playing a game with your grade 7 students. As you start to put them into teams, they beg to play "boys against girls." One student calls out: "If we play 'boys against girls,' Riley won't fit on either team!" How do you respond? Why?

Scenario 4: You are a teacher who identifies your sexuality and/or gender as "queer." Should you labor to hide your identity at school? Why? In order to "pass," what kinds of (extra) work would you have to do? Be specific.

The preservice teachers have indicated that they appreciate this opportunity to "stray from the case" and consider a broader range of how the case issues play out in schools. It shows them that they already have many of the tools they need to respond sensitively, confidently, and effectively. The workshop is also useful, because its investigation of foundational terminology and critical incidents addresses concerns that in past years have come to dominate our class time together. In doing so, the Workshop Series frees up our subsequent meeting time to work through the actual issues of the case.

Conclusion

As the discussion of *Day of Pink* and *Stinky Lunch* demonstrates, the role of the subject area resource specialist in TELL though PBL is to design learning experiences that spark the preservice teachers' curiosity about and passion for the curriculum themes that have been embedded in each case. As a resource specialist charged with exploring social justice education, my task is to help them deepen their engagement with the complex and difficult themes of privilege and oppression. I continue to be excited about my work with the TELL through PBL cohort, because it is so well suited to supporting these ends. As this chapter explores, the PBL pedagogy is an excellent vehicle for teaching for social justice, not only because of its complexity, authenticity, and flexibility, but also because of the meaningful, ongoing connections that it enables across curriculum areas and among both preservice teachers and instructors.

References

British Columbia Ministry of Education. (2008). *Making space: Teaching for diversity and social justice throughout the K-12 curriculum*. Retrieved from https://www.bced.gov.bc.ca/irp/pdfs/making_space/makingSpace_full.pdf

Bruner, J. (1960). *The process of education*. Cambridge: Harvard University Press.

Daniel, B. (2009). Conversations on race in teacher education cohorts. *Teaching Education, 20*(2), 175–188.

Dei, G. J. S., & Calliste, A. (2000). Mapping the terrain: Power, knowledge and anti-racism education. In G. J. S. Dei & A. Calliste (Eds.), *Power, knowledge and anti-racism education: A critical reader*. Halifax: Fernwood Publishing.

Derman-Sparks, L. (1995). How well are we nurturing racial and ethnic diversity. *Rethinking schools: An agenda for change, 17–22*.

Kelly, D. (2012). Teaching for social justice: Translating an anti-oppression approach into practice. *Our Schools/Our Selves, 21*(2), 135–154.

Kelly, D. M., & Brooks, M. (2009). How young is too young? Exploring beginning teachers' assumptions about young children and teaching for social justice. *Equity & Excellence in Education, 42*(2), 202–216.

Kelly, D., & Minnes Brandes, G. (2001). Shifting out of "neutral": Beginning teachers' struggles with teaching for social justice. *Canadian Journal of Education, 26*(4), 437–454.

Kumashiro, K. K. (2000). Toward a theory of anti-oppressive education. *Review of Educational Research, 70*(1), 25–53.

Lambda Legal and the National Youth Advocacy Coalition. (2008). *Bending the mold: An action kit for transgender youth*. "Designed to help you make your school a safer place." Retrieved from http://data.lambdalegal.org/publications/downloads/btm_bending-the-mold.pdf

Luhmann, S. (1998). Queering/querying pedagogy? Or, pedagogy is a pretty queer thing. In W. F. Pinar (Ed.), *Queer theory in education*. Mahwah: Lawrence Erlbaum Associates.

McIntosh, P. (1990). White privilege: Unpacking the invisible knapsack. *Independent School, 49*(2), 31–36.

Pride Education Network of BC. (2011). *The gender spectrum: What educators need to know*. Retrieved from http://pridenet.ca/wp-content/uploads/the-gender-spectrum.pdf

Public Health Agency of Canada. (2010). *Questions and answers: Gender identity in schools*. Retrieved from http://www.sieccan.org/pdf/phac_genderidentity_qa-eng.pdf

Raby, R. (2004). 'There's no racism at my school, it's just joking around': Ramifications for anti-racist education. *Race, Ethnicity & Education, 7*(4), 367–383.

Schmidt, S. L. (2005). More than men in white sheets: Seven concepts critical to the teaching of racism as systemic inequality. *Equity & Excellence in Education, 38*(2), 110–122.

Solomon, R. P., Portelli, J. P., Daniel, B., & Campbell, A. (2005). The discourse of denial: How white teacher candidates construct race, racism and 'white privilege'. *Race, Ethnicity & Education, 8*(2), 147–169.

Style, E. (1988). Curriculum as window and mirror. In M. Crocco (Ed.), *Listening for all voices: Gender balancing the school curriculum*. Summit: Oak Knoll School.

United Nations Association of Canada. (2002). *The kit: A manual by youth to combat racism through education*. Retrieved from http://www.unac.org/yfar/The_KIT.pdf

Young, I. M. (1990). *Justice and the politics of difference*. Princeton: Princeton University Press.

Chapter 12
The Place of Problems in Problem Based Learning: A Case of Mathematics and Teacher Education

Cynthia Nicol and Fil Krykorka

Introduction

I [coauthor Fil] remember my first month of teaching well. I had just graduated from a problem based learning [PBL] cohort for my teacher education degree. My PBL cohort was structured around researching problems through teaching cases. Here is my first month of teaching, told as a teaching case:

> You are a beginning teacher in a small rural K-12 school in an isolated community in British Columbia. The school operates under a unique partnership arrangement between the First Nations Band and the local school district. Almost all of the 60 students are First Nations or of First Nations ancestry. A priority of the School District and the community is to incorporate local culture and language into school curriculum and pedagogies in order to better support the success of all students in the district.
>
> You are not originally from this community, but were drawn to this teaching position for the opportunity to live in this beautiful remote mountain valley, close to the land and surrounded by wilderness. Like many teachers throughout the province you had few opportunities as an elementary or secondary student to learn about Canadian Aboriginal history, culture and language. During your PBL teacher education program, at least one of your PBL cases focused on rural education and Indigenous education that gave you an opportunity to begin to research Indigenous content, pedagogies, and epistemologies. You understand this is a start but also know it is inadequate for you as a beginning teacher.
>
> You notice the effects of colonization, specifically the horrific legacy of residential schools on your students and their families. Your combined Grades 5/6/7 class of 17 students brings these scars with them to class everyday. Parents are distrusting of a school system that has historically done little to prepare their children for active life within the community or for further schooling outside the community. Although all parents are

---

C. Nicol (✉)
Department of Education, Curriculum and Pedagogy, University of British Columbia, Vancouver, BC, Canada
e-mail: cynthia.nicol@ubc.ca

F. Krykorka
School District 74, Lytton, BC, Canada

interested in education for their children, many find it difficult to support schooling in its current form. As a result maintaining high school attendance is challenging for you and your colleagues.

After the first month of teaching you feel overwhelmed as you try to figure out how to teach a class that is the polar opposite of your practicum experience and far from your own personal experience as a student. You wonder how to teach the curriculum and integrate local culture and language in meaningful ways, as well as meet the emotional and social needs of your students. You look to the land for inspiration.

Fil's vignette or PBL teaching case provides the context for our chapter. Although written from his perspective as a beginning teacher, it draws upon issues, questions, and challenges similar to those discussed during his PBL teacher education program. As a teacher educator (Cynthia) and graduate, now teacher (Fil) of a PBL program, we examine what it means to learn about teaching through PBL pedagogy from both the teacher educator and preservice teacher perspectives.

Our experiences with PBL are in a specific post-baccalaureate teacher education degree program that is designed around PBL. Preservice teachers in this program encounter 11 teaching cases, similar to Fil's, and work in small tutor-lead groups to explore and research their questions related to the case issues. During a two-week cycle, preservice teachers work with curriculum specialists to learn more about the case through specific content areas and end the two-week cycle with presentations of their research to peers. Returning to Fil's teaching case that describes the context of his first month of teaching, we could explore the case with the following questions: How does PBL prepare preservice teachers to teach in contexts or places different from their personal and practicum experiences? What aspects of PBL for learning to teach can be used in the classroom for learning school subject matter such as math and science? How can land and place be inspirations for problem based learning and pedagogical inquiry?

In this chapter, we begin by introducing ourselves and our relationship to problem based learning. As teachers we focus on the importance and challenge of designing good PBL problems for our students and preservice teachers. Next, we examine the literature on place-conscious pedagogies and provide examples of case problems from our practices of teaching and learning through PBL. Finally, we conclude with ideas, thoughts, and challenges for designing problems for PBL that can have the potential to engage students, teachers, preservice teachers, and teacher educators in pedagogical and mathematical inquiry.

Importance of Place in Considering Tasks: Place as Problem and Possibility

I (coauthor Cynthia) grew up in a small mountain town in Kootenay territory of British Columbia. The town, nestled among mountain peaks and valleys of the Selkirk range, was, and still is, home to about 3000 people. Mountains frame the town, and together with surrounding glacier-fed streams, rivers, and lakes, they bound the area from the Interior Plateaus. The mountains were, and to some extent still are, the community resource. They offer food (hunting and fishing) and economic (mining and smelting) and recreational (skiing, hiking, and snowshoeing) activities. Their massive presence humbles those who live within the mountain shadows. The spiritual beauty of this place extends from the land to the sky and includes a variety of weather systems. From towering vertical columns to wispy stretches across the horizon, clouds, thunder, and storms occupied that space in between the sky and mountain. For those who grew up in this place, the land and sky were intimately connected to personal experience.

Yet, the land and our experience of it were often left outside the classroom door. Although we lived amidst the Selkirk range, our Geography 12 class study of rock formations such as glacial carved peaks, mountain scree, and alluvial fans was grounded in a textbook. A glance out the classroom window would provide immediate experience with cumulus or cirrus clouds that feathered the mountain peaks, yet we kept our eyes on textbook diagrams of cloud descriptions. Memories and wisdom located in this land were not made available for school inquiry. Our studies were disconnected from the cultural, historical, and physical knowledge of this land and our own experiences of our local place.

Like Cynthia, I (Fil) am the product of an educational system fixated on keeping the real world away from the classroom. Outside, real-world problems were seen as too open ended and messy and tended to "interrupt" the flow of knowledge from the source (teacher) to the receptacle (student). I experienced this top-down, fact-centered approach in various schools as a student in both Europe and North America. Later, in an attempt to get closer to the "real world," and away from the regurgitation of facts, I chose to study physics and then, for the next 10 years, spend as much time as possible outside, exploring things that had been shut out of my classrooms. How could the beauty of the world, I wondered, be at once so obvious to children and yet so obscure to teachers?

When I began my teacher education program within the PBL cohort, I, like many of my classmates, knew little about the principles of learning and even less about elements of PBL pedagogy. Once I became familiar with these in a broad sense, I welcomed the apparent flexibility of the PBL model, as well as the emphasis on social and collaborative learning. Interestingly, though, I did not see a parallel between learning through PBL as a preservice teacher and learning to teach through PBL in my future school classrooms. That is, this connection was not explicitly addressed in my coursework or through our case investigations. In other words, we learned about teaching using a PBL approach; however, the specific elements of the pedagogy were not necessarily unpacked and deconstructed for use in our classroom practice. Interestingly, I did not consider opportunities – nor, to my knowledge, did any of my PBL cohort peers – to try teaching using a PBL approach during my practicum. In short, problem based learning was something that I left behind after graduating.

For many of us, school learning may have considered place as a problem that interfered with required learning and thus was ignored. How might place be a possibility for learning and teaching? Educators and researchers in the area of place-conscious education, advocate for place to be a central starting point for education. Arguing for place-conscious education as a more holistic conceptualization of education, Smith and Sobel (2010) state it is not a new curriculum. Instead, it is "a way of thinking broadly about the school's integral relationship to the community and the local environment" (p. ix). It is a process, they write, that "begins with the local and that draws children into real-time participation in civic life and decision-making [which] can help children and youth begin to see themselves as actors and creators rather than observers and consumers" (p. viii).

Similarly, Gruenewald (2008) citing Clifford Geertz (1996) writes: "No one lives in the world in general" (p. 145). How then can the local be an inspiration for teaching and learning within a place called school? What kinds of tasks might help students learn to listen to the land and to ask with Gruenewald (2003) "What are our places telling us and teaching us about our possibilities?" (p. 639). Furthermore, what kinds of tasks might help teachers be open to an approach to teaching that takes place seriously and heightens awareness of place-conscious possibilities? In this chapter, we explore these questions from the perspective of teacher educator (Cynthia) and preservice teacher (now practicing teacher – Fil) in the context of problem based learning and pedagogical inquiry.

Nature of Tasks/Problems for Learning to Teach and for Teaching/Learning Mathematics

There are varied interpretations of what counts as worthwhile tasks for learning to teach and for teaching/learning in school math and science classrooms. Henningsen and Stein (1997) argue that high-level tasks have the potential for high cognitive demand by students. Good questions, on the other hand, are, according to Sullivan and Lilburn (2002), more than recall, educative and may have many possible acceptable solutions. From the perspective of addressing student diversity and differentiation, good questions are culturally responsive and related to students' interests and lives (Gutstein 2006; Gruenewald 2003) or provide students with pedagogical choice (Small 2009).

Worthwhile tasks are those that share characteristics of being inquiry or problem based. They can offer students some degree of choice and require self-direction and motivation for completion. As a beginning teacher, creating such tasks can be a challenge, especially if teachers have few opportunities as students themselves to experience learning mathematics or science in this way. How can teachers learn the practice of posing, creating, and adapting worthwhile problems?

Teacher Educator Perspective (Cynthia): Designing Place-Based Pedagogical Problems

As a mathematics teacher educator within a problem based learning (PBL) elementary teacher education cohort, I provide opportunities for preservice teachers to experience both mathematical and pedagogical inquiry. With the guidance of a

PBL tutor, preservice teachers discuss, frame, and research various issues, including the teaching and learning of mathematics, that they identify in a given written case. For example, one case featured an elementary teacher who agrees to try using math journals with her students but is skeptical of their value in developing her students' mathematical understanding, while another focused on a teacher wondering how to integrate the study of mathematical concepts across multiple subject areas.

As a mathematics teacher educator and mathematics education resource person for the PBL cohort, I provide resources for preservice teachers to respond to and inquire into their own questions. However, as many preservice teachers have had few experiences living mathematics through inquiry or problem-based approaches, I also devote class time for them to engage in mathematical inquiry. This then can provide a background for preservice teachers to collaboratively adapt, design, and explore their own mathematical tasks. As with Gadanidis and Namukasa (2009), these tasks provide opportunities for teachers to explore mathematics and to "disrupt and reorganize [their] views of what it means to do and learn mathematics" (p. 114). In addition, drawing upon Gruenewald (2003), the tasks described in the following section focus on challenging preservice teachers to consider teaching through inquiry using place-conscious education where an understanding of place is necessary to understanding "the nature of our relationship with each other and the world" (p. 622).

Pedagogical Inquiry Task 1: Social Justice Issues from Global to Local

> Between 1990 and 2005, Brazil cleared 42,329,000 hectares of forest – an area larger than Germany. The main cause of Brazil's deforestation is cattle ranching. Brazil is the biggest beef exporter in the world and has the largest cattle herd on the planet, 40 % of which is located within the Amazon basin. Land-use change and deforestation – which is mostly done fire – make up 75 % of Brazil's greenhouse gas emissions (Branbrook Design 2010, p. 34–35).

A number of cases within the problem based learning cohort include opportunities to discuss social justice and environmental issues. Although it may appear that mathematics likely doesn't play a role in such discussions, an understanding of mathematics is actually necessary to gain deeper insight into the issues and to consider possible actions to the problems. In our PBL mathematics education classes, we therefore explore various local and global issues with mathematical eyes. In one class we begin with the problem described above reporting information on deforestation in Brazil from *The Little Book of Shocking Global Facts* (Branbrook Design 2010). The reported facts provoke PBL preservice teachers to ask further questions: Has the rate of deforestation in Brazil increased or decreased since 2005? Which countries import Brazil's beef and how much is imported? What are the effects of such deforestation and how does this compare to logging practices in British Columbia?

Working in small groups, PBL preservice teachers explore other facts and consider how such information could be placed for mathematical investigations with their students:

- 848 million people in the world are malnourished. 1,600 million people in the world are overweight (Branbrook Design 2010, p. 65).
- There are over 15 million refugees worldwide, many living in long-term camps. The 1990 World Declaration on Education for All (UNESCO 2001) states that all children, including refugee children and youth, have the right to education. As of 2011 a large number (40 % of 181,533) of refugees in the Dadaab camp in Northeast Kenya are of school age (5–17 years of age), yet less than half are enrolled in school (UNHCR 2012, 2011).
- [There are] 6.8 billion people living on planet earth; 5.6 billion people living in less developed regions (Branbrook Design 2010, p. 76–77).

Some preservice teachers begin by engaging in the ethical and political issues of the problem and can be heard asking: Why are so many people worldwide displaced? Why is only half the number of children in the Dadaab refugee camp receiving education? How has Canada responded to the refugee situation? How many refugee children are in my school? Those preservice teachers, who focus on the numbers, do so to better understand the context. These preservice teachers tend to compare the information given with others that require research to find: What is the rate of population growth on the planet? How has the population increased? What percentage of people are living in less developed regions and what percent are living in more developed regions? Where are these regions in the world? Can we graph population growth for various countries?

When preservice teachers are engaged in both the context of the problem and the mathematics, they bring their passions and interests to teaching and learning mathematics. Although it is often challenging for preservice teachers to pose problems for their students that are also interesting and exciting problems for themselves (Bragg and Nicol 2008; Nicol and Bragg 2009), problems located in social justice issues often peak preservice teachers' interests. In the PBL mathematics education class, they are asked to start with an interesting global fact, consider other questions inspired by the fact, and develop a mathematics problem for students using the facts as inspiration. Preservice teachers work in small groups to design a problem and share their problems with the whole class. One class decided to follow up on a small group's presentation on disposable diapers, and this problem spurred questions and activities for two classes:

> It is estimated that 90 % of babies in North America use disposable diapers. In Canada there are 1,877,095 children under the age of 4 (Canada Census 2011) how many diapers are disposed in Canadian landfills each year?

The class, in this case, estimated that 938,547 [half of 1,877,095] children in Canada were under the age of 2 and assumed that by the age of 2 many children were toilet trained. Assuming that 90 % of babies in Canada use disposable diapers, their calculation represented about 844,692 children. They estimated that for a child under the age of 2, an average of 42 diapers is used in a week. This leads to: 42 diapers/week x 52 weeks/year x 844,692 children or about 1,800,000,000 [1.8 billion] diapers per year. One teacher candidate asked:

> "But how large is that? That's a large number but, really, how big is it?"

The class continued and was encouraged to find a way of making this large number understandable and related to students' experiences. Understanding large numbers can be a challenge for children and adults. "How many swimming pools or soccer fields would 1.8 billion disposable diapers fill?" Ten? One hundred? Five hundred? Estimates indicated that preservice teachers themselves struggled with making sense of this large number. One group quickly searched online to find that an Olympic-size swimming pool has a volume of about 2500 m^3, and, working in their small groups, teacher candidates found that the number of disposable diapers disposed of in landfills in 1 year across Canada could fill about 720 swimming pools. For some teacher candidates, this number was still difficult to conceptualize, so they worked to determine the amount of land needed to spread the diapers out one-layer thick. Would this area cover the Vancouver landfill at Burns Bog? If the layer was a meter thick, how much area would be covered? How many soccer fields would it cover?

This task was mathematically challenging for many PBL preservice teachers but it also surprised them:

> My most memorable aspect of the course was math for social justice. I hadn't thought about using social justice issues to teach math [before this course]. I'm so excited to try this in my practicum class.

Tasks focused on global issues can lead teacher candidates to develop problems focused on local issues. The task of exploring these issues from a mathematical perspective provided opportunities for preservice teachers to experience learning mathematics through problem solving. Opportunities for PBL preservice teachers to design mathematical problems for their students around social issues engaged them in pedagogical inquiry that was located in places and issues important to them. As a result, preservice teachers sought to explore contexts and strategies for making mathematical content meaningful and engaging to their students. For example, some stated interest in designing lessons for their students focused on:

- Surveying recycling practices and dispositions of school and community members
- Studying streams near the school for their water quality and graphing the results
- Understanding and responding to the degree of homelessness around the school community area
- Developing culturally responsive lessons that connected students to the land and First Nations Peoples of the land

Pedagogical Inquiry Task 2: Historical, Graphical, and Mathematical Studies of Land through Geocaching

> Emphasizing hands-on, real-world learning experiences, this approach to education increases academic achievement, helps students develop stronger ties to their community, enhances students' appreciation for the natural world, and creates a heightened commitment to serving as active, contributing citizens.
> (Sobel 2004, p. 7)

A second mathematical and pedagogical task elaborated in the PBL case materials focuses on using mathematics to better understand the places and land in which PBL preservice teachers will be teaching. This task involves historical, graphical, and mathematical studies of place.

There are multiple ways of learning about place that include: (1) talking to elders and community members, (2) learning stories of place, (3) learning the issues and concerns of community members, (4) learning the language of place, and (5) being a community member. Listening to place can be at the center of efforts to develop meaningful experiences for students learning mathematics (Cajete 1994). One way to learn more about place and mathematics is through the context of a worldwide hide and seek activity commonly referred to as geocaching.

Geocaching involves use of a global positioning system (GPS) device to hide or find various caches stashed in places around the world. A geocacher can hide a cache, use the GPS to determine its location, share the location online with others, and then wait for others to try to find it. A typical cache can contain a logbook for seekers to sign once they've found the cache and small objects such as buttons, pencils, and markers for seekers to take and replace with some other kind of object. A website and app allow geocachers to post hidden caches, clues to their whereabouts, and comments on their finds (see www.geocaching.com).

There are multiple ways to approach the event of geocaching. For some the event can become one of collecting and reporting the most caches found. For others the event provides opportunities to explore, walk, and learn about new areas. For PBL preservice teacher candidates, a geocaching activity provides strategies to learn more about the history, culture, and stories of places as well as the mathematics of positioning and locating. After sharing maps of different areas near and outside the university where caches were hidden, preservice teachers discuss in small groups which caches would be interesting to find and why.

Preservice teachers ask questions of each other to explore how the maps, titles of the caches, and cultural knowledge of the place could be opportunities for their students to learn more about the stories of the land in which the geocache was hidden. There were not ready answers to the questions PBL teacher candidates asked. Instead, they researched responses themselves. Some researched the historical stories connected to the street names of the area; others researched the important attributes of the land for local Indigenous people and how the place names were reflected in the stories; still others researched the names settlers gave to particular areas. Activities inspired by Bragg and Skinner (2011) lead to explorations of longitude and latitude mapping position and determining location on inflated balloons representing the earth. Learning more about direction and orientation was also included. Due to time constraints, searching for a geocache was left to preserve teachers to follow outside of class time. However, time was given to consider how the class might design their own geocache, where it would be placed, the kinds of hints that could be given so that others could find the cache, and how it would be named. This activity brought preservice teachers together to learn more about the historical and cultural contexts of the places around their practicum schools and how they might engage their future students in designing their own class geocache.

Teacher Perspective (Fil): Designing Place-Based Problems for Students

I often wonder what things might look like had I considered more purposefully to follow PBL methods in my classroom from day one. Now, 4 years into my teaching practice at a provincial school, having gained some experience with ministry, district, and school-wide programs, acronyms and learning outcomes, and having gained confidence with classroom management, I now feel I'm able experiment with different approaches to learning and teaching. My approach so far can best be described as a loose, if not coincidental, intersection of PBL and place-based, culturally relevant education. By no means would I consider my practice to adhere to any coherent well-defined principles, and I freely admit that I've been loosely stepping near and at times blindly stumbling around what could be termed a consistent pedagogical problem based learning or problem-based education approach.

This spring, in Oregon, I happened upon an improvisational gathering. At first, I considered the group to be a random collection of eccentric individuals. However, after a few days, I began to see their improvisational jam not as a collection of individuals doing separate tasks or talking in ways that announced their individuality, but instead more as a codependent group where group harmony mattered. One individual started a task or conversation, and others responded in their own ways. The response evolved as it undulated through the group and flowed like a dance or improvisational jam. In a way, this response to stimulus is how living things function in ecosystems. David Sobel (2008) argues that classrooms, viewed through a complexity lens, are much more like fluid ecosystems than top-down hierarchies frozen in time. Is a classroom then a sort of improvisational jam, where students and teachers are learning from each other, reacting to each other, like a conversation, in the holistic ("wholistic") sense?

Providing a meaningful, engaging, real-world problem for students is a challenging task for a teacher. A quick glance at the prescribed learning outcomes for any grade, and any subject, reveals that integration and improvisation are both difficult and challenging. If I think of my classroom as a sort of in-the-moment improvisational act where I react to students and they react to me, how can I design worthwhile problems for students that are both meaningful for them in this place and satisfy the ministry-prescribed learning outcomes?

The challenge is not trivial: In order to provide real-world, integrated problems of which the students in a multigrade classroom are a part, then I as the teacher need to access a deep understanding of the learning outcomes across several grades and all subject areas in order to be able to identify, combine, and deconstruct learning outcomes and to recognize when the learning outcomes are met. I need a willingness to experiment and support from my administrators to do so. My pedagogy needs permission to get messy and, perhaps, the freedom to teach with no preconceived notion of where it will all end up. It is difficult to play around with outcomes when they are, literally, prescribed. In short, it is much easier to systematically tick off boxes of learning outcomes in terms of whether the students "get it" or not, than to walk out on the limb of a tree with little support. As I reflect on the memorable teaching and learning moments of my past several years, they have all been, without exception, messy, open ended, and designed in ways that could be described as building the scaffolding while at the same time building the tower. The gwenis problem is a good example of my attempt to offer my grades 5, 6, and 7 students PBL and be open to the unpredictable mess that PBL teaching can bring.

Problem Based Learning Task: Gwenis

The gwenis problem began as a brief mathematics lesson. It evolved into the sort of improvisational jam that can get messy and which I've seen little evidence of in curriculum resources. Gwenis (pronounced wa-neesh) is a small landlocked kokanee salmon that is found in only a handful of lakes in the world. One such lake is in our community, and gwenis was an important traditional food source in the winter months. People emerged from their siskins (underground pit homes) to gather the fish that had washed up on shore. I had taken a recent photo of a gwenis and so began my lesson by sharing this photo with my students. I invited our cultural language teacher to the class to provide a cultural context for the photo, and together we used the story of the gwenis to form the context of the math lesson and also the cultural language lesson.

As we discussed the gwenis and studied the photo, I realized that I had forgotten to collect the measurements of the fish I had photographed while at the beach. Examining the photo more closely, I wondered if the students could use the Douglas fir tree cone lying beside the fish as a way to figure out the measurements of the fish. I posed the problem. I hadn't planned to pose this problem. It was purely an accident, but it was a genuine problem.

The class talked about it. I knew that the problem was not easy, because when I asked, "how could you find out how big the fish is?" some of the grade 5 students stretched their palms apart to about shoulder width and said "this big." I knew, from our PBL classes in our teacher education program, and in particular Cynthia's open-ended teaching, to simply say, "Ok, what do others think?" Other students stated that the fish was over a meter in length, since that is how big the image appeared projected on the whiteboard. I smiled gently, knowing this was a good problem, and, although I hadn't anticipated posing it, knew that it offered us a good place to explore some mathematics. A grade 7 student noticed that if length were determined by how large the fish was when projected on the screen, then the length would change depending on how far the projector was from the screen. We tested that conjecture by moving the projector closer and further from the screen. I became aware of many implicit lessons in that picture: ratio and proportion, magnification, object/image relationships, measurement, scale, dimensionality, etc. Which ones should I focus on in this moment? How much guidance should I provide? Should I let the students decide?

I recognized that for grade 5 students, the photo could offer a measurement lesson, whereas for older students, it could be an introduction to ratio and proportion. The students requiring more support could have specific roles in their groups, such as "fish illustrator, materials gatherer, or ruler operator." At this point, my mind was racing with ideas. In some ways, this immediacy became not only a mathematics problem for students but also a pedagogical inquiry problem for me as well. Ironically, I wondered if I should have planned it better. Perhaps with more planning, I could have addressed many more learning outcomes and could have provided more scaffolding for students. On the other hand, I couldn't help but think about my overplanned lessons and how such planning sometimes narrows the possibilities for exploration, noticing the unexpected, and genuine, problem posing and solving.

From this whole-class brainstorm and discussion, during which I tried to make sure every student understood the problem, I explained that they had everything in the classroom at their disposal including our class collection of ponderosa pine and Douglas fir cones as well as needle clusters (from which they could work out average length). I grouped the grade 7 students in pairs and encouraged them to work together, while the grade 5 and 6 students were assigned to multigrade groupings and given large pieces of paper and their math journals.

Conclusion

As our cases of teaching with and from problem based learning illustrate, creating tasks for students or for preservice teachers can form rich contexts for pedagogical and/or mathematical inquiries. However, at the teacher education level, Fil's case indicates that learning to teach through PBL and through tasks such as those shared by Cynthia doesn't necessarily provide explicit approaches for how PBL might be used by teachers in classrooms with their students. In addition, although teaching cases used in the PBL program highlight issues of teaching in rural and Aboriginal contexts, it was the practicum experience that seemed to dominate as a resource during the first year of teaching. The experiences of researching case issues provided opportunities to gain knowledge of the issues outside the classroom; however, it was teaching experience itself that grounded and extended this knowledge.

Providing increased opportunities for preservice teachers to design tasks or problems that are inspired by context place or land in which they are teaching during their practica may provide the support needed for them to, as Fil states, take the invitation for improvisational jamming and problem based learning in their own classrooms. The fact that Fil had opportunities to experience and study math and learning to teach through problem solving in his teacher education program, but that these experiences were not necessarily a prominent resource for him in his first years of teaching, remains significant. Although these social justice issues were recognized as interesting and important, finding the balance between posing these kinds of problems, teaching through problem based learning, and meeting the Ministry intended learning outcomes was challenging.

For the gwenis problem, it has become a thematic entry into other subject areas such as science, social studies, language and culture, fine arts, language arts, and math. Working with the cultural language teacher Fil has developed an awareness of language, culture, and subject matter that provides confidence that some, not all, of the required Ministry intended learning outcomes can be met. However, recognizing that problems such as the gwenis problem were meaningful for students comes more from the reverberations to the greater community, the discussions around family dinner tables about traditional cultural practices and the resulting interest in elders sharing their knowledge in the classroom, and the extended discussions about Aboriginal fishing technologies, seasonal awareness, food sources, nutrition, and history. The land and place provide inspiring problem based learning tasks and engage our students in subject matter content, social justice issues, and culturally responsive education.

References

Barnbrook Design. (2010). *The little book of shocking global facts*. Hong Kong: Fiell Publishing.
Bragg, L., & Nicol, C. (2008). Designing open-ended problems to challenge preservice teachers' views on mathematics and pedagogy. In O. Figueras, & A. Sepúlveda (Eds.), *Proceedings of the joint meeting of the 32nd conference of the international group for the psychology of mathematics education [PME] and the XXX North American Chapter Vol 2* (pp. 256–270). Morelia: PME.
Bragg, L., & Skinner, M. (2011). *Geocaching: Math in the environment: Grades 4–8*. Bayswater: Teachers First Choice Pty Ltd.
Cajete, G. (1994). *Look to the mountain: An ecology of Indigenous education*. Durango, Colo.: Kivaki Press.
Canada Census. (2011). *Statistics Canada*. Available at http://www12.statcan.gc.ca/census-recensement/index-eng.cfm
Gadanidis, G., & Namukasa, I. (2009). Teacher tasks for mathematical insight and reorganization of what it means to learn mathematics. In B. Clarke, Grevholm, & R. Millman (Eds.), *Tasks in primary mathematics teacher education: Purpose, use and exemplars* (pp. 113–130). New York: Springer.
Geertz, C. (1996). The Java question. *The Wilson Quarterly, 20*(4), 58–68.
Gruenewald, D. (2003). Foundations of place: A multidisciplinary framework for place-conscious education. *American Educational Research Journal, 40*(3), 619–654.
Gruenewald, D. (2008). Place-based education: Growing culturally responsive teaching in geographical diversity. In D. Gruenewald & G. Smith (Eds.), *Place-based education in the global age* (pp. 137–153). New York: Routledge.
Gutstein, E. (2006). *Reading and writing the world with mathematics: Towards a pedagogy for social justice*. New York: Routledge.
Henningsen, M., & Stein, M. (1997). Mathematical tasks and student cognition: Classroom-based factors that support and inhibit high-level mathematical thinking and reasoning. *Journal for Research in Mathematics Education, 28*, 524–549.
Nicol, C., & Bragg, C. (2009). Designing problems: What kinds of open-ended problems do preservice teachers pose? In M. Tzekaki, M. Kaldrimidou, & H. Sakonidis (Eds.), *Proceedings of the 33rd conference of the international group for the psychology of mathematics education [PME] Vol 4* (pp. 225–232). Thessaloniki: PME.
Small, M. (2009). *Good questions: Great ways to differentiate mathematics instruction*. New York: Teachers College Press.
Smith, G., & Sobel, D. (2010). *Place and community-based education in schools*. New York: Routledge.
Sobel, D. (2004). *Place-based education: Connecting classrooms & communities*. Great Barrington: Orion Society.

Sobel, D. (2008). *Childhood and nature: Design principles for educators*. Portland: Stenhouse Publishers.
Sullivan, P., & Lilburn, P. (2002). *Good questions for math teaching: Why ask them and what to ask*. Sausalito: Math Solutions Publications.
United Nations Educational, Scientific and Cultural Organization (UNESCO). (2001). *Monitoring report on education for all*. Retrieved August 2012, at http://www.unesco.org/education/efa/monitoring/monitoring_rep_action.shtml
United Nations Humanitarian Council for Refugee (UNHCR). (2011). *Year of crisis UNHCR global trends*. Available at http://www.unhcr.org/4fd9e6266.html
United Nations Humanitarian Council for Refugee [UNHCR]. (2012). *Refugees in the horn of Africa*. Available at http://data.unhcr.org/horn-of-africa/region.php?id=3&country=110

Chapter 13
Measures of Success in Problem Based Learning: Triple Jump Assessments and E-Folios

Anne Zavalkoff

Introduction

How best to formatively and summatively assess preservice teachers is an ongoing and evolving conversation in the Teaching English Language Learners through Problem Based Learning (TELL through PBL) cohort of UBC's Bachelor of Education. These conversations have been driven partly by our own self-inquiries into our cohort's purposes and practices and partly by program changes within the broader B.Ed. program. More than just idle conversation, our inquiries in the 8 years I have worked with this cohort have resulted in three distinct shifts in our summative assessment criteria. Each shift has moved us toward more coherent and achievable examinations that prioritize problem-solving abilities and reason-giving over information retention and recitation. They have also moved us toward a more integrated, ability-based approach that better reflects the professional competency sought by our cohort and the UBC B.Ed. program as a whole.

The three summative points of assessment used by our cohort are structured as "Triple Jumps," a form of assessment common to many PBL programs (MacDonald and Savin-Baden 2004).[1] The Triple Jumps take place at the end of each of the three academic school terms; three terms translate to three successive "jumps." According to Macdonald and Savin-Baden (2004):

> [T]he 'Triple Jump' exercise has three phases: hop, step and jump. In the hop phase the tutor questions the student, thus they are caught on the hop. The step phase allows the student time to research the findings and hypotheses that have emerged from the

---

[1] While this chapter focuses on the summative assessment of our TJs, much of the assessment that we do in TELL through PBL is integrated into the preservice teachers' learning that unfolds over the 2-week case cycle. For an exploration of these forms of formative assessment, please see Chap. 8.

A. Zavalkoff (✉)
Department of Educational Studies, University of British Columbia, Vancouver, BC, Canada
e-mail: anne.zavalkoff@ubc.ca

hop phase. In the jump phase they are expected to provide the tutor with a written report of their findings. (p. 11)

Our cohort's first two Triple Jumps are most true to this original structure. They assess how well the preservice teachers have learned to ask questions of a case, draw out its complexities, conduct collaborative research, and make good individual judgments about how to proceed. The final Triple Jump differs in that the preservice teachers are required to construct a professional portfolio that includes a Statement of Educational and Teaching Philosophy. While the Triple Jump formats vary, there are strong links across their purposes and practices. Each one gives the instructors a snapshot of where the preservice teachers are on their journeys toward becoming teachers, while also providing the preservice teachers an opportunity to explore and demonstrate their professional growth over time.

In the discussion that follows, I will explain the purposes and practices of our Triple Jumps (TJ) using MacDonald and Savin-Baden's (2004) principles of PBL assessment. These principles help clarify how our cohorts' current framings of these exams enable meaningful summative assessments of our preservice teachers' growth toward becoming teachers. I also discuss the evolution of the TJs, demonstrating how our cohort's ability to be reflective and responsive has enabled us to align our TJs more closely with MacDonald and Savin-Baden's principles.

Principle 1 *"As lecturers, we need to ensure that there is alignment between our objectives and the students' anticipated learning outcomes, the learning and teaching methods adopted, and the assessment of learning – strategies, methods, and criteria"* (MacDonald and Savin-Baden 2004 p. 7).

The first two TJs mimic the structure of the biweekly case cycles that catalyze preservice teacher learning throughout the year.[2] All follow a case-research-response format where preservice teachers unpack problematic cases through collective inquiry that culminates in their individual responses and syntheses. These shared formats and markers of success align our methods of learning and demonstrating learning.

This alignment begins with our integrated approach to TJ planning. Tutors and instructors meet to craft our cases. For the TJ, we review the themes addressed in the preceding class meetings and research packages. We fine-tune previous TJ cases and assessment rubrics to ensure that they align with the arc of the preservice teachers' learning and our evolving course objectives.[3] We also canvass each other's ideas for how the TJ case narratives might be altered to evoke increasingly complex and cross-curricular responses from the preservice teachers. This collaborative process continues the kind of case refinement and responsiveness that our cohort strives toward throughout the rest of the year.

The day of the TJ exam itself then compresses the typical case cycle into a single morning and afternoon. In the morning, the preservice teachers pick up a case pack-

---

[2] For a fuller description of the biweekly case cycle, please see Chap. 8.

[3] In response to cohort-inquiry and programmatic change, the assessment rubrics have shifted substantially over time. The details and rationales of this evolution are explored in the section discussing Principle 5.

age that includes the TJ case: a narrative comprising many ill-defined yet true-to-life themes. For roughly five hours, they work together in their tutorial groups to enact the already familiar PBL pedagogy. They identify and puzzle through the case issues. They look back at previous research packages. They access library resources for review and further inquiry. Drawing from their collective work, they then develop their own interpretations and responses.

In the afternoon, each preservice teacher sits down for a 30 minute dialogue with one of the TELL through PBL instructors. The preservice teachers offer their analyses and plans of action. The instructors continue the Socratic questioning used throughout the rest of the term to help draw out the preservice teachers' meanings, rationales, and practical strategies. The strongest responses generally draw from a combination of the content knowledge, practical experience, and research strategies that the preservice teachers have developed and culminate in responses that align with their emerging sense of themselves as teachers.

The first two TJs assess the extent to which the preservice teachers can embody the cycle of inquiry that has grounded their learning throughout the year.[4] How well can they trouble a school-based context, identifying possible issues and research questions? How well can they refine their questions as their academic and practical knowledge base grows? How well can they take up critical theory to ask and answer: who/what is framed as the problem; whose perspectives are represented and whose are marginalized or absent; and what questions am I asking and what questions or possibilities don't I see? How well can the preservice teachers identify what they know, what they don't know, what they need to know, and where to find it? How well can they synthesize a well-justified response that draws from their diverse knowledge bases and results in a specific, context-embedded plan for action?

By constructively aligning our methods of learning and assessment, the first two TJs attempt to encourage deep, as opposed to surface, approaches to learning (Biggs 2007; MacDonald 2005). They attempt to assess the growing content knowledges and competencies that the preservice teachers have been working to develop and which they will need to become effective, engaged educators.

Principle 2 *"Assessment should reflect the learner's development from a novice to an expert practitioner and so should be developmental throughout the program of studies"* (MacDonald and Savin-Baden 2004, p. 7).

The TJs are structured to reflect the increasing level of sophistication and self-reflection we expect to see as the preservice teachers progress from one term to the next. While the first Triple Jump (TJ1) and the second Triple Jump (TJ2) share the same "hop-skip-jump" process described above, TJ1 attempts to recognize that the preservice teachers are still early in their development as teachers. It is structured to review and reconsider many of the case issues and broad themes of the first academic term. These themes might include building classroom community amidst diverse cultures, linguistic backgrounds and learning styles, teaching for social jus-

---

[4] In this section, I discuss only the first two TJs, as they most closely embody all elements of Principle 1. While the third TJ also assesses the products of learning, its e-folio employs a different format for assessment. I explore this format in the sections discussing Principles 2 and 3.

tice and anti-oppression education, teaching math through problem-solving, developing a balanced literacy reading program, and integrating Indigenous knowledges into classroom planning and practice. By asking the preservice teachers to synthesize and apply their prior content learning in response to familiar issues, TJ1 recognizes their still novice status.

At the same time, TJ1 is not a straight repetition or regurgitation of prior content learning. "The triple jump not only assesses what the students learned, but how they learned it" (McTiernan et al. 2007 p. 117). It is a test of process as well as product. To explore how well the preservice teachers have learned to use the PBL pedagogy, we play with the narrative contexts in which the TJ case issues play out. We might alter the grade level in which the TJ case is set and therefore the developmental stages of the learners. We might alter the class or community composition and with that the strengths and challenges for both learners and teacher. The case also includes one broad, previously unresearched theme. This addition assesses the preservice teachers' growing abilities to problematize and inquire. It evaluates their abilities to transfer and apply their growing knowledges to new circumstances. It gauges their abilities and dispositions to respond with flexibility, collaboration, and perseverance to the unexpected challenges of teaching. Finally, it extends their learning, spurring on the development of their professional judgment and identities.

The differences between TJ1 and TJ2 are designed to account for the preservice teachers' gradual movement from novice to expert. TJ2 follows the same case-research-response format as the first, but asks both the preservice teacher and the examiner to enter into a more formal role-play for their dialogue. As the rubric makes clear, examiners may choose to be a parent of one of the case study students or the principal of the case study school.[5] While parents and principals may ask different types of questions of preservice teachers, both role-plays introduce even more unpredictability into the second TJ, assessing the preservice teachers' abilities to think on their feet. The preservice teachers must loosen their expectations of being able to stick to a fully formed plan, making this experience and exam even closer to authentic professional contexts. By inviting the preservice teachers to practice using their professional voices in an extended exchange about education, TJ2 is designed to help move them toward articulating more clearly their own teaching philosophies and practices.

The rubrics for TJ1 and TJ2 also attempt to account for the developmental nature of the TJs and the preservice teachers' journeys. While we work within a pass/fail system, we have designed the rubric to allow us to recognize gradations of performance and directions for future growth. For each criterion within the rubric, the preservice teachers receive an assessment of how well they have met the expectations of the exam: "exceeding" (**), "meeting" ($\sqrt{}$), and "not yet meeting" (−). These more nuanced gradations allow the preservice teachers to pass onto the next phase of their program, with the understanding that their continued develop-

---

[5] As the rubric states: "The pre-service teacher dialogues with the examiner in a situated role-play (examiner as parent and/or principal; pre-service teacher as classroom teacher)."

ment as professionals is required.[6] While the TJs are summative, we do not want them to stand completely apart from the iterative, formative process of the 2-week case cycle.

Many instructors make use of the "comment section" of the rubric to provide the preservice teachers suggestions for how to build on their developing strengths, shore up their current weaknesses, and chart possible paths forward toward continued improvement. As an example of what this feedback can look like in practice, I have included some of my own:

Example 1 Try to incorporate a richer discussion of the theories of learning and development that ground your pedagogical objectives, rationales, and practices. While you made good references to Ministry documents (e.g., Focus on Bullying), you had difficulty linking to academic theorists, even when asked to do so directly. During the next Triple Jump, try to trace the origins of the educational concepts that you employ, situating your discussion in a more explicit (CALP!) academic context. Or to borrow again from the TELL focus of TELL through PBL, and try to better match your responses to the register of the Triple Jump.

Example 2 Try to think through the concrete application of your educational goals. You clearly have a general game plan of what you want to do, but your strategies are still a little fuzzy. While you responded to my prompts for further explanation (your discussion of using a ceramic tile art project to help build classroom community is a case in point), you sometimes struggled to explain what your objectives would look like in actual elementary classrooms (e.g., how you might use literature circles and specific books to counteract bullying). Fear not, I am certain that the required assimilation to practice will come as you spend more concentrated time in the classroom this coming term.

Example 3 Try to articulate your ideas more clearly and robustly. While I know that part of your difficulty in expanding on your thinking was the result of Triple Jump nerves, as you progress through Term 2, you must develop the confidence and depth with which you relay your commitments about teaching and learning. Consider joining an organization like Toastmasters. They provide time-tested techniques for effective communication and a supportive community in which to practice. Perhaps you also can make speaking out in our large group discussions at UBC a goal for your practice in Term 2. You might try jotting down what you want to say before speaking to help you find your voice. Learn to trust your knowledge and yourself.

The third and final TJ (TJ3) has the explicit intention of inviting the preservice teachers to trace and present their movement from novice to (more) expert practitioner. How have the preservice teachers developed as teachers and people throughout the course of the program? What fundamental pedagogical commitments have come

---

[6] As the TJs mark the end of discrete academic terms and coursework, the preservice teachers cannot continue on to the next phase of their program without passing these summative points of assessment. Despite our developmental approach to these exams, some do not.

to underpin their professional priorities, planning, and practice? How do they understand their greatest, ongoing strengths and challenges? This broader reflective piece is designed to allow the preservice teachers to reflect on their growth over time. As such, I will present its format and purposes later in the discussion of Principle 3.

Principle 3 *"Students should be able to engage in self-assessment, evaluation, and reflection as the basis for future continuing professional development and self-directed learning"* (MacDonald and Savin-Baden 2004 p. 7).

The self-assessment practices woven into our TELL through PBL cohort pedagogy are carried through to each of the TJs.[7] The first two TJs ask the preservice teachers to complete a self-assessment using the same TJ rubrics and criteria for success that the examiners use. This element supports them in evaluating their own strengths and challenges as learners and professionals.

Currently, we are in the process of integrating an additional reflexive element into the first two TJs. This element builds from the case syntheses generated by the preservice teachers at the end of each case cycle.[8] In the 2013–2014 school year, we have asked the preservice teachers to review their past syntheses and come to the TJ ready to talk about how their understandings have changed from the time of their original writings. This looping back is meant to impress upon the preservice teachers that the process of "becoming teacher" is perpetual and ongoing. It also underlines the importance of the self-reflective, biweekly syntheses. So far, it is too early to assess formally how this new reflexive practice is impacting the preservice teachers' professional development or self-directed learning. We anticipate that it will achieve the end described by Macdonald and Savin-Baden (2004): "it is through peer, self and collaborative assessment that [PBL] students are able to make judgments about how well they are learning and not just how much they have learned" (p. 5).

Building upon the opportunities for self-assessment included within TJ1 and TJ2, TJ3 encourages deeper reflection focused on retrospective and potential growth. It is built around the production and presentation of a professional e-portfolio. This e-folio includes a Statement of Educational and Teaching Philosophy, as well as the preservice teachers' analyses of their strengths and challenges in relation to the Standards for the Education, Competence and Professional Conduct of Educators set out and enforced by the British Columbia Teachers Regulation Branch.[9]

---

[7] For a more detailed discussion of these varied points of self-assessment, please see Chap. 8.

[8] These syntheses are individual projects that demonstrate each preservice teacher's ability to consolidate and apply the sum of the group's collective learning in a personal response to the case issues. For a more thorough description of case syntheses and their roles in PBL pedagogy, please see Chap. 8.

[9] These standards were previously upheld by the British Columbia College of Teachers. When this self-regulatory body was disbanded in 2012, the newly formed, government-based Teacher Regulation Branch took over the oversight and disciplining K-12 educators in British Columbia (https://www.bcteacherregulation.ca/AboutUs/AboutUs.aspx).

In some contexts, professional portfolios are framed as employment-searching tools, becoming a pro forma exercise designed to highlight assets and demonstrate competencies. While preservice teachers may choose to frame their e-folios in this way, we encourage them to understand this final TJ as a tool for continued development, where they may explore the contradictions and challenges inherent in both their professional journeys and the teaching profession itself. Regardless of which framing the preservice teachers choose to pursue, the e-folios are an extension of the self-reflective work they have undertaken throughout the year, giving them a final opportunity to pause and assess who they are becoming as teachers and people.

At the center of the e-folio is the Statement of Educational and Teaching Philosophy. In it, the preservice teachers articulate the "whats, whys, and hows" of their most fundamental pedagogical commitments.

What What should be the proper aims of schooling and education? What is "good" teaching? What do they want their students to learn, do, or know as a result of having known them? The strongest responses define the language used with exceptional clarity. They also convey a deep understanding of what the preservice teachers' pedagogical commitments mean to them, set within a context of how others might interpret differently the purposes of schooling and education.

Why Why are the preservice teachers' larger pedagogical aims valuable? Why do their classroom goals serve their students, both during and after their schooling? The strongest responses offer ample, well-supported justifications for the preservice teachers' stated educational and pedagogical objectives. They build a compelling case grounded in deep, passionate, and original commitments.

How How will they implement their educational and pedagogical aims? How will they attempt to influence the practices, relationships, and contexts of their classrooms, schools, and communities? The strongest responses include brief yet specific examples that paint vivid portraits of what their practices actually look, sound, and feel like. Not only do they help to illuminate the statement of philosophy, but they also demonstrate that the preservice teachers' have thought through the complexities of schooling.

Despite having worked all year with the "what, why, and how" framework, the preservice teachers are often challenged by the focus and honesty required of this concise piece. Writing the statement requires them to deeply and sincerely contemplate their professional and personal development. It requires them to identify, articulate, and synthesize the fundamental pedagogical commitments that are coming to ground their work as teachers. As such, it supports them in developing explicit and well-supported frameworks for their own decision-making. It prepares them to enter into public debates about education with multiple, varied stakeholders. Their statements of philosophy give the preservice teachers a sound foundation for ongoing reflection and dialogue, whether they are encountering contradictions in their own practices, being called upon to defend their professional choices, or advocating for their fundamental values.

The reflexivity inherent in writing their statements of philosophy also provides a strong grounding for the other written element of TJ3: their responses as critical educators to the Standards for the Education, Competence and Professional Conduct of Educators. To construct a response, the preservice teachers choose artifacts from their course and practicum work, linking each artifact to one of the eight standards.[10] They then write a minimum 200-word reflection on how their chosen artifacts demonstrate personal growth, professional competency, and engagement with the standard. To help them build more coherent pictures of who they are becoming as teachers, we encourage the preservice teachers to integrate the commitments expressed in their statements of philosophy into the artifacts they choose and the reflections they write.

Preservice teachers may choose to frame their responses highlighting only their strengths, successes, and full compliance with each standard. However, we ask them to consider aiming for a more complicated conversation. How do they understand the wording and meaning of each standard? In what ways do they, or others, think each standard is important? We suggest that they apply a critical lens to the standards, considering what is at stake in and assumed by each. We ask them to imagine what the standards might look like in practice. When so located, what tensions emerge within and between the standards? How might they act in response? The strongest responses demonstrate the preservice teachers' efforts to understand and appreciate what is at stake in the standards and their complexities, while also clearly voicing their own passions, journeys, and challenges as developing teachers. Thus, while the e-folio signals a reflexive end to their programs, it also involves looking forward toward the inspirations and tensions that will continue to face them throughout their careers.

Principle 4 *"Assess what the professional does in their practice, which is largely process-based professional activity, underpinned by appropriate knowledge, skills, and attitudes"* (MacDonald and Savin-Baden 2004 p. 7).

In crafting the structures, processes, and activities of the TELL through PBL cohort, we continually return to the professional knowledges, competencies, and dispositions required in the context of elementary teaching. What do we hope the preservice teachers will come to know and be able to do? Who do we hope they will be as people and teachers? Good teachers possess well-informed, well-supported, and ever-growing knowledge bases. They adapt and apply their knowledges in chaotic, ever-changing environments. They exercise good judgment supported by good reasons. They inquire into the curriculum, the world, and themselves. They see complexity in their classrooms, schools, and communities. They problem-solve col-

---

[10] In fact, a commitment to reflexive, lifelong learning is itself one of the eight standards. "Educators engage in career-long learning: Educators engage in professional development and reflective practice, understanding that a hallmark of professionalism is the concept of professional growth over time. Educators develop and refine personal philosophies of education, teaching and learning that are informed by theory and practice. Educators identify their professional needs and work to meet those needs individually and collaboratively" (https://www.bcteacherregulation.ca/Standards/StandardsDevelopment.aspx).

laboratively. To assess these processed-based professional activities, the TJs seek to assess the preservice teachers' knowledges, skills, and attitudes.[11]

Curricular knowledges form the foundations in which the good judgments and practices of professional educators are based. How best to assess these subject-specific knowledges in a cohort that uses an integrated, competency-based approach to assessment? How best to assess individual content areas when our rubrics do not include subject-specific, content-based course objectives?

To encourage a serious engagement with the curricular knowledges associated with every programmatic content area, we use a "you choose two, we choose one or two" model for exploring the TJ case issues.[12] Preservice teachers first choose two of the issues to be unpacked, working from strength and building confidence. Based on the gaps that seem to be emerging from the dialogue, instructors then choose one or two issues for continued exploration. This flexibility ensures breadth in the examination. Depth is achieved through the concession that not every issue can be formally taken up during the exam. However, as the preservice teachers don't know in advance which of the issues will be explored, they come prepared to discuss the content of all.

The development and assessment of knowledges is only the first step. The TJs also assess the skills, abilities, or competencies that underpin what elementary teachers do in practice. At the heart of our competency-based assessment is the "what, why, and how" framework described above.[13] For every case issue taken up during the first two TJs, the preservice teachers demonstrate their professional competency by explaining the specific meanings of the concepts they employ, the reasonings that supports their analyses, and the concrete implementations of their action plans.

To satisfy the "what," preservice teachers must be able to explain how they understand the content knowledges they have acquired. They must be able to express the complex, academic concepts in plain language. They must be clear about what their language means when taken up in the literature and school system, as well as in their own use. Finding conceptual clarity helps the preservice teachers to imagine what these concepts look like in practice. Moreover, speaking accessibly and succinctly is an essential part of effective communication with parents and fellow educators. Fixed ideas about what concepts mean, along with assumptions about how others are using them, can lead to profound disagreements within educational debates. Finding a way through the murkiness of abstract language and oft-used buzzwords is an essential part of finding common ground with others and constructive paths forward.

---

[11] I leave the discussion of attitudes or dispositions to Chap. 3, which is devoted to their place within the TELL through PBL cohort.

[12] As the rubric states, "the pre-service teacher dialogues with the examiner on three (or four) of the issues identified. Two issues will be selected by the student and one (or two) will be selected by the instructor."

[13] Please see the discussion of the statement of philosophy in Principle 3.

To satisfy the "why," preservice teachers must be able to articulate good reasons in support of the content knowledge they have acquired, as well as their ensuing pedagogical judgments. It is not enough for teachers to know what they want to do in a classroom; they must also know why they want to do it. Developing good reasons that synthesize the insights of academic literatures and professional experiences helps to clarify commitments and provide frameworks for decision-making. It helps ensure greater consistency between professional priorities and practices. Moreover, for preservice teachers to be successful in the highly political and contested arena of public schooling, they must be able to convince others that their judgments are wise and their actions are well justified. These abilities are the basis for arguments in support of the professional autonomy of teachers.

To satisfy the "how," preservice teachers must be able to apply the content knowledge they have acquired in specific, ever-changing contexts. They must move beyond a general understanding of abstract principles to the concrete details of educational practice. It is not enough for teachers to vaguely know what they want to do in classrooms; they also must work through what such a plan looks, sounds, and feels like. Knowing concretely how to implement educational and teaching objectives is the difference between a well-meaning teacher and an excellent one.

This "what, why, and how" framework is also at the heart of the assessment rubrics for the first and second TJs. As the rubrics state, for each issue discussed, preservice teachers are expected to:

- Communicate ideas and understandings in a clear, coherent, and articulate manner.
- Provide well-justified rationales for their responses/action plans, as well as for the pedagogical commitments that inform them. Rationales should demonstrate an understanding of both academic and professional knowledges.
- Articulate concrete responses or action plans to the issues. These descriptions should apply academic and professional knowledges to elaborate what the response would look like in practice.

Each element of this "what, why, and how" framework is interdependent, with the strongest TJ performances displaying a deep understanding of and consistency between them all.

In a 1-year teacher certification program, even the most effectively structured course of studies cannot equip preservice teachers with all of the knowledge they will need throughout their careers. They also must emerge from their studies with particular ways of knowing, abilities, and attitudes. The first two TJs assess how the knowledge acquired is held, applied, and transformed in response to evolving contexts: The final TJ also foregrounds understanding, reasoning, and application.[14] Taken together, the three TJs test what teachers actually do in practice.

---

[14] Please see the discussion of the statement of philosophy found in the section for Principle 3.

Principle 5 *"Assessment should be based in a practice context in which students will find themselves in the future – whether real or simulated"* (MacDonald and Savin-Baden 2004, p. 7).

Our pursuit of assessment that simulates the realities of professional practice is perhaps best demonstrated by the evolution of the TJ toward an increasingly competency-based, open-ended, and dialogical format. Elementary school teachers tend to work in complex, ever-changing contexts that require flexible responses grounded in consistent goals for purpose and practice. Over time, the TJ cases and rubric have been updated to better emulate these messy, real-life contexts, thereby better supporting the authentic and meaningful assessment toward which Principle 5 strives.

When I first came to PBL in 2006, the TJ emphasized the assessment of content knowledge. The rubric was a pastiche of subject area objectives that had been plucked straight out of the course outlines used in the rest of the B.Ed. program. For example, the content-based criteria related to just two of the nine subject areas included:

EDUC 317 Education Psychology: Special Education

- Identifies a variety of pathways to learning that take into account a variety of learners
- Addresses many challenges of, and strategies, for working with children with exceptionalities within the regular class, including working with supportive services, parents, and communities and making specific visual and sensory adaptations designed to help a student with autism be successful in learning
- Identifies challenges of involving some parents in the special educational needs of their children, highlights social factors that impact parental involvement (e.g., English language proficiency in immigrant communities, working conditions for both high- and low-income parents)

LLED 310 Language and Literacy Education

- Identifies the components of a balanced reading program, describing and discussing a wide variety of components and their implications for teaching, including guided reading and literature circles
- Identifies appropriate and diverse tools for the ongoing assessment of student reading, including running record
- Identifies how the reading program could be adapted to meet the needs of individual students

The lengthy, itemized list that resulted was unwieldy. Examiners could not reliably keep track of how well the preservice teachers had met the multiple objectives of each standalone course. Moreover, a 30-min exam simply wasn't enough time for the preservice teachers to demonstrate both breadth and depth of content learning. Not to mention that acquiring content knowledge is only a very preliminary first step toward professional competency. In the real world of teachers, how knowledge is held, applied, and transformed in response to evolving contexts is equally essential.[15]

Not only was the rubric geared more toward information retention and recitation than competency-based processes like problem-solving and reason-giving, so was the framing of the TJ cases. An excerpt from TJ1 in 2008 reads:

> This fall your goal is to put in place a *balanced literacy program* that will meet the needs of all your students. The reading levels in your class range from emergent to fluent. How would you assess your struggling readers and adapt your teaching to meet their needs? You are also looking into *teaching math through problem* solving as a way to engage all your students and develop their thinking. (Emphasis added)

In naming specific pedagogies, like a balanced literacy program or a problem-solving approach to math, the TJ cases unnecessarily foreclosed the methods and rationales that the preservice teachers might choose to explore in their responses.

To correct these limitations, the TJ cases were rewritten as murkier, open-ended narratives that challenge the preservice teachers to find their own paths forward. The parallel revised excerpt used in 2009 reads:

> The reading levels in your class range from emergent to fluent. This fall your goal is to replace the current reading program with one that will meet the needs of all your students. You are also looking into ways to teach math to develop their thinking and get them more engaged.

Opening up the case in this way creates space for variable responses. It invites the preservice teachers to voice their own priorities, rationales, and practices. As such, the exam more closely mirrors the experiences of practicing teachers.

To further enhance the "realness" of the first two TJs, we have shifted the emphasis of the oral components from presentation to dialogue. The original rubric made no explicit mention of the form of exchange envisioned. As a result, what often resulted was more independent preservice teacher monologue than dynamic, responsive dialogue. However, in the practice context of teachers, who are public professionals accountable to diverse stakeholders, exchanges are often open-ended and unpredictable, requiring flexibility and responsiveness.

The dialogical format now specified in the TJ rubric simulates these realities. While the preservice teachers start off the exchange by briefly presenting how they understand the big ideas and issues of the case, examiners quickly enter into the mix with questions that grow out of the analyses offered. If a preservice teacher says she would use a problem-solving approach to math, I might ask how to explain to parents this approach, along with its benefits and its challenges. If describing the implementation of a guided reading program, I might ask for clarification about its specific strengths and weaknesses for Indigenous students or English language learners. As an examiner, this Socratic dialogue is very exciting; I can often see in-the-moment learning taking place as the preservice teachers integrate or extend a piece of their prior learning.

---

[15] For a discussion of the knowledges, skills, and attitudes assessed in the current TJ format, please see the section outlining Principle 4.

The TJs have evolved not only in response to our self-inquiries into our cohort's purposes and practices,[16] but also as a response to shifts in the realities of the broader UBC and British Columbian contexts. In 2012, UBC introduced a fully revamped B.Ed. program. Concurrent with this programmatic change, the Problem Based Learning cohort merged with Teaching English Language Learners cohort, becoming "TELL through PBL." With this merger came the challenge of how to infuse the priorities and practices of TELL into the learning and assessment structures of PBL.[17]

Moreover, concurrent demographic shifts within British Columbia are bringing tangible changes to the working conditions of K-12 educators. According to the BC Ministry of Education (1999, updated 2013), "Students for whom English is a second or additional language (or dialect) are a growing segment of British Columbia's K-12 school population. Over the past 10 years, the number of students identified as needing ELL services in BC has more than tripled" (p. 4). Similarly, the Vancouver School Board notes that within its district "25 % of K-Grade 12 students are designated ELL [and] 60 % speak a language other than English at home."[18] These demographic realties are having a profound impact on the practice contexts in which our preservice teachers find themselves now and into the future, where "many students are unfamiliar with the English alphabet or with Canadian traditions, history, culture, education systems, and lifestyles" (BC Ministry of Education 2009, updated 2013, p. 5).

These programmatic and demographic shifts gave rise to the most recent evolution of our TJ assessments. In both the first and second TJs, there is now a requirement that the preservice teachers address the opportunities and challenges inherent in school communities populated by English speakers of various proficiencies.[19] The strongest TJ responses infuse the principles and practices of TELL into the discussion of every case issue, demonstrating how the cultural and linguistic resources of ELLs can assist all learners.

In sum, the TJ cases and rubrics have evolved toward increasingly competencies-based, open-ended, and dialogical formats that better represent and respond to the changing realities of professional educators in BC. The flexibility inherent in the TELL through PBL structure, where modes of learning and assessment are programmatically independent but internally integrated, has enabled us to better simulate these messy, real-life contexts, enabling us to better assess the professional

---

[16] For example, in 2009, an assessment review subcommittee was struck to inquire into the myriad forms of PBL assessment, both within our cohort and as it is practiced elsewhere. The changes described above come largely out its recommendations.

[17] For a discussion of these changes, please see Chap. 4.

[18] http://www.vsb.bc.ca/programs/supporting-ell-students, accessed March 14, 2014

[19] The TJ1 rubric states, preservice teachers are expected to "dialogue with the examiner on three (or four) of the issues identified… Of these 3–4 issues, at least one must take up concerns for ELLs." The TJ2 rubric states, preservice teachers are expected to "dialogue with the examiner in a situated role-play…At least one of the issues that is taken up in the role play must include English Language Learners."

competencies sought by the TELL through PBL cohort, as well as the UBC B.Ed. program as a whole.

Principle 6 *"Students should begin to appreciate and experience the fact that in a professional capacity they will encounter clients, users, professional bodies, peers, competitors, statutory authorities, etc. who will, in effect, be 'assessing' them"* (MacDonald and Savin-Baden 2004, p. 7).

Assessment rooted in multiple, diverse standpoints takes place throughout the program, so that preservice teachers can learn to understand and respond to competing perspectives, purposes, and practices within educational contexts.[20] Likewise, the TJs require the preservice teachers to develop an appreciation of how differences in personal standpoint, institutional constraints, and professional responsibilities will impact both how others position them and how they attempt to position themselves. As the TJ1 and TJ2 rubrics state, preservice teachers are expected to "identify the key issues of the case and articulate the reasoning that frames these situations as issues. *This involves considering from the perspectives of multiple stakeholders why the situation deserves contemplation. For whom do these issues matter and why*" [emphasis added].

TJ2 explicitly integrates this engagement with ever-widening perspectives by adding the role-play element described above.[21] Examiners choose to inhabit their principal or parent roles in very different ways across many different preservice teacher interviews. In the past, I have played the parent of a myriad of (imagined) children, including a highly imaginative English language learner who plays piano by ear, but has difficulty focusing and lacks organizational skills; an academically gifted but socially shy child whose aunt has a similar-sex partner; a born performer who loves to sing and dance, but struggles with written output and seat work; and a gender-nonconforming child who asks big picture questions, but has trouble with reading comprehension. Sometimes, I am helpful and cooperative. Other times, I present nothing by challenges. Every character requires different quick-witted adaptations from the preservice teachers. The role-plays of TJ2 require the preservice teachers to understand how diverse populations perceive and assess them, so that they can anticipate and respond effectively.

For TJ3, the diversity of assessment standpoints expands yet again. In constructing their e-folios, the preservice teachers must respond explicitly to the Standards for the Education, Competence and Professional Conduct of Educators that are monitored by the BC Teacher Regulation Branch.[22] In demonstrating their appreciation of how these standards might be intended, interpreted, and complicated, they effectively enter into a dialogue with their profession.

During this TJ, the preservice teachers' peers also enter into the assessment process from their unique standpoints. The final piece of the e-folio is a public interview conducted between pairs of preservice teachers. Interview questions might

---

[20] For a description of how multiple voices are integrated in the case cycle, please see Chap. 8.

[21] This role-play is explored further in the sections discussing Principles 2 and 5.

[22] The preservice teachers' engagement with these standards is explored in the section discussing Principle 3.

include the following: how has the process of selecting artifacts, creating reflections, and articulating a philosophy of education transformed you; what reflection was most difficult to write; or what do you still wonder about the standards? An open question period follows, where the entire cohort and all prior instructors are invited to enter the conversation. The feedback for this element of TJ3 rests with the preservice teachers themselves: Each interview pair receives structured peer feedback. Thus, this final celebration of the preservice teachers' growth further extends the diversity of perspectives with which they must engage.

Not only is each TJ internally structured to vary the perspectives and priorities to which the preservice teachers must respond, but they also are so structured across the TJs. We take special care to ensure that different instructors and tutors assess each preservice teacher at each TJ. In a similar vein, tutors never examine any of the preservice teachers from their own small tutorial groups.[23] We also do not disclose the examination pairings ahead of time, so that the preservice teachers will not tailor their TJ review to their expectations of how particular examiners may focus their questions. Moreover, many instructors chose to focus their exam questions outside of their specialties, because we generally already have sufficient data about the preservice teachers' performance in our own areas. As Principle 6 suggests, narrow preparations serve well neither the current learning of the preservice teachers nor their future careers; the TJs aim to ensure that assessment is located in a wide variety of standpoints.

Conclusion

Every TJ experience is unique. Examiners come from different areas of specialization with different understandings of good teaching. They assess different preservice teachers who come with their own distinct experiences and assumptions. These shifting positionalities provide preservice teachers opportunities to practice navigating social locations, identities, and the competing demands made of professional educators.

Every TJ is also the same, shaped by the same principles of good assessment. Macdonald and Savin-Baden (2004) provide one way of articulating these principles in relation to TELL through PBL's current and evolving practices. Our TJ cases, rubrics, and activities strive to capture the deep professional competencies sought by problem based learning and requisite for good teaching. In the process of continuing to inquire into and improve our assessment practices, our cohort enacts the kinds of knowledges, abilities, commitments, and self-reflexive development that we encourage in preservice teachers.

---

[23] This arms-length standard also helps to better ensure fairness across examinations by preventing the prior knowledge and close connections developed between the tutors and their tutees from unduly influencing the TJ assessment.

References

BC Ministry of Education. (1999, updated 2013). *English language learning : A guide for classroom teachers*. Special Programs Branch. Retrieved from http://www.bced.gov.bc.ca/ell//policy/classroom.pdf

BC Ministry of Education. (2009, updated 2013). *English language learning: Policy and guidelines* Special Programs Branch. Retrieved from http://www.bced.gov.bc.ca/ell//policy/guidelines.pdf

Biggs, J. (2007). *Teaching for quality learning at university* (3rd ed.). Buckingham: SRHE/Open University Press. Retrieved from http://docencia.etsit.urjc.es/moodle/pluginfile.php/18073/mod_resource/content/0/49657968-Teaching-for-Quality-Learning-at-University.pdf

MacDonald, R. (2005). Assessment strategies for enquiry and problem-based learning. In T. Barrett, I. Mac Labhrainn, H. Fallon (Eds.), *Handbook of enquiry & problem based learning*. Galway: CELT. Retrieved from http://www.nuigalway.ie/celt/pblbook/

Macdonald, R., & Savin-Baden, M. (2004). *A briefing on assessment in problem-based learning* (LTSN Generic Centre assessment series; 13). York: Learning and Teaching Support Network (LTSN).

McTiernan, K. et al. (2007). The 'triple jump' assessment in problem based learning: An evaluative method used in the appraisal of both knowledge acquisition and problem solving skills. (2007). In G. O'Neill, S. Huntley-Moore, & P. Race (Eds.), *Case studies of good practice assessment of student learning in higher education (*pp. 116–119). Dublin: AISHE. Retrieved from http://www.aishe.org/readings/2007-1/

Part IV
Reflections

> Reflection involves not simply a sequence of ideas, but a consequence – a consecutive ordering in such a way that each determines the next as its proper outcome, while each in turn leans back on its predecessors. The successive portions of the reflective thought grow out of one another and support one another; they do not come and go in a medley. Each phase is a step from something to something – technically speaking, it is a term of thought. Each term leaves a deposit which is utilized in the next term. The stream or flow becomes a train, chain, or thread.
>
> ~John Dewey, 1993

Problem based learning involves taking into account dispositions for inquiry, asking questions, finding out, and engaging in ongoing reflection. Educating teachers is not the work of technocrats, and knowledge about teacher education is not something deliverable in propositional form. Rather it is relational, immersed in the world, and constantly changing according to current school contexts. PBL's emphasis upon habits of mind and critical stances are applicable to teacher educators as they are to preservice teachers. By engaging in writing and ongoing reflection, multiple and varied perspectives of PBL team members over a period of 15 years demonstrate our "lived PBL curricula" and commitment to professional learning. Our goals are to enact professional judgments of greatest benefit for preservice teachers' learning while offering insights of potential benefit for other teacher educators.

In this part, we pose difficult questions and introduce difficult knowledge about PBL, not only to pique our own desire to learn more but to draw upon the curiosity and creativity of other teacher educators. We have chosen to consider the continuing challenges and resistance to problem based learning in teacher education as a "problematized case" and use the inquiry cycle to share and annotate relevant research literature, identify primary issues and questions, and conclude with three individual syntheses. Regrettably, the unique voices, rich dialogues, and compelling conversations of our team about the case are missing. However, each reader is invited to

---

Dewy, J. (1933). How we think. (EBook #37423) Accessed at: http://www.gutenberg.org/files/37423/37423-h/37423-h.htm

engage with the case and become part of the dialogue. In the end, it is our thinking about why "problem based learning" is a significant pedagogy in teacher education that is of consequence. We want to continually examine how a PBL cohort may help fulfill the promise of more meaningful teacher learning and result in educating more effective teachers.

Chapter 14
Continuing Challenges and Resistance

Margot Filipenko, Jo-Anne Naslund, and Lori Prodan

Introduction

In this chapter, the continuing challenges and resistance to problem based learning (PBL) and TELL are problematized in a case called "continuing challenges." This case, of all our cases, is probably the most important. Through an examination of the case issues, the reader is invited to engage in critical reflection about the TELL through PBL cohort. It would be ideal if a Socratic dialogue could take place between all of our key stakeholders – preservice teachers, tutors, faculty, school advisors, librarians, practicum placement officers, and director of teacher education. However, as we plan for the coming year this case and its issues will provide a starting point for our critical dialogue and advocacy.

We have tackled this case in the time-honored way of problem based learning. That is, we have followed as far as possible the problem based learning inquiry cycle: we first identified the primary issues in our case, created a list of resources in the form of a bibliography[1] which can be found at the end of this chapter, and finished by offering three syntheses, each of which offers the perspective of a PBL member (student, coordinator, and tutor). These syntheses serve a two-fold purpose. They are meant to illustrate the variety of ways preservice teachers' understandings

---

[1] The bibliography comes at the end of the chapter and was developed by the contributors to this text.

M. Filipenko (✉)
Department of Language and Literacy Education, University of British Columbia,
Vancouver, BC, Canada
e-mail: margot.filipenko@ubc.ca

J. Naslund
Education Library, University of British Columbia, Vancouver, BC, Canada
e-mail: joanne.naslund@ubc.ca

L. Prodan
Vancouver School District 39, Vancouver, BC, Canada

and syntheses of a case may be represented; and for us they synthesize and explicate the upcoming issues and challenges that face our TELL through PBL cohort in our teacher education program. It is our hope that when you, the reader, connect with an issue embedded in this case, it may be possible for you to contextualize it to your institution, program, students, and community.

Case 13: Continuing Challenges

You have been working with PBL cohorts for over a decade, and it has now been 2 years since the cohort was linked with the teaching English language learners cohort. This has been a period of transition. All the cases and case cycle procedures were reexamined to ensure there is a consistent, meaningful engagement with the concerns of English as an additional language (EAL) education.

The merging of the two cohorts has been reinvigorating in some ways and challenging in others. You have found that attitudes about EAL as not being the work of regular teachers persist, among both preservice teachers and some instructors. The continual work of making language visible often seems to compete with the desire for a more content-based focus. And, as the team has discovered, as "elastic" and adaptable as the case method is, there is a limit to how many issues preservice teachers can meaningfully take up within each 2-week cycle.

Since many preservice teachers enter the program with "commonsense" ideas about language learning, your continual questioning of their assumptions is necessary. Sometimes you question your effectiveness, especially since for many preservice teachers, the belief in monolingualism within the school system, for example, stubbornly persists. Just the other day in tutorial, a preservice teacher said she didn't want students writing in other languages because she wouldn't be able to evaluate their work.

In terms of the PBL program itself, many of the institutional challenges remain – not the least of which is operating on a 2-week schedule when the rest of the faculty operates on a 1-week schedule. In a program that employs a range of people as instructors – PhD candidates, seconded teachers, sessional instructors, tenured faculty members – the turnover rate for subject area resource specialists and tutors can be frustrating. For a person new to PBL, often not of their own choosing, the method can be daunting, and it definitely requires pedagogical "buy-in."

This year in particular, you've really been heartened by the work the preservice teachers have been producing, by the insightful questions they have been raising, and by the high level of respectful debate occurring in the tutorials. But this wonderful culture of inquiry seems misunderstood by many of your colleagues. Questions persist – how are the preservice teachers being

(continued)

assessed? How do you know they have met the requirements of each course syllabus? Where is the rigor? Frustrating as these questions are, you know that you need to find new ways to articulate and celebrate the value of the PBL approach with the wider institution.

Your belief in the value of PBL as more than a pedagogical approach has been reinforced year after year as you see preservice teachers leave the program with true dispositions toward inquiry and agency as emerging professionals. You continue to draw your inspiration from them.

Primary Issues and Questions within "Case 13: Continuing Challenges"

After examining the case, several primary issues and questions were identified that could be clustered around four major themes. The first theme included content issues concerning curricular content, subject-specific knowledge, and the need for preservice teachers to be well versed in language, literacy, and pedagogy. The second theme focused on problem based learning issues about the very nature of problem based learning itself, key characteristics of this pedagogy, and essentials for implementation. The third theme considered institutional issues, those matters that revolved around institutional realities of implementing a PBL program – number of instructors, timetabling, etc. The fourth theme related to school and university partnership issues such as clear communication, use of meaningful terminology, and shared goals and vision for a successful practica. The primary issues and questions are summarized below:

1. *Content issues*

    - Developing robust cases that reflect core content and processes

        – Can enough background knowledge be learned through investigating issues in a single case?
        – Will preservice teachers find "wrong information" that could distort their understandings?
        – Do tutors have enough specialized knowledge for each case to contribute to building background knowledge of the preservice teachers?

    PBL preservice teacher's comment:

    Our cases were good in the fact that they did present issues that were famous like bullying cases so they addressed the whole spectrum of issues from bullying to racism to homophobia. I think probably it was the curriculum courses that could – the teachers tried to cross over what they were teaching with the case but it just – what they were teaching really didn't seem relevant or useful. So I think I would really make sure there is better communication between the tutorial groups and the subject teachers.

PBL preservice teacher's comment:

I think the whole case study process identify the issues, create a bibliography, present and synthesize – that whole case cycle is very good in the beginning but I don't know if it needs to be done for all ten cases. I think it needs to be adapted as we mature and get more adept at it. By the sixth case it became less about inquiry … it became a pattern. I think role plays and all that sort of thing and or creating tangible products for our practicum is better. (2012)

- Understanding the language and literacy needs in multilingual/multicultural classrooms
    - What is the knowledge base needed for teachers working in complex multilingual/multicultural classrooms?
    - What do preservice teachers need to know about L1 and L2 learning that they cannot find out through interrogating cases?
    - What has been shown to be effective language and literacy teaching practice in multilingual/multicultural classrooms?
- Background knowledge of language and language acquisition
    - Is there a need for front-loading of knowledge regarding language and language acquisition before preservice teachers can engage with PBL cases?
    - Should a textbook be a required research resource?

PBL preservice teacher's comment:

I think in the beginning it [instruction] could be a little bit more concrete. I know there was a lot of questions about what are were doing. Begin to pull back as students get familiar with content and PBL. Certainly just being slightly more explicit at the beginning gradually allowing [pre- service teachers] more freedom to do the work…. (2012)

2. *Problem based learning (PBL) issues*

    - Problem based learning and its pedagogical principles
        - What are the principles that underlie PBL?

PBL preservice teacher's comment:

… The PBL cohort is a bit confusing to people they can't really understand what it is about even some of us don't understand. (Preservice teacher 2012)

    - Is there only one approach to PBL?
    - Is a PBL approach suitable for all preservice teachers?

PBL subject area resource specialist's comment/question:

Is PBL for the quiet educator? What about students who do not gravitate to oral communication as their first choice? (2012)

    - Resistance to PBL
        - What are the most common misconceptions about PBL?
        - How can we help new faculty learn about PBL?

3. *Institutional issues*

    - How do you move forward and go beyond implementation especially after a PBL program has existed for many years?
    - In what ways does a PBL approach disrupt instructional efficiency in a predominantly traditional teacher education program?
    - How can organizational change be facilitated?
    - In what ways does the notion of institutional/administration ownership impact the future longevity of the PBL cohort?
    - How can there be flexibility in a PBL program, and have it still remain true to the principles of PBL and not experience curricular drift? Who ensures the integrity and content of the program?
    - Is a PBL program cost-effective?

4. *School and university partnership issues*

    - Shared understanding of the PBL program by school advisors, principals, specialist teachers, and school district administrators
        - Do school advisors understand how the PBL program works?
        - Will school principals recognize that preservice teachers in the PBL program will not be taking specific courses?
    - The impact of a PBL model of teacher education on professional practice
        - What do the schools need to know about the affordances of PBL as an approach to teaching and learning in the K-12 classroom?

    PBL preservice teacher's comments:

    …But some of them [school advisors] I think weren't really sure how to take [problem based learning] into the classroom or even if that was what they were supposed to do. (2012)

    PBL preservice teacher's comments:

    I was lucky in Richmond [Richmond School District] in our school particularly they do believe in inquiry learning and teaching so my school advisor was really good with showing me techniques to start open ended questioning to put the onus back on the student for them to get that intrinsic motivation to want to find out more. (2012)

    - Does PBL make any difference in the practicum experiences that the preservice teachers have?
        - Are they better able to teach or less able?
        - Are they better at job interviews and at taking on unusual teaching assignments?

Annotated Bibliography and Syntheses for Case 13

Within the problem-based inquiry cycle, the first stage is to create an annotated bibliography of the research literature that was consulted, and then it is shared with the tutorial group. For Case 13, our annotated bibliography can be found at the end of this chapter. When this bibliography is shared online, any omissions are duly noted, and a discussion occurs about the literature that was found. Many of these resources are used to create information packages for the primary issues in the case. For purposes of brevity, we have not included the information packages or presentations that are typical of the inquiry cycle.

The final stage of the inquiry cycle is that of creating an individual synthesis in response to the case. Three individual syntheses were prepared for Case 13. The first synthesis by a preservice teacher is written in the form of a news release entitled *Growing BC's Future Teachers – Case by Case*. The second synthesis is by the PBL Program Coordinator in the form of a journal entry. The third synthesis is that of a tutor in the PBL program and is written as a guide for tutors.

Synthesis 1: News Release

As a preservice teacher in the program I have chosen to write my synthesis as a news release.
Vancouver, British Columbia

Growing BC's Future Teachers – Case by Case

Overlooked and Underserved English Language Learners in BC Classrooms
Real-life classrooms or at least scenarios from them are being used to prepare teachers at the University of British Columbia. The success of "teaching English language learners through problem based learning" according to Filipenko, Talmy, and Early, professors in the Faculty of Education, hinges on addressing some current realities of BC classrooms.

According to the BC Ministry of Education, some 25 % of BC K-12 students speak a language other than English at home. In Vancouver, that number is greater than 50 % and includes some 150 different languages. Talmy and Early want all youngsters in our city's public schools to experience success. For that to happen, they are adamant, "Classroom teachers really need to understand second language learners and become culturally responsive." For them problem based learning offers all sorts of possibilities to do this well.

Problem based learning isn't new. It has been used in fields such as medicine, nursing, dentistry, and engineering. Filipenko reports that at UBC,

(continued)

problem based learning in teacher education has been around since 1998. What has changed is that two cohorts, problem based learning is now linked with teaching English language learners. The merger, a one of a kind in Canada, makes certain that issues of English language learners will not only be added to the mix but will be central so that new teachers are equipped to meet the needs of many kids in BC classrooms.

In this program, no formal courses are taught. No course outlines or course texts are required. "Often, this comes as a bit of shock for new instructors in the program," says Filipenko. "However, once new instructors and students get used to it, they love the fact that they learn on their own and find out for themselves. It means they use the UBC library and web resources a lot."

In reality, the student teachers are not left totally to learn on their own. I saw them in their tutorial groups where they met with experienced teachers, their tutors. They examine cases and are guided through their discussions. They learn from one another and also from "resource specialists" – faculty experts in different teaching areas such as special education, mathematics, science, literacy, and social justice. One day a week, they visit their practice teaching schools in Vancouver and Richmond. What they learn is researched, talked about, shared, and sometimes debated. In the end, it comes back to "what do I do in the classroom?"

One tutor I spoke with who was a very experienced teacher and former school principal from North Vancouver was happy with the program. For him, they begin with a case that focuses on teaching practice and what are the issues teachers are struggling with. The inquiry seeks out the best ideas and concludes with what am I going to do?

The ultimate litmus test comes for these student teachers during their 3-month practice teaching and eventually will be played out on the job. The time is right to ask, "What kind of change is occurring in BC teacher education to ensure that all children succeed at school?"

It's time to move away from traditional ways of preparing teachers. Problem based learning has been shown to be effective in the field of education. And, if Ipsos pollsters Darryl Bricker and John Wright* are correct, then added to the 6 million people who have come to Canada from another place already and given that immigrants to this country are needed on a continuing basis, our schools will only grow in linguistic diversity.

What Lies Ahead?

To find out, we asked six of our preservice teachers from different backgrounds to give us their take on PBL and teaching English language learners.

One young woman commented if you are a good student you sort of get shaken up. The process of continuously learning and having to synthesize means there is no way to cram. It's a completely different way of learning and obviously more effective.

Another stated that she liked reflecting on the approaches she used with her students and thinking about how she could do better. When she reviewed what had gone well and what flopped, it made for her best learning. She valued those times when her sponsor teacher didn't just leave her to flounder, but she loved being left to roll with it as well.

One male described problem based learning as a little bit mysterious like a big powerful energy. A lot of teachers who are not very independent or don't have some experience with it, he thought, would find it difficult.

Another commented about teachers often complaining about being alone. For her, what actually ended up happening is that she collaborated with the librarian, another teacher in her school, and with her sponsor teacher. "I started to branch out, and I don't think I would have done it if I had not been encouraged to collaborate so much with my peers in problem based learning."

As others looked ahead to teaching careers, they mentioned that successful educators have to always expand their knowledge. To achieve the BC Teacher Regulation Branch standard of engaging in career-long learning, you can't think you know everything – that's being closed-minded. There is really no substitute for a real-life case study where your students literally need something and you need to be able to fulfill it.

Quite possibly, UBC's teacher education program is a change in the right direction.[2]

Synthesis 2: Coordinator's Journal

As the Coorindator of the program, I have chosen to write my synthesis as a diary entry.
I keep a diary because it keeps my mind fresh and open. Once the details of being me are safely stored away every night, I can get on with what isn't just me…
~Gail Godwin[3]

I'm exhausted! Yet as the academic year draws to an end, I know that we have made progress in building a problem based learning community and revisioning our cases to not only reflect the complexity of our public school classrooms but also to engage our preservice teachers in issues that will face them in their teaching practice. Much of this was accomplished through strengthening the strands woven through our cases. I'm particularly proud of the way in which our cases have provided an educational space for discussion and reflection regarding the possibilities for non-indigenous peoples to transformatively learn from indigenous knowledges, perspectives, and pedagogies in a mainstream educational space through problem based learning. The social and ecological justice strand also continues to be an area of strength, and I have been blown away by the subject area resource specialists who this

(continued)

---

[2] Jutras, L. (2014, Jan 04). And now a word from Canada's future. *The Globe and Mail*

[3] From Gail Godwin (1991). A Diarist on Diarists. *Writers on Writing*, edited by Rober Pack and Joy Parini. University Proess of New England. Accessed at: http://grammar.about.com/od/advicefromthepros/a/Twelve-Reasons-To-Keep-A-Writers-Diary.htm

year seemed to have taken to the PBL model like ducks to water. Specifically, these subject area specialists have indicated how much they enjoy the interdisciplinary/integrated approach of our cohort. Several resource specialists got together to give integrated, hands-on workshops, and the physical education resource specialist integrated PE with both social justice issues (gender and bullying) and educational psychology (motivation). I am particularly heartened by feedback from all the resource specialists who have indicated they would like to return to teach with PBL next year.

Yet, while I take much satisfaction from the progress we have made this year, there is still much to be accomplished. Particularly worrying is how we can strengthen the TELL focus of our cohort. All students including ELL students are expected to meet the learning objectives of the BC curriculum. Yet, many teachers still lack key knowledge regarding language acquisition and teaching ELLs. There is so much to understand about the students we refer to as ELL. These students come to our classrooms with a wide range of language/literacy profiles (e.g., "ELL" is not one thing, it is a profile):

- Interrupted formal schooling
- Lack of L1 literacy
- Generation 1.5/Canadian-born ELLs[4]
- Refugees
- Survivors of trauma/war
- Poverty

There is obviously a need for us, as a cohort, to have a more explicit focus on the complex issues related to ELL academic success. To that end, I'm considering a weeklong TELL orientation for the PBL preservice teachers to introduce/front-load language content. I hope this might give the preservice teachers some background knowledge that they can bring to their research into case issues related to language and teaching ELLs.

Given the importance of meeting the needs of ELLs in our community, possibly against my better judgment, I'm also thinking about having Dr. Talmy and Dr. Early identify a textbook on language as a resource for the preservice teachers. I predict that since we have always been firm that preservice teachers identify their own resources rather than rely on course textbooks, this will be a very thorny issue particularly with the tutors and some of our long-term resource instructors … thin edge of the wedge!

With a declining number of students applying to the teacher education program, there have been and continue to be cuts in the cohorts offered to those applying to our B.Ed. program. The threat to the TELL through PBL cohort is

---

[4] The term *Generation 1.5* refers to immigrants who arrive in the new country in their teens and bring with them language and culture from the home country but continue with assimilation in the new country. Thus, they are referred to as halfway between the first generation and second generation of immigrant communities.

(continued)

real. This makes me very anxious. We know that in the twenty-first century the emphasis should be on knowing how to find and evaluate pertinent information in collaboration with others in order to construct and communicate new understanding. The BC Ministry of Education writes in its BC Education Plan:

...for the future there will be more emphasis on key competencies like self-reliance, critical thinking, inquiry, creativity, problem solving, innovation, teamwork and collaboration, cross-cultural understanding, and technological literacy.[5]

This could be a description of problem based learning, yet I continue to struggle to convince administration of the relevance and robustness of PBL as a vehicle for twenty-first-century learning.

While we have a long way to go before a PBL model of teaching and learning is taken up in the school districts where our preservice teachers complete their practica, increasingly these schools are implementing an inquiry approach to learning. I was cheered by a preservice teacher who reported:

> I was lucky in Richmond [Richmond School District] in our school particularly they do believe in inquiry learning and teaching so my school advisor was really good with showing me techniques to start open ended questioning to put the onus back on the student for them to get that intrinsic motivation to want to find out more. (2012)

So, dear diary, next year I have my work cut out for me:

- To strengthen, support, and build the ELL focus of our cohort
- To work toward administrative buy-in and understanding of and a sense of ownership of our cohort
- To build stronger bonds with the schools in which our preservice teachers complete their practica

While I find the above overwhelming, I take solace in the knowledge that I work with an extraordinary group of committed individuals who always give of their best. Our preservice teachers are among the best I have ever worked with – they embody the principles of PBL: they are curious and self-reliant yet collaborative; they challenge yet have the capacity to understand multiple perspectives; they are critical thinkers able to make sense of complicated real-world classroom contexts; and finally, PBL preservice teachers are motivated active learners able to discern their learning needs.

---

[5] Accessed at http://www.bcedplan.ca/assets/pdf/bc_edu_plan.pdf

Synthesis 3: TELL Through PBL Tutor Guide

**As a tutor my synthesis for the case "continuing challenges," I've chosen to write the introduction to an imaginary tutor guide for our PBL program.*

Welcome to our team! In this package you will find a brief introduction to the philosophy of problem based learning as well as important principles about the teaching of English language learners. In addition, there is a "Frequently Asked Questions" section based on questions posed by previous tutors. Finally, there is a glossary at the end of the guide where we have tried to explain the terms that may be exclusive to our cohort or used differently by us (e.g., triple jump, synthesis). Please note, like most things in our TELL through PBL program, this document is meant to be continually adapted to the changing needs of our teacher candidates and our instructor team. We hope that this guide is a helpful resource for your upcoming work as a tutor.

Problem Based Learning

PLB can be practiced in a variety of ways. In our program, we have developed the following core practices:

- Small group learning creates an environment of trust.
- Preservice teachers work with different partners over the course of the case cycles, cultivating a sense of interdependence and professional collegiality.
- Preservice teachers teach each other throughout the year, providing ongoing practice in presentation skills and learning through teaching.
- Assessment is continuous and based on multimodal expressions of understanding. It is a responsibility that is shared among the instructor team.
- All learning is based on inquiry – with tutors' guidance, preservice teachers pose and refine the questions – putting the preservice teachers' evolving needs at the center of the learning.
- Tutors are also faculty advisors, allowing for a continual integration of the weekly practicum experience with "on-campus" work.
- For all areas of inquiry, preservice teachers are asked to specifically consider issues of language and the needs of English language learners.

(continued)

Teaching English Language Learners

Teaching English language learners is a constant thread throughout the 11 cases. The following are some of the core principles about English language learning that are held by our team:

- Linguistic and cultural diversity is a resource within classrooms and school communities and should be explicitly treated as such.
- Teachers need to plan and implement ways to make language visible in all content areas.
- Teachers need to understand the significant individual differences within the category of "English language learner."
- Identity and language are interwoven.
- First languages play a vital role in additional language learning.

Frequently Asked Questions

Can tutors answer preservice teachers' questions?

There is no one way to answer this question. The tutor calls upon his/her educational experience and judgment. Within PBL, there is room for a tutor to direct discussion, pose questions, and provide "quick" answers to prevent misunderstandings. It may also be advisable to provide the group with some specific terms that may be helpful during their research about a particular topic. However, the focus of the tutorials remains on the preservice teachers' inquiries, ideas, and overall agency.

Why are there no textbooks?

Knowledge and understanding is not presented as static or bound. Preservice teachers, through their inquiries, create and recreate their own knowledge and understanding. They are required to seek out answers from a variety of voices, including academic research, government documents, and publications by practicing teachers.

With so much emphasis on learning through discussion, what about quiet students?

Students who tend to be quiet in groups in fact may benefit greatly from the small group work and supportive environment of PBL tutorials. In addition, through biweekly presentations, quiet students gain valuable public speaking practice, which is of great benefit during their practicum. Tutors may choose

(continued)

to open tutorials with a round table or talking circle format where everyone is given a choice to speak and the responsibility to listen.

Are there any drawbacks to PBL?

No single pedagogy is perfect or perfectly suited for all learners. We believe that with its emphasis on learner agency, inquiry, and integrating content and process, PBL is suited for helping develop beginning teachers with dispositions toward inquiry, lifelong learning, and openness toward multiple perspectives.

Why the consistent emphasis on English language learners?

In British Columbia, a significant number of the students in any given classroom are English language learners (20 % in Kindergarten through Grade 4). This number is expected to rise. These learners are given additional support for only a maximum of 5 years. The extent of this support may vary, but it is very rarely "full time." Thus, classroom teachers are professionally responsible for the vast majority of these students' learning needs. As a profession, elementary teaching requires an explicit focus on the complex issues related to English language learning and on the diversity of these learners. Language is the means through which all content knowledge is constructed and shared. It is at the center of education.

How do you know that all preservice teachers have covered all the material for all of the courses in the B.Ed. program?

Our use of continuous assessment (criterion-referenced feedback for two individual assignments and two partner assignments every 2 weeks) and end-of-term oral exams provides both formative and summative assessments. The 11 cases have been planned out to include the key outcomes from all the relevant syllabi. All instructors are invited to provide input into the cases, which are revised each year in response to student need.

Tutor Mentorship

Becoming a TELL through PBL tutor can be a steep learning curve, requiring flexibility and curiosity. As we have all been "the novice" at one point, we know how necessary mentorship is for this role. Your fellow tutors will be interested in answering your questions and providing any guidance they can throughout this year. Being a tutor is an intense and exhilarating role. Enjoy your first year!

Conclusions

New teachers graduating from teacher education programs will "juggle many goals as they coordinate pedagogical actions with various kinds of knowledge, such as subject matter knowledge, pedagogical content knowledge, and knowledge of individual students. "For experts, teaching is a problem solving context … " (Hmelo-Silver and Barrows 2006, p. 21). A recent activity required of preservice teachers in our PBL teacher education program was to describe their school-based practicum classrooms. Their descriptions illustrate complex and diverse classroom contexts and point to the need for teachers to be problem solvers. The three descriptions below are typical of those classrooms detailed by many of our preservice teachers:

1. For my practicum placement, I am in a Grade 2 classroom. Even though it is a straight Grade 2 class, there are a wide range of abilities and talents. There are eight students that receive pullout support. The support includes aboriginal education, English language learning, numeracy, reading, and writing. This particular school district is fairly homogenous, but there are a high percentage of low-income families and single-parent families. In my placement, there is no in-class support, so it is important to have adaptations in each lesson. There is a table at the back of the room that is always available for students that would like some extra support. Because I have a lot of students who struggle with reading and writing, I try to plan as many collaborative and experiential activities as possible. I also try to incorporate different modalities into each lesson to play on each student's strengths.
2. My class is composed of 9 girls and 12 boys, many of whom live with their extended family. There is a high level of English language learners (ELL) within the group, with over 80 % of the students speaking a language other than English at home. Three students visit a language support teacher (LST) on a regular basis in order to augment their conceptual underpinnings of the English language. As such, the unit has been adapted to address ELL needs throughout its entirety. In particular, I will provide language support and graphic organizers to accompany informational texts in order to scaffold students' understanding of Canadian animals.
3. The class also contains one student who is on an Individual Education Plan (IEP). Another with attention-deficit/hyperactivity disorder (ADHD) diagnosis, this student often requires additional prompts regarding appropriate behavior during lessons. In response to his condition, I will ensure each lesson is organized in smaller chunks of time with scheduled "brain breaks" to maintain his attention. This adaptation also benefits other high-energy students in the class.

Diverse classrooms like those described by our preservice teachers require them to be *constructive solution seekers* (Savery 2006, p. 18). From our perspective, problem based learning, which takes a learner-centered instructional approach that supports "higher level thinking skills, self-regulated learning habits, and problem-solving skills" (p. 18), is the ideal model for educating preservice teachers to become *constructive solution seekers*. Yet, if our cohort is to remain viable and robust, we must tackle some real challenges including:

- Within a PBL model, how can we ensure preservice teachers develop a deep understanding of language acquisition and effective teaching strategies with ELLs?
- Those of us who work in the TELL through PBL cohort in teacher education recognize the challenges that the program raises for our administration: How can we work more closely with our administration to foster collegiality and commitment to a model that is not easily administered?
- How can we strengthen bonds with the school districts where our preservice teachers are engaged in their practica?

In conclusion, as a group of faculty, seconded teachers, resource specialists, and librarians knowledgeable about and dedicated to the PBL model, we will continue to problem-solve the issues that face us as a cohort in a teacher education program. We believe that the strength of our PBL cohort is its flexibility and its ability to adapt to the changing needs of our disciplines and the realities of current school contexts.

Annotated Bibliography

Content Knowledge Issues

Clouston, T. J., Westcott, L., Whitcombe, S. W., Riley, J., & Matheson, R. *Developing problem-based learning curricula* (pp. 35–50). Oxford: Wiley-Blackwell. Available at: http://dx.doi.org/10.1002/9781444320541.ch4
  A focused discussion about curriculum design and PBL cases. Important considerations include subject matter; practice of educators; teacher regulation standards and so on. Scaffolding content in a manner that provokes deep thinking is essential.
Cummins, J. (2007). Rethinking monolingual instructional strategies in multilingual classrooms. *Canadian Journal of Applied Linguistics, 10*, 221–240.
  Current research/theory, support the interdependence of literacy-related skills and knowledge across languages. Thus, teachers should reinforce effective learning strategies in a coordinated way across languages rather than following those assumptions that tend to dominate best practices in most second/foreign language classrooms.
Gibbons, P. (2002). *Scaffolding language, scaffolding learning: Teaching second language learners in the mainstream classroom*. Portsmouth: Heinemann.
  English as Second language (ESL) students can no longer be thought of as a group apart from the mainstream – they are the mainstream. This book describes the ways to ensure that ESL learners become full members of the school community with the language and content skills they need for success. (http://www.heinemann.com/products/E00366.aspx)
Harper, C., & de Jong, E. (2004). Misconceptions about teaching English-language learners. *Journal of Adolescent & Adult Literacy, 48*, 152–162.
  Four popular misconceptions regarding the teaching of English Language learners (ELL) outlined are: exposure and interaction will result in English language learning; All ELL's learn

English in the same way and at the same rate; good teaching for native speakers is good teaching for ELL's; effective instruction means nonverbal support. There is a need for explicit instruction that focuses on the genres, functions, and conventions of the language. Teachers must learn to look at language used in the classroom in order to understand the linguistic demands of their content areas and carefully structure learning tasks according to ELLs' needs.

Hung, W. (2011). Theory to reality: A few issues in implementing problem-based learning. *Educational Technology Research and Development, 59*(4), 529–552. Available at: http://dx.doi.org/10.1007/s11423-011-9198-1

A compelling discussion about the design of cases and includes some revealing statistics that demonstrate why problem based learning is successful in the field of education. They also demonstrate why it is so hard to who that cases uncover what could be considered traditional course content.

Problem Based Learning

Boud, D., & Feletti, G. (1997). *The challenge of problem based learning* (2nd ed.). London: Kogan Page.

This is a major work on PBL. It identifies resistances to PBL that often arise irrationally as reactions to evangelistic presentations associated with claims of PBL's benefits or by means of insufficient concern with staff induction and development. PBL is mistakenly considered an approach to curriculum design with the teaching of the problem solving. PBL disrupts the habitual and comfortable patterns of work and PBL outcomes are criticized for not being tangible. PBL does attempt to "develop highly competent practitioners who will continue to learn effectively throughout their lives." (p. 6)

Hung, W. (2011b). Theory to reality: A few issues in implementing problem-based learning. *Educational Technology Research and Development, 59*(4), 529–552. Available at: http://dx.doi.org/10.1007/s11423-011-9198-1

This is a review of PBL literature; what it takes to implement a PBL approach, its effectiveness and issues faced by institutions. Variable degrees of self-directedness and problem structuredness are factors and may vary by discipline and according to the cognitive readiness and self-directed learning skills of the students. Six representative models of PBL are described: pure PBL, Hybrid PBL, anchored instruction; project based learning; case based learning; and instruction with problem solving activities.

Johnassen, D. H., & Hung, W. (2008). All problems are not equal: Implications for problem-based learning. *Interdisciplinary Journal of Problem-Based Learning, 2*(2), 6–28. Available at: http://dx.doi.org/10.7771/1541-5015.1080.

McPhee, A. D. (2002). Problem-based learning in initial teacher education: Taking the agenda forward. *Journal of Educational Enquiry, 3*(1), 60–78.

Institutional Issues

Barrett, T. (2005). Understanding problem-based learning. (2005). In T. Barrett, I. Mac Labhrainn, & H. Fallon (Eds.), *Handbook of enquiry & problem based learning* (pp. 13–25). Galway: CELT. Available at: http://www.nuigalway.ie/celt/pblbook/

Dykes, F., Gilliam, B., Neel, J., & Everling, K. (2012). Peeking Inside Pandora's Box: One University's Journey into the Redesign of Teacher Educator Preparation. *Current Issues in Education, 15*(2), 1–8.

Teacher education reform at the University of Texas at Tyler integrated three instruction divisions (regular, special education and ESL) in order to dispel the idea that educators could excuse themselves from teaching all students. The restructuring was aided by key personnel, open communication, gradual phase in and feedback by student/faculty advisory groups throughout the process.

Savin Baden, M., & Howell, C. (2004). *Foundations of problem based learning.* Blacklick: McGraw-Hill.

An excellent read for faculty/tutors involved in PBL as it considers the nature of institutional cultures and resistance to change. A move to PBL involves complex disciplinarity shifts and although higher education institutions embrace PBL, it enhances "employability and graduateness" and suggest it as a change from a traditional instructional paradigm to a learning paradigm, critical administrative oversight shows a lack of understanding, leads to curricula drift and "facilitator burnout". PBL therefore remains challenging and misunderstood.

Yin, H. S. *Problem-based learning: An institutional perspective.* Available at: www.tp.edu.sg/files/centres/pbl/pbl_hee_soo_yin.pdf

While PBL is reported to have positive effects on student learning, many institutions remain hesitant about implementing a PBL approach. Impediments to change, are not educational but organizational. It is easier to continue with the status quo than to learn something new. Yin outlines strategies for developing understanding of PBL through capacity building and *buy-in*.

School University Partnership Issues

Barron, L., Clarksville, T., & Wells, L. (2013). Transitioning to the real world through problem-based learning: A collaborative approach to teacher preparation. *Learning in Higher Education, 9,* 13–18.

Research indicates that students in teacher education either did as well as or better than their lecture based counterparts. They tended do better when using a PBL approach in subject matter that was outside of medical education.

Delisle, R. (1997). *How to use problem-based learning in the classroom.* Alexandria: Association for Supervision & Curriculum Development (ASCD).

This is a practical guide for teachers about how to use problem-based learning in the classroom. PBL can replace passive listening and rote memorizing with active investigation, participation, and problem solving. It is a practical book that includes methods on how to engage students in independent learning.

Macdonald, D., & Isaacs, G. (2001). Developing a professional identity through problem-based learning. *Teaching Education, 12*(3), 315–333.

Hung, W., & Holen, J. (2011). Problem-based learning: Preparing pre-service teachers for real-world classroom challenges. *ERS Spectrum, 29*(3), 29–48.

Findings of this study show that pre-service teachers' in a PBL program developed key abilities and dispositions vital to their success in teaching. Their perceptions of PBL were highly positive and they displayed resilient dispositions and problem solving skills when faced with authentic classroom situations and tasks.

Hattie, J. (2012). *Visible learning for teachers: Maximizing impact on learning.* New York: Routledge.

This book provides a very useful model for reflecting upon our PBL program. It is evident that our primary goal is to help our students become their own teachers.

Afterword

As Associate Dean of Teacher Education, I was invited to write this afterword most appropriately after the chapters were written and as part of the call for a Socratic dialogue between the Problem-Based Learning (PBL) cohort's key stakeholders, including faculty in the Teacher Education Office. It was a pleasure to read about PBL's history and follow the very honest accounting of successes and challenges recorded from many perspectives. I noted some inarguable benefits to the approach, a number of dichotomies – some real and some perhaps less distinct than described – and an interesting evolution in which I am now playing a role. In this brief epilogue, I shall not attempt to weave together the work of others into a succinct summary as this might disrupt the intentions of the book to celebrate the interplay of unique perspectives. Rather, I hope to highlight some of the strengths and tensions from the perspective of the 'established' UBC teacher education program as well as some important parallels between PBL and tenets of the larger program and, in so doing, uncover where current and future synergies may enhance a somewhat reimagined and evolving PBL cohort.

The current cohort, Teaching English Language Learners (TELL) through Problem-Based Learning, has overcome many of the initial challenges articulated in Chap. 4 and catalyzed a new era in PBL's history, mirroring to some extent a revised era in UBC's reimagined BEd program. TELL's tenets are predicated on viewing languages, cultures and content through a cross-curricular lens. This perspective, imbued through frontloading at the start of the academic year, allows preservice teachers to begin to understand their cohort's conceptual framework in a meaningful way, a process that can take more time in some of the other cohorts. Initiating the year with a week of orientation to TELL, led by Steven Talmy and Margaret Early, has made a difference in establishing a TELL identity as has their direct involvement with local school district English language learner education initiatives. Faculty involvement of this nature, it should be noted, was a key recommendation in the revised BEd program, implemented in 2012, and something we value greatly in the Teacher Education Office.

Strong district-university relationships, as those described in Chaps. 6 and 7, are important to all cohorts and have been in place since the early 1990s with a geographically based cohort in Surrey, followed by thematic cohorts, the first being the Community of Inquiry in Teacher Education (CITE) and then PBL. District and university funds were designated to nurture these partnerships and continue today with five cohorts and four districts. The TELL-PBL partnership has been well received in schools and with new developments underway working with district-based TELL educators, we hope to strengthen and expand these district links.

UBC's teacher education program has also undergone a recent renaissance. The 6-year process of reimagining the BEd program was undertaken by the Community to Reimagine Alternatives for Teacher Education (CREATE), led by Associate Dean Rita Irwin and in which both Margot Filipenko and I took an active part. It allowed for a new way forward, and there is no question that some of its key tenets were informed by PBL's approach to teacher education, most notably, helping new teachers develop a disposition for inquiry and collaboration essential in increasingly diverse classrooms as well as an ability to problematize. Some facets of the previous program, including organization by cohort, strong district partnerships and adjunct instructors who provide rich, current practitioner expertise, were woven together with an increased emphasis on inquiry, teacher research, collaboration and a dialogic approach to teaching and learning.

The established teacher education program has been characterized in a number of chapters as 'traditional', 'dissemination-oriented' and at times predicated on 'institutional efficiencies' in contrast to PBL's 'constructivist, real-world approach' intended to inculcate 'inquiry-oriented dispositions'. Even if one were to overlook for a moment the tenets of the revised BEd program and compare to earlier iterations of the programme, there is much evidence of innovative and constructivist approaches to educating new teachers in the Faculty of Education's history. In fact, the current teacher education program is based on the understanding that traditional conceptions of teaching and learning need to be more flexible since we must educate in and for a world that, as Arendt (cited in CREATE 2007) reminds us, is 'out of joint' (p. 1). Anne Phelan, a key CREATE collaborator, articulated the purpose of teacher education as needing to 'not only educate teacher candidates to what has been or is but to do so in such a way that preserves their capacity to act in ways that might renew the world and their profession' (cited in CREATE, p. 2).

Every course was reimagined with certain conceptual touchstones and curricular strands intended to be woven throughout:

- Rich and varied field experiences
- Systematic research and inquiry
- Dialogues in social and ecological justice in local and global contexts
- Problematics in curriculum, pedagogy and assessment
- Explorations in language and learning as social practice

With varying degrees of success, the program and those who work within it have done their best to realize CREATE's intentions. Through ongoing evaluation, consultation and monitoring by a working group, we endeavour to respond to stakeholders' experiences and refine and adapt wherever possible. It is a work in progress.

Some of the 'instructional challenges' involved in incorporating the PBL approach mentioned in Chap. 14 are very real, such as integrating a two-week case cycle within a 13-week semester in a system where there is enormous demand for classroom space, so that if a room (or gym space) is not used every week, other faculties claim it. Allocating what methodology instructors consider half the class contact time they have with other cohorts makes some wonder about the extent to which preservice teachers can learn what they need to know by interrogating cases: will preservice teachers acquire the same foundational knowledge or insights as those in other cohorts? The revised BEd program underscored this question when methodology courses shifted from three credits (normally 39 contact hours) to two credits (26 contact hours). What we have learned in this book is that, in fact, preservice teachers do *not* acquire the same knowledge and insights but, rather, follow a very different path with different outcomes. These are articulated eloquently by a number of authors who argue that the whole does not equal the sum of the parts.

My own experience with the PBL cohort started in 2001 with French workshops I was invited to deliver because there was no French methodology course for preservice teachers in the BEd program unless enrolled in the French Specialist cohort. A series of workshops was organized, and each cohort received one 3-hour session. These were offered quite out of context and, certainly for the PBL cohort, were not integrated into any of the cases. It was an in-service on how to engage one's students using even a small amount of French one might possess. It was an enjoyable few hours, but I doubt that preservice teachers felt any more prepared as a result. A decade later, when the new BEd program was implemented, along with a two-credit French methods course for all elementary and middle year preservice teachers, PBL's section was scheduled in the last summer session, well after the final practicum. Again, it was decontextualized from the cases and, it seemed, the program itself.

This year, a series of four workshops was organized to integrate teaching French as a second language (FSL) within Cases 7 to 9. I delivered one of the workshops and two French methodology instructor colleagues the other three. I uploaded a number of resources to the cohort's Connect site, provided input to three cases (adding links to FSL teaching and learning), attended one research package presentation that focused on FSL, provided written feedback for this and another package and participated in a triple jump session. As much as I appreciated the opportunity to infuse some French as well as FSL for ELL perspectives, I echo Steven Talmy's and Margaret Early's concerns in Chap. 4 about the need to frontload concepts and methodologies specific to this curriculum area because the preservice teachers are, as they describe, 'simply ill-equipped to undertake informed and critical inquiries into .... the demands of the language of schooling for ELLs ... [because] they must have a basic understanding of how language works in schools in order to *inquire* about it, to investigate it, and interrogate it on their own' (p. 61). I would like to move preservice teachers beyond a recounting of the issues related to teaching French as a generalist teacher in BC or a list of resources around which to develop lessons to a more nuanced view of the role other languages play in additional language learning, not to mention the sociopolitical aspects of learning both of Canada's official languages, especially for ELLs (Carr 2013; Mady 2012, 2013). I would also like them to understand that current methodologies have evolved beyond a focus on vocabulary and grammar to one based on literacy (Anderson et al. 2011) and continuum learning (Council of Europe 2011). My hope after this first year is that the spirit of collaboration described in the introduction to Part II and that we experienced in finding FSL connections will prevail in the ongoing integration of multilingual perspectives into the case-based inquiries.

What was evident from my involvement this year was the preservice teachers' very strong ownership of their work in the TELL-PBL cohort. They took charge of the cases' messy, multiple perspectives of real-life classrooms, unpacked them and grappled with a wide range of integrated problems. Preservice teachers took a stand on particular educational issues and defended their positions by referencing research they had undertaken just as they will ultimately do as educators with their colleagues, students' parents, administrators and others. As Halbert and Kaser (2013) point out in *Spirals of Inquiry*, a resource used to support teacher (and preservice teacher) inquiry in the teacher education program, 'These are critically important and confusing times for K-12 educators in Canada and across the world'; the authors endorse transformative approaches to learning, which they term as 'wise, strong and new ways' (p. 12).

As an administrator who oversees all cohorts in UBC's teacher education program, it is my responsibility to see that they flourish and respond to the needs of preservice teachers as well as to the field, that the instructor teams work well together and that each of the cohorts evolves over time. There are many forces at work in a teacher education program: competing interests, time and space constraints, workload and budgetary limitations and so on. There have been some instances in PBL's recent history where instructors have challenged the approach and preservice teachers have questioned it (as mentioned in several chapters), but there has also been a willingness on the part of the cohort's key faculty members to acknowledge some of the institutional pressures and to work with administration to ensure sustainability. To this end, a very recent evolution has taken place that now highlights cross-curricular case-based inquiry, and this resonates very well with where the field is moving.

British Columbia's curriculum renewal process, *BC's Education Plan: Focus on Learning* (BC Ministry of Education, 2015), with an emphasis on core competencies that cross curricular boundaries, provides a natural invitation for TELL-PBL to bring to the fore its cross-curricular inquiry approach to case-based learning. I enthusiastically encourage this next phase of the cohort's evolution because the degree of resonance with developments in the field seems not only appropriate but also sustainable over time. As Margot Filipenko et al. notes, "the strength of our PBL cohort is its flexibility and its ability to adapt to the changing needs of our discipline" (p. 245). One of the key recommendations of the *BC Education Plan* is the need to view curriculum, pedagogy and assessment from interdisciplinary perspectives, which is a hallmark of the case-based inquiry approach described throughout this book. PBL incorporates important pedagogical approaches that have inspired and are compatible with advances made in the revised BEd program to develop dispositions in preservice teachers that equip them to be the kind of professionals and make the kind of judgements necessary for a complex and rapidly changing future.

References

Anderson, B., Carr, W., Lewis, C., Salvatori, M., & Turnbull, M. (2008). *Effective literacy practices in FSL: Making connections*. Toronto: Pearson Education.

BC Ministry of Education. (2015). *BC's education plan: Focus on learning*. Accessed from http://www.bcedplan.ca/assets/pdf/bcs_education_plan_2015.pdf

Carr, W. (2013). Learning French in British Columbia: English as additional language learner and parent perspectives In. K. Arnett & C. Mady (Eds.), *Minority populations in Canadian second language education* (pp. 22–37). Bristol: Multilingual Matters.

Committee to Reimagine Education and Teacher Education (CREATE). (2007). *Envisioning a culture of teacher education: Conceptual touchstones and curriculum strands – Draft*. Available http://teach-educ.sites.olt.ubc.ca/files/2013/07/CREATE-Faculty-Meeting-Sept-2009.pdf

Council of Europe. (2011). *The European framework of reference for languages: Learning, teaching, assessment*. Available http://www.coe.int/t/dg4/linguistic/source/framework_en.pdf

Halbert, J., & Kaser, L. (2013). *Spirals of inquiry: For equity and quality*. Vancouver: British Columbia Principals' and Vice Principals' Association.

Mady, C. (2012). Official language bilingualism to the exclusion of multilingualism: Immigrant student perspectives on French as a second official language in "English-dominant". Canada. *Language and Intercultural Communication, 12*(1), 74–89.

Mady, C. (2013). Adding languages, adding benefits: Immigrant students' attitudes toward and performance in FSOL programs in Canada. In K. Arnett & C. Mady (Eds.), *Minority populations in Canadian second language education* (pp. 3–21). Bristol: Multilingual Matters.

Phelan, A. (2009). The ethical claim of partiality: Practical wisdom, the disciplines and teacher education. *Journal of Curriculum Studies, 41*(1), 93–114.

Dr. Wendy Carr, Associate Dean
Teacher Education, Faculty of Education,
University of British Columbia, Vancouver, BC, Canada

Contributors

Frank Baumann worked for 34 years in School District 44, North Vancouver. During the last 18 years, he was an elementary school principal. For the past 9 years he has been a faculty associate at the University of British Columbia, and for seven of those years, he has been a tutor with the Problem-Based Learning cohort. Frank received his master of education degree and bachelor of arts degree from Simon Fraser University. In recent years he has been involved in the Imaginative Education Research Group at Simon Fraser University.

Kathyrn D'Angelo Assistant Superintendent, Richmond School District No. 38, is district principal and student services and district liaison regarding student transition into school and coordinates extra support needs. Her portfolio reflects her interest in district partnerships where teaching and learning opportunities involve technology and diverse learner needs.

Margaret Early is an associate professor in the Department of Language and Literacy Education at the University of British Columbia, where she teaches graduate and undergraduate courses in teaching in multilingual classrooms. She has conducted large-scale collaborative teacher action research studies on content-based language teaching and multi-literacies.

Margot Filipenko is a professor of teaching in the Department of Language and Literacy at the University of British Columbia, Canada. She worked as an early childhood educator for 12 years at the Child Study Centre at the University of British Columbia. Her research interests focus on problem-based learning, teacher education, early literacy and the texts and materials of reading. Her current research projects explore the integration of digital pedagogies in a new teacher education programme at the University of British Columbia.

Nicky Freeman earned her bachelor of arts degree with a major in English literature at UBC. Nicky enrolled and graduated with a bachelor of education degree in the Problem-Based Learning cohort and completed her practica in a Grade One classroom in the Richmond School District. She is now an enrolling Grade 2 teacher in the Richmond School District.

Catherine Johnson is currently a programme coordinator of teacher education at Simon Fraser University where she continues to enjoy supporting and motivating teacher candidates during their professional year. She focuses specifically on teaching and learning with English as additional language learners and physical education.

Jeannie Kerr is an emerging scholar in educational studies and is currently working as an adjunct teaching professor and faculty associate with TELL-PBL at the University of British Columbia. For the last 4 years, Jeannie has been teaching undergraduate and graduate classes that examine ethics, social issues and philosophy in educational studies. Prior to her academic career, she was an elementary school teacher with the Vancouver School Board for 12 years and was also involved in research with multi-literacies and related pedagogy in the school district. Since completing her PhD in 2013, her current research is focused on understanding the experience of resistance in educational contexts as the substance of curriculum.

Gail Krivel-Zacks is a member of the Faculty of Education at Vancouver Island University and has a private paediatric and adolescent practice that focuses on children with exceptionalities. She completed her doctorate at the University of British Columbia and a research study on Problem-Based Learning and teacher education.

Fil Krykorka is a graduate of the PBL teacher education cohort at the University of British Columbia. He currently teaches a combined 5/6/7 class in a community school located on St'at'imc territory in southwestern British Columbia.

Jo-Anne Naslund is an education librarian at the University of British Columbia. She has worked as a teacher and teacher-librarian in schools in Alberta, British Columbia and Melbourne, Australia. Her research interests focus on information literacy, problem-based learning, teacher education, school libraries, Canadian children's literature and adolescent reading interests. She has authored library publications and taught library courses in teacher-librarianship at the Universities of Melbourne, Alberta and British Columbia. Her education includes a bachelor of arts, bachelor of education, master's of education and a master's in library and information science.

Cynthia Nicol is an associate professor of mathematics education in the Department of Education, Curriculum and Pedagogy at the University of British Columbia, Canada. Her research focuses in the areas of teacher education, mathematics education, Aboriginal education and culturally responsive research ethics and teaching practices. She is particularly interested in the methodologies of participatory action research, self-study research and community-based action research for the transformative possibilities they offer in researching mathematics, teacher and Aboriginal education. Her current research projects explore the nature of problem-based learning, culturally responsive education and place-conscious learning.

Lori Prodan holds a bachelor of arts from McMaster University in Hamilton, Ontario; a bachelor of education from the University of Western Ontario in London, Ontario; and a master's of arts from Simon Fraser University in Burnaby, British Columbia. She has taught Kindergarten to Grade Five with the Vancouver School Board, primarily in the inner city. Lori worked as a teacher educator in Ethiopia for 2 years at the Awassa College of Teacher Education where she helped develop new curriculum for the education of English teachers in the Southern Region. Lori is an adjunct teaching professor in the Department of Literacy and Language Education at the University of British Columbia where she currently works with the 'Teaching English Language Learners through Problem-Based Learning' cohort.

Carolyn Russo is an elementary teacher at Currie Elementary School in the Richmond School District. She received a bachelor of education degree from the University of British Columbia in 2004 and recently completed a graduate diploma in education from Simon Fraser University. Carolyn is a sponsor teacher mentoring pre-service teachers from the Problem-Based Learning cohort. Carolyn values the importance of providing pre-service teachers with opportunities to explore and discover themselves as educators and collaborating with them through this process.

Linda Siegel is the Dorothy C. Lam Chair in Special Education and a professor in the Department of Educational and Counselling Psychology and Special Education at the University of British Columbia, Vancouver, Canada. She was a professor at the McMaster University Medical School from 1968 to 1984 and worked in various capacities in problem-based learning. She developed and directed a Problem-Based Learning cohort in teacher education at the University of British Columbia. She had conducted research on dyslexia, reading development, mathematical concept learning, mathematical learning disabilities and children learning English as a second language. She has been the president of the Division of Learning Disabilities of the Council on Exceptional Children. In 2010, she was awarded the Gold Medal for Excellence in Psychological Research from the Canadian Psychological Association.

Steven Talmy is an associate professor in the Department of Language and Literacy Education at the University of British Columbia, where he is involved in both graduate education and K–12 teacher education/certification. His research has focused on English language learners in K–12 public school settings, and he is new to PBL.

Monika Tarampi is currently a district teacher in the Langley School District supporting the integration needs of students with exceptionalities. She taught in the Richmond School District for 21 years. She received a bachelor of education degree from Simon Fraser University in 1991 and a master of education degree from the University of British Columbia in 2001 in special education, specializing in students with developmental disabilities and challenging behaviour. Throughout her career, Monika has held multiple roles, beginning as both a classroom teaching and a learning assistance/resource teacher, 5 years as head teacher and 7 years as a teacher-consultant in the area of special needs at the district level. In her district role, Monika supports teachers, educational assistants and others in the educational community in meeting the needs of a diverse group of learners. This is her second year as adjunct teaching professor (educational psychology and special education), tutor and faculty advisor (Teaching English Language Learners Through Problem-Based Learning) in the teacher education programme at UBC.

Anne Zavalkoff is a member of the University of British Columbia's Department of Educational Studies. She has a doctorate in philosophy of education with a focus on gender, sexuality and critical thinking. Anne has worked with the University of British Columbia's PBL bachelor of education cohort since 2006. She is the resource instructor primarily responsible for helping the teacher candidates explore the social justice dimensions of each case. She also supports them through the process of thinking through and writing their teaching philosophies. In consultation with the PBL team, Anne has worked to revise the cohort's assessment strategies and has worked twice with the group charged with rebuilding the TELL-PBL cases.

Index

A
ADHD. *See* Attention-deficit/hyperactivity disorder (ADHD)
Amador, J.A., 124, 126, 131
Aoki, T., 12
Attention-deficit/hyperactivity disorder (ADHD), 218

B
Barrows, H., 13
Barrows, H.S., 129
Basic interpersonal communication skills (BICS), 70
Baumann, F., 7, 103–121
BC Ministry of Education, 214
BICS. *See* Basic interpersonal communication skills (BICS)
Biesta, G., 19
Blumberg, P., 140
Bonstead-Bruns, 67
Boyd, 165
British Columbia College of Teachers, 192
British Columbia Ministry of Education, 92
British Columbia Teachers Regulation Branch, 192
Britzman, D., 19, 126
Brooks, M., 152
Bruner, J., 157

C
CALP. *See* Cognitive academic language proficiency (CALP)
CCT. *See* Client-centered therapy (CCT)
Client-centered therapy (CCT), 14
Cognitive academic language proficiency (CALP), 70
Communication
  and collaboration, 91
  comparative evaluation, 80
  program responsiveness, 81
  stress level, 88
  teaching strategies, 88
  transparency, 78
Content knowledge, 217, 218
Continuing challenges and resistance
  annotated Bibliography and Syntheses, 210
  bibliography, 205
  constructive solution seekers, 218
  coordinator's journal
    educational psychology, 213
    inquiry learning and teaching, 214
    language/literacy profiles, 213
    meeting, 213
    preservice teacher, 214
    social and ecological justice, 212
    social justice issues, 213
    teaching and learning, 214
    teaching practice, 212
  core content and processes, 207
  cost-effective, 209
  diverse classrooms, 218
  EAL, 206
  effectiveness, 206
  emerging professionals, 207
  institutional/administration ownership, 209
  institutional challenges, 206
  instructors, 206
  language and language acquisition, 208
  language learning, 206
  multilingual/multicultural classrooms, 208

Continuing challenges and resistance (*cont.*)
  news release, 210–211
  practicum experiences, 209
  problem based learning and pedagogical principles, 208
  professional practice, 209
  resistance, 208
  teacher education program, 206
  traditional teacher education program, 209
  tutorials, 206
Critical thinking, 27, 42, 58, 90
  inquiry (*see* Inquiry)
Curriculum designer, 141, 142

D
D'Angelo, K., 6, 73–82
Daily physical activity (DPA), 72
Day of Pink
  anti-oppression education, 167
  dialectical learning, 166
  flash mobs, 168
  gender identities and expressions, 166–168
  PBL instructional team, 166
  play in schools, 171
  popularity, 168
  preservice teachers, 166, 170
  resource specialist in PBL, 171
  response and supporting rationales, 171
  scenarios, 171
  school curriculum, 169
  social justice teaching, 169
  teaching and learning, 166
  variance, gender, 167
  workshop, 170
Designing cases
  B.Ed. Program, 58–70
  bullying, 62
  cases and dilemma, 61
  developing effective problems
    building classroom community, 65
    documents case, 63, 64, 66
    first nations enhancement education, 65
    kindergarten program guide, 65
    orality and language acquisition, 65
    preservice teachers, 65
    principles, 63
    social justice, 65
    value of play, 65
  developing, matrix
    content knowledge, 59
    course objectives and course topics, 59, 60
    Education Curriculum and Pedagogy (EDCP), 59
    educational psychology (EPSE), 59
    educational studies (EDST), 59
    process, 59
    scenarios, 58
    students' learning activities, 58
  grade 3/4, 62
  grade 4/5, 62
  grade 5/6, 62
  inquiry and research, 62
  K/grade 1, 62
  kindergarten and elementary classrooms, 61
  planning for instruction, 62
  primary grades, 62
  research packages
    classroom community, 67
    issues of language, 68
    Kindergarten curriculum, 67
    orality andlliteracy, 67, 68
    play-based learning, 66
    social justice and aboriginal education, 66, 67
  resource-based coastal community, 62
  special needs education, 62
  student, 62
  technology, elementary classroom, 62
  thematic strands
    curriculum development team, 61
    curriculum, pedagogy, and assessment, 60
    diversity and social justice, 60
    field experiences, 60
    inquiry and dialogical understanding, 61
    interdisciplinary curriculum team, 59
    languages, literacies, and cultures, 60
  theory and practice, 62
Dewey, J., 14
Dispositions for Inquiry Research Project (DIRP), 26
Dispositions, inquiry
  "culture of inquiry", 23
  DIRP, 26
  faculty and tutors, 28
  inquiry-based learning, 36
  PBL approach, 35
  pedagogical approaches, 28–30
  personal and professional investment, 23
  pre-service teachers, 23, 36
  primary data sources, 26
  problematisation, 28
  professional practice, 25–26
  social learning networks, 23
  teacher learning and stories, 23

Index

District Coordinator
    PBL meeting, 75
    roles and responsibilities, 76, 77
Dolmans, D., 57, 58
DPA. *See* Daily physical activity (DPA)

E

EAL. *See* English as an additional language (EAL)
Early, M., 6, 41–79
Educational and Counseling Psychology and Special Education (EPSE), 79
Educational psychology (EPSE), 59
Educational studies (EDST), 59
Education Curriculum and Pedagogy (EDCP), 59
English as an additional language (EAL), 206
English as a second dialect (ESD), 110
English language learners (ELL), 93
ESD. *See* English as a second dialect (ESD)

F

Faculty advisor
    PBL, 105
    pre service teachers, 106
    reflection, 107, 108
    research, 106
Filipenko, M., 1–7, 57–70, 205–221
Freeman, N., 85–98

G

Gadamer, H.G., 15
Geertz, C., 176
Gijselaers, W., 13
Global positioning system (GPS), 180
Godwin, G., 212
GPS. *See* Global positioning system (GPS)

H

Hao, 67
Hendry, G.D., 123, 126
Hmelo-Silver, C.E., 129

I

IEP. *See* Individual Education Plan (IEP)
Individual Education Plan (IEP), 218
Information literacy
    connectivity and networked environment, 146
    educational research and teaching, 143
    librarians, 143
    PBL cohort, 142
    pre service teachers, 142
    tutors/even co-tutors, 143
Inquiry
    learning types, 34
    pedagogy, 33
    problem based learning teacher education, 24–25
Inquiry cycle, 109

J

Johnson, C., 6, 73–82

K

Kelly, D.M., 162
Kemmis, S., 43
Kerr, J., 6, 11–21
Klette, K., 144, 145
Krivel-Zacks, G., 73–82
Krykorka, F., 7, 173–185

L

Language support teacher (LST), 218
Learning management system (LMS), 111
Librarians
    curriculum designer, 141, 142
    information literacy, 142, 143
    resource consultant and collection developer, 140, 141
Library, 136, 143
    PBL (*see* Problem-based learning (PBL))
    reshaping (*see* Reshaping, library services)
Linguistic diversity, 41, 42, 46
The Little Book of Shocking Global Facts, 177
LMS. *See* Learning management system (LMS)
LST. *See* Language support teacher (LST)

M

Mathematics and teacher education
    designing place-based pedagogical problems, 176–177
    geocaching
        activities, 181
        event, 180
        GPS, 180
        learning, 180

Mathematics and teacher education (*cont.*)
    mathematical and pedagogical
        task, 180
    real-world learning experiences, 180
    learning school subject matter, 174
    place-conscious pedagogies, 174
    postbaccalaureate, 174
    preservice teachers, 174
    problem and possibility
        arguing, 176
        classroom door and window, 175
        classroom practice, 175
        coursework, 175
        educators and researchers, 175
        food and economic and recreational
            activities, 175
        Interior Plateaus, 174
        interrupt, 175
        mountains frame, 174
        and pedagogical inquiry, 176
        rock formations, 175
        social and collaborative learning, 175
        teaching/learning mathematics, 176
        top-down, fact-centered approach, 175
    social justice issues
        classes, 178, 179
        context of problem, 178
        deforestation, Brazil, 177
        and environmental issues, 177
        ethical and political issues, 178
        inspiration, 178
        interesting and exciting problems, 178
        mathematical investigations,
            students, 178
        opportunities, 179
        students focus, 179
        task, 179
    students
        dance/improvisational jam, 181
        eccentric individuals, 181
        gwenis, 182–184
        learning and teaching, 181
        memorable teaching and learning
            moments, 182
        ministry-prescribed learning
            outcomes, 182
        multigrade classroom, 182
        willingness, 182
    teaching, 173, 174
Mayo, 129, 130
McCaughan, K., 14, 15
McTaggart, R., 43
Mohan, B., 43
Multilingual, 43, 44, 46
Murray-Harvey, R., 125–127

N
Naslund, J., 205–219
Naslund, J.-A., 1–7, 23–45, 135–149
Nicol, C., 7, 173–185

P
PBL. *See* Problem-based learning (PBL)
PBL methodology, 85
PBL programme, 37
PBL teacher education
    in 2015, 5
    bimonthly meetings, 2
    case-based tutorial approach, 4
    collaborations, 6, 7
    constructivist approach, 5
    develop dispositions, 1
    dispositions for inquiry, 6
    educational issues, 3
    experience and shared values, 2
    experiences, 5
    faculty member, 3
    fostering active learning, 7
    goals, 2
    inquiry and collaboration, 3
    learning, 3
    reflections, 7
    resistance, 4
    schools and classrooms, 3
    strengths and tensions inherent, 5
    student-centered learning, 2
    students need, 3
    thoughts and feelings, 3
    tutors, 4
    University of British Columbia, 1
Phelan, A., 18
Place-Based Relational Educational
    Autobiography, 19
Planning
    adaptations/modifications, 95
    energy and commitment, 95
    imaginative writing and representations, 94
    lesson, 95
    multicultural/multilingual students, 93
    Nicky's teacher education programme, 89
    problem based learning pre-service
        teacher, 90
    writing activity, afternoon, 88
Pourshafie, T., 125–127

Index

Practicum, school-based
  classroom population, 92–96
  collaborative learning, 98
  educational research, 97
  parent-teacher meetings/conferences, 96
  pre-service teacher, 85
  School Advisors, 85
  student teacher-sponsor teacher relationship, 97
  teacher education programme, 85
Pre service teachers
  assigned standing, 120
  classroom management, 88, 120
  communication, 120
  Educational Psychology courses, 87
  field-based practicum, 117
  instructional implementation, 119, 120
  instructional planning, 118, 119
  introductory comments, 118
  learning disabilities, 87
  Nicky Freeman, 87–89
  professional qualities, 118
  synthesis, tutor feedback, 114–116
Problem-based learning (PBL)
  academic libraries, 138, 139
  Art and Music resource specialists, 69
  Asperger's syndrome and autism spectrum disorders (ASD), 69
  augment faculty and tutor competencies, 139
  client-centered therapy, 21
  cohorts, 151
  course objectives, 57
  curriculum-as-lived, 12
    activity of teaching, 19
    complex and uncertain enterprise, 18
    complications, 18
    constructivist theory and pedagogy, 16, 19
    disciplinary context, 16
    disequilibrium, 20
    educational commitment, 17
    emotional/intellectual landscape, 19
    experiential learning theory and collaborative learning, 16–17
    facilitator, 20
    inquiry, 17
    instructional paradigms, 19
    instructors, 18
    medicine/engineering, 17
    metacognitive dimensions, 17
    philosophical hermeneutics, 16
    resource specialists, 20
    systematic and methodical approaches, 17
    taught, 19
    technical-rational approaches, 18
    tutorial sessions, 20
  curriculum-as-plan, 12
    CCT, 14
    constructive and metacognitive process, 13
    constructivist learning theory, 15
    constructivist pedagogy, 15
    Dewey's inquiry and problem-solving process, 15
    encounter, 16
    experiential learning, 15
    experiential learning theory, 14
    Gadamer emphasizes, 16
    interdisciplinary educational approach, 14
    learning, 13
    medical education program, 13
    pedagogical practices, 15
    practices/dimensions, process, 13
    scholarship, 15
    social and contextual factors, 14
    Socratic method, 14
    transformation, 15
  curriculum development team, 57
  disciplinary context, 21
  diversity and social equity, 11
  educational studies/curriculum theory, 11
  explorations
    cohort, 183
    instructors teaching, EDST course, 184
    interactions, preservice teachers, 156
    pre-assessment tool, 156
    programming, 183
    social justice education, 156
    themes, 183
  facilitating explorations
    face-to-face meeting, 156
  faculty advisor, 125
  holistic nature, 124
  inquiry-centered program, 21
  instructional model, 57
  instructors and tutors, 21
  instructor teaching, 11
  journey, 123
  librarians (*see* Librarians)
  library, 138
  North American multilingual/multicultural classroom environment, 69
  Physical Education, 69

Problem-based learning (PBL) (*cont.*)
　preservice teachers, 124
　reading assessment, 69
　resources and services, 138
　resource specialist
　　content learning, 153
　　conventional tools, 152
　　meetings, 152
　　privileges, 153
　　student, 152
　　support pre service teachers, 152, 153
　　teaching, cohort, 152
　self-directed learning, 139
　social and economic needs, 124
　social experience and complications, 11
　student learning, 57
　synthesis, 131
　teacher education program, 69
　teacher education reform, 58
　transformative learning, 21
　trust
　　climate setting, 126
　　community, 127
　　experience and knowledge, 125
　　frustration and disorientation, 125
　　institutional requirements, 126
　　preservice teachers, 125
　　research package, 126
　　teaching and learning, 126
　tutor (*see* Tutor)
　tutor and faculty advisor, 11
　UBC education library, 136, 137
　University of British Columbia (UBC), 57
　well-designed cases, 57
Problem solving
　team work cohesiveness, 34
Prodan, L., 6, 7, 23–45, 103–121, 123–132, 205–221
Professional learning and knowledge society
　characteristics, 145
　community, 145
　information literacy, 145
　library services, 145
　preservice teachers, 145
　relevant library services and instruction, 144
Professional practice
　dispositions and relationship, 25–26
　research packages, 31, 32
Program responsiveness
　governance practices, 73
　phronesis, 74
　practice teaching, 74
　problem based learning, 74
　teacher education program, 73, 74
　theory and practice, 74
The Project for Learning Resources Design, 13

R
Raby, R., 165
Reshaping, library services
　benefits, 143
　connectivity and networked environment, 146
　inquiry and PBL, 147, 148
　preservice teachers, 144
　professional learning and knowledge society, 144–146
Resource specialist
　PBL faculty, roles and relationships
　　on campus, 78
　　District Coordinator, 76, 77
　　school advisor/sponsor teacher, 77
　　school coordinator, 77
Richardson, V., 15
Richmond School District, 4
Richmond School District policy
　of inclusion, 95
Russo, C., 7, 85–98

S
Savery, J.R., 128
Savin-Baden, M., 14, 16
Schön, D., 17
School advisors
　Carolyn Russo, 86
　organizational responsiveness, 82
　PBL pre-service teachers, 86
　school district and the teacher education program, 79
　teaching pedagogy, 86
Second language, 42, 51, 52
Siegel, L., 1–7, 136
Smeby, J., 144, 145
Sobel, D., 181
Social justice and anti-oppression education, 154–156, 165
　components, 151
　Day of Pink (*see Day of Pink*)
　PBL (*see* Problem based learning (PBL))
　privileges, 158
　　face to face meetings, preservice teachers, 156

Index

research and self-reflection, 158
Stinky Lunch case (*see The Stinky Lunch*)
revised UBC program, 151
teacher (*see* Teacher education)
Socratic method, 29
Socratic questioning, 104
Solomon, R.P., 159
Standards for the Education, Competence and Professional Conduct of Educators, 194
Statement of Educational and Teaching Philosophy, 193
The Stinky Lunch
   anti-racism education, 165
   aromatic variations, 160
   classroom community, 159
   composition of groups, 160
   concept, class activity, 160
   concepts, 163
   differences, home and school life, 159
   Egg Station, 161
   grouping, 160
   PBL, 161
   PBL process, 163, 164
   preservice teachers, 159
   privileges, 159, 160
   professional practice and judgment, 162
   research, 164
   schools, 162
   self-reflections, 163
   social justice education, 159, 165
   teachers function, 162
   variability, 163
Student-centeredness, 14

T
Talmy, S., 6, 41–79
Tarampi, M., 7, 103–121
Teacher education
   anti-oppression and multicultural education, 154
   anti-oppression education, 154
   language, 155
   preservice teachers, 155
   resistance to any knowledge, 155
   social justice work, 154
   tourist approach, 154
Teacher education program, 18
Teaching English language learners (TELL)
   audio and video recordings, 44
   awareness, media influences, 77

BC schools, 42
CALP and BICS, 70
challenges
   frontloading, 48–49
   knowledge mobilization, 50
   loss, PBL identity, 50–51
   process of working, 49
   tutors and instructors, 49
children's academic achievements, 70
classroom, 64
classroom activities, 78
classroom community, 65
clusters, 44
collaboration and communication, 48
comparative lack of research, 44
components, 76
critical media education, 78
cross-cultural and cross-linguistic exchange, 41
cultural and linguistic diversity, 42
designs, learning, 74–75
diversity, 64
DPA, 72
education system, 42
effectiveness, 78
email communication, 44
ethical issues, 77, 78
face to face interactions, 77
forms of data, 44
Frontloading, 51, 52
global economy, 41
globalization and immigration, 41
guided reading program, 69
guided reading program and students' independent reading, 71
implementation, 42
indigenous knowledge systems, 68
infusion, 45–46
integration, 47, 72
knowledge-based economy, 41
knowledge mobilization and innovation, 43
language and communication, 64
language issues, 67
literature circles, 72
low-income neighborhood, 72
modes of expression, 76
motivation, 76
"nature-connect" learning, 77
new cases, 52
out-of-school reading, 65
parent-teacher conferences, 65, 66
plan and facilitate learning experiences, 78
population, 76

Teaching English language learners
      (TELL) (*cont.*)
   private institution, 79
   projections, 41
   public school teaching, 53
   radical economic and social changes, 42
   refugee students, 72
   resource teacher, 71
   resource-based coastal community, 67
   school principal, 70
   staff meeting, 70
   staffroom, 69
   stakeholders, 51
   students, 73, 75
   subject area classrooms, 52
   teacher education curriculum, 42
   teachers' experiences, 69
   teaching, 75
   teaching journal, 71
   technology and children, 78
   tensions experience, 51
   time, 47
   time and effort, 51
   tutors, 52
   way of thinking, 74
   workshops, 53
TELL. *See* Teaching English language
      learners (TELL)
Timetabling, 207
Todd, S., 20
Transformative learning, 21
Triple jump assessments and E-folios
   academic school terms, 187
   balanced literacy program, 198
   benefits and challenges, 198
   competency-based processes, 198
   content learning, 197
   context of teachers, 198
   diversity of assessment, 200
   EDUC 317 education psychology, 197
   educational contexts, 200
   expectations, 201
   experiences, practicing teachers, 198
   flexibility, 199
   formatively and summatively assess, 187
   instructors, 188
   instructors and tutors assess, 201
   interview questions, 200
   K-12 educators, 199
   limitations, 198
   LLED 310 language and literacy
      education, 197
   parent, 200
   preservice teachers, 188

principle
   abilities and dispositions, 190
   alignment, 188
   case-research-response
      format, 188, 190
   class/community composition, 190
   class meetings and research
      packages, 188
   classroom, 196
   classrooms, schools
      and communities, 194
   collaborative process, 188
   comment section, 191
   competencies, 189
   competency-based assessment, 195
   content-based criteria, 197
   content knowledges, 189, 195, 197
   context of elementary teaching, 194
   course objectives, 188
   curricular knowledges, 195
   decision-making, 196
   development and assessment, 195
   educational debates, 195
   educational practice, 196
   effective communication, 195
   elementary school teachers, 197
   expectations, 190
   explicit, 191
   explicit and well-supported
      frameworks, 193
   flexibility, 195
   framing, 193
   hop-skip-jump process, 189
   identify and puzzle, 189
   inspirations and tensions, 194
   learner's development, 189
   learning and demonstrating
      learning, 188
   pass/fail system, 190
   pedagogical commitments, 191, 193
   preservice teachers' efforts, 194
   prior content learning, 190
   processed-based professional
      activities, 195
   process of integrating, 192
   product, 190
   professional and personal
      development, 193
   professional contexts, 190
   professional portfolios, 193
   professional practice, 197
   professional priorities
      and practices, 196
   public schooling, 196

reflection, 192, 193
reflexivity inherent, 194
self-assessment practices, 192
Socratic questioning, 189
sophistication and self-reflection, 189
subject-specific knowledges, 195
teacher certification program, 196
themes, 189
tutors and instructors, 188
proficiencies, 199
programmatic and demographic shifts, 199
role-play element, 200
self-inquiries, 199
summative assessment, 187
TELL, 199
Tutorial's Learning Journey, 32–37
Tutors, 114
B.Ed. program, 217
drawback, PBL, 217
educational experience and judgment, 216
english language learners, 217
evaluator, 130, 131
expert, 127, 128
facilitation, 129, 130
faculty advisor, 105–108
learning environment, 104
mentorship, 217
PBL, 103
pre service teachers (*see* Pre service teachers)
problem based learning, 215
quiet students, 216
teaching english language learners, 216
two-week cycle (*see* Two-week cycle)
Two-week cycle
bibliography, 111
criteria, 112
dialogue versus debate, 105
ESD, 110
"fun" activities, 109
independent inquiry, 111
inquiry, 109
in-service teachers, 113
integration, indigenous knowledge, 110
literacy program, 110
materials, 111
place-based learning, 110
pre service teachers, 108, 112, 113
professional development, 109, 110
research package, 112
resource-based coastal community, 109
social and ecological justice issues, 110
synthesis, 113
teacher education program, 108
visuals and graphic organizers, 112

U
UBC education library
authentic and messy, 137
innovative direction, 136
PBL program, 136
pre service teachers, 136, 137
problem-based learning, 137
strategies, 136
UBC Teacher Education Program (UBC-TEP), 16, 17
Ungerleider, C., 3
University of British Columbia, 1

W
Walsh, A., 124, 126, 129, 131

Z
Zavalkoff, A., 7, 151–171, 187–201

CPSIA information can be obtained
at www.ICGtesting.com
Printed in the USA
LVOW01*2146300116
473006LV00007B/193/P

9 783319 020020